INFORMATION
SUPPORT,
PROGRAM
BUDGETING,
AND THE
CONGRESS

Information Support, Program Budgeting, and The Congress

Edited by

ROBERT L. CHARTRAND,
Library of Congress

KENNETH JANDA,
Northwestern University

MICHAEL HUGO,
American Enterprise Institute

SPARTAN BOOKS
New York

CONTENTS

vi

BIOGRAPHICAL NOTES

ANDREW A. AINES

Executive Secretary (Acting Chairman), Committee on Scientific and Technical Information (COSATI) of the Federal Council for Science and Technology, since 1964.

Technical Assistant to the Director, Office of Science and Technology, Executive Office of the President (current).

Colonel, U.S. Army (current).

Staff, Office of Director of Defense Research and Engineering, Department of Defense.

Director, Army Technical Information, Office of Research and Development, Department of Army.

University of Maryland, M.S., Experimental Psychology; George Washington University, M.A., International Affairs; Boston University, degree in Business Administration; Command and General Staff College; Army War College.

PAUL ARMER

Associate Head, Computer Sciences Department, RAND Corporation.

RAND Corporation, 1947 to present.

Member, Mayor's Space Advisory Committee, City of Los Angeles; Committee Lecturer on Computers, Theodore von Kármán Lecture Series, 1967.

Consultant, Presidential Commission on Technology, Automation, and Economic Progress, 1965.

Member, U.S. Computer Delegation to the Soviet Union, 1959.

Executive Board, SHARE (scientific users of large-scale IBM computers), 1955–58, and 1960.

Vice President, American Federation of. Information Processing Societies, 1966–; Chairman, Committee on the Social Implications of Information Processing Technology, 1965–66.

Vice Chairman, National Joint Computer Committee, 1959–60; Member, National Council of the Association for Computing Machinery, 1958–60, and 1964–68; Lecturer, ACM National Lectureship Series, 1966–67; ACM Representative to National Joint Computer Committee, 1958–61.

Member, Association for Computing Machinery, American Association for the Advancement of Science, Institute of Electrical and Electronics Engineers, Mathematical Association of America.

University of California at Los Angeles, graduate, 1946.

Publications include: "Social Implications of the Computer Utility," in *Computers and Communications—Toward a Computer Utility*, Englewood Cliffs, Prentice-Hall, April 1968; "The Systems Gap," in *Datamation*, Vol. 13, No. 8, August 1967; "Computer Aspects of Technological Change, Automation, and Economic Progress," in *Technology and the American Economy*, Appendix, Vol. 1, The report of the National Commission on Technology, Automation and Economic Progress, Washington, D.C., U.S. Government Printing Office, November 1965, also in *Automation and Economic Progress*, Howard R. Bowen and Garth L. Mangum, Eds., Englewood Cliffs, Prentice-Hall, 1966.

JOSEPH BECKER

Director of Information Sciences, Interuniversity Communications Council (EDUCOM).

Lecturer, Automation of Library Services, Catholic University.

Coordinator, Computer/Library exhibits, American Library Association, Seattle and New York World's Fairs.

Member, Association for Computing Machinery, American Library Association, American Documentation Institute.

Research Fellow, Computer Sciences, Western Data Processing Center, University of California at Los Angeles.

Catholic University, M.A., Library Science; Polytechnic Institute of Brooklyn, B.S., Aeronautical Engineering.

Publications include: *Information Storage and Retrieval,* co-author with Robert M. Hayes; numerous articles on Library Automation.

WILLIAM M. CAPRON

Senior Staff, The Brookings Institution.

Assistant Director, U.S. Bureau of the Budget, 1964–65.

Senior Staff, Council of Economic Advisers, 1962–64.

Professor of Economics, Stanford University, 1956–62.

Economist, The RAND Corporation, Santa Monica, California, 1951–56.

Assistant Professor of Economics, University of Illinois, 1949–51.

Research Associate, Harvard Economic Research Project, 1948–49.

U.S. Bureau of Budget, 1945–46.

Member, American Economic Association, Econometric Society, Commerce Technical Advisory Board, Social Science Research Advisory Council to Arms Control and Disarmament Agency, Research Advisory Committee to Economic Development Administration.

Harvard University, graduate work in Economics, M.A., 1948; Harvard University, Littauer Fellow, Graduate School of Public Administration, 1946–67, MPA, 1947; Swarthmore College, A.B., 1942.

Publications include: "Cost-Effectiveness Analysis for Government Domestic Programs," in *Cost-Effectiveness Analysis: New Approaches in Decision-Making,* Thomas A. Goldman, Ed., Washington Operations Research Council, 1967; "The Impact of Analysis on Bargaining in Government," in *The Politics of American Public Administration,* Alan Altshuler, Ed., 1968.

WILLIAM E. CASSELMAN II

*Legislative Assistant to Representative
Robert McClory of Illinois.*

Member, Young Republicans; Secretary, Capitol Hill George
Washington Law Association.

George Washington University Law School, LL.B., 1968; Uni-
versidad de Madrid, 1963; Claremont Men's College, B.A.,
Government, 1963.

ROBERT L. CHARTRAND

*Information Sciences Specialist, Legisla-
tive Reference Service, Library of Congress.*

Senior Staff, Science Policy Research Division, Legislative
Reference Service, Library of Congress.

Manager of Applications Development, Planning Research
Corporation.

Federal Systems Division, IBM Corporation.

Technical Staff, Ramo-Wooldridge Division, TRW, Inc.

Intelligence Analyst, Central Intelligence Agency.

Lecturer, University Seminars, Brookings Institution.

Member, American Society for Information Science, Association for Computing Machinery; Washington Operations Research Council, American Society of Photogrammetry.

University of Missouri, M.A.; Louisiana State University,
graduate work.

Publications include: "Automatic Data Processing for the
Congress," a general study for the Congress, reissued Janu-
ary 3, 1967; "The Systems Approach: A Tool for the Con-
gress," a general study for the Congress, March 9, 1967;
"Computer-Oriented Information for the U.S. Congress," in
Law and Computer Technology, Vol. 1, No. 2, February 1968.

RICHARD F. FENNO, JR.

Professor of Political Science, University of Rochester.

Professor, University of Rochester, 1964–; Associate Professor, 1960–64; Assistant Professor, 1957–60.

Assistant Professor, Amherst College, 1956–57; Instructor, 1953–56.

Instructor, Wheaton College, 1951–53.

Teaching Fellow, Harvard, 1949–51.

Member, Committee on Governmental and Legal Processes, Social Science Research Council, 1964–.

Fellow, Rockefeller Foundation, 1963–64; Social Science Research Council, 1960–61, summer, 1962.

Amherst College, A.B., 1948; Harvard University, Ph.D., 1956; Phi Beta Kappa.

Publications include: *The President's Cabinet,* Harvard, 1959, New York, Knopf, Vintage Books, 1962; *Federal Aid to Education and National Politics,* with Frank Munger, Syracuse, 1962; *The Power of the Purse: Appropriations Politics in Congress,* Boston, Little Brown, 1966.

ROBERT N. GROSSE

Deputy Assistant Secretary for Program Systems, Office of the Assistant Secretary for Program Coordination, Department of Health, Education, and Welfare.

Head, Economics and Costing Department, Research Analysis Corporation, 1963–1966.

Visiting Professor on Defense Economics, Industrial College of the Armed Forces; Lecturer, Armed Forces Staff College, Army War College, National War College.

Director, Bethesda Office, The RAND Corporation, in charge of project helping Assistant Secretary of Defense (Comptroller) develop the Department of Defense Program-Budgeting System; Chief, Factors and Estimates Branch, Cost Analysis Department, RAND Corporation, 1954–61.

Economist, Office of Statistical Standards, Bureau of Budget, 1951–53.

Economist, Harvard University Research Project on the Structure of the American Economy, 1949–51.

Instructor and Staff Member, Bureau of Business and Economic Research, Rutgers University, 1947–49.

Instructor in Economics, Bates College, 1946–47.

Research Assistant, Harvard University, 1945–46.

Harvard University, Ph.D., 1948; M.A., Economics, 1946; Columbia University, A.B., Economics, 1944.

Publications include: "The Program Budget; Its Value to Education at Federal, State and Local Levels," in *Occupational Education: Planning and Programming*, A. Kotz, Ed., Stanford Research Institute, September 1967; "Are Cities Ready for Systems Analysis," *WORC Newsletter*, January 1968; "Planning, Programming, and Budgeting," *Bulletin of the New York Academy of Medicine*, February 1968.

WERNER Z. HIRSCH

Professor of Economics and Director, Institute of Government and Public Affairs, University of California at Los Angeles.

Consultant, RAND Corporation; Bureau of the Budget, Executive Office of the President.

Trustee, Midwest Research Institute, Kansas City, Missouri.

Professor of Economics and Director, Institute of Urban and Regional Studies, Washington University, St. Louis, Missouri, 1953–63.

Consultant, Administrator of the National Aeronautics and Space Administration, 1960–66.

Member, Economic Advisory Panel, National Science Foundation, 1961–63.

Consultant, Internal Revenue Service, 1960–62; Joint Economic Committee of Congress, 1959.

Vice President, Midwest Economic Association, 1960–61.

Economist, Resources for the Future, Inc., 1958–59.

Assistant Research Director and Chief Economist, St. Louis Metropolitan Survey (study financed by Ford Foundation), 1956–57.

Vice President, American Statistical Association (St. Louis), 1954–56.

Economist, The Brookings Institution, 1952–53.

Economic Affairs Officer, United Nations, 1951–52.

Instructor in Economics, University of California at Berkeley, 1949–51.

University of California at Berkeley, Ph.D., 1949; B.S., 1947 (Phi Beta Kappa, Sigma Xi).

Member, Committee on Urban Economics, Resources for the Future, Inc.; Chairman, Committee on Regional Accounts, Resources for the Future, Inc.; Conference on Research in Income and Wealth; American Economic Association; American Farm Economic Association; Regional Science Association; American Statistical Association.

Publications include: *Introduction to Modern Statistics*, New York, The Macmillan Company, 1957; *Exploring the Metropolitan Community*, with others, Berkeley, University of California Press, 1961; *Natural Resources Activities in the Program Budget*, The RAND Corporation, 1965; *Integrating View of Federal Program Budgeting*, The RAND Corporation, 1965; *Regional Accounts for Public Decisions*, ed. and contributor, Baltimore, Johns Hopkins Press, 1966.

KENNETH JANDA

Associate Professor, Department of Political Science, Northwestern University.

Consultant, State of Illinois Commission on the Organization of the General Assembly, 1966.

Participant, National Science Foundation Institute on the Role of Mathematics in Social Science Theory Building, Yale University, 1965; Social Science Research Training Institute in Mathematics for Political Scientists and Sociologists, 1964.

Chairman, "Computer Aids for Congressmen," Conference at the Survey Research Center, University of Michigan, 1966; "Solving Problems That Hinder Data Use," Panel at the Third Technical Conference of Council of Social Science Data Archives, Ann Arbor, Michigan, May 10–12, 1966.

Member, Information Retrieval Committee of the Council of Social Science Data Archives, American Council of Learned Societies Committee on Information Technology, Northwestern University Computing Center Committee, Editorial Board, Midwest Journal of Political Science, Inter-University Consortium for Political Research, 1965–67, AFIPS-ACM Government Advisory Committee.

Indiana University, Ph.D., Government, 1961; Pre-Doctoral Fellow, in residence, Survey Research Center, University of Michigan, 1959–60; Illinois State University, B.S., 1957.

Publications include: *Cumulative Index to the American Political Science Review, Volumes 1–57, 1900–1964*, Evanston, Northwestern University Press, 1964; *Data Processing— Applications to Political Research*, Evanston, Northwestern University Press, 1965; "Information Systems for Congress," in *Congress: The First Branch of Government*, Washington, American Enterprise Institute, and Garden City, Doubleday Anchor Books, 1966; *Information Retrieval: Applications to Political Sciences*, Indianapolis, Bobbs-Merrill Company, 1968.

LESTER S. JAYSON

Director, Legislative Reference Service,
Library of Congress.

Deputy Director, Legislative Reference Service, Library of Congress, 1962–66; Senior Specialist in American Public Law and Chief of American Law Division, 1960–62.

Special Assistant to Attorney General, Department of Justice; Chief, Torts Section; Vice Chairman, Interdepartmental Federal Tort Claims Committee; Member, Committee Executive Privilege; Representative, Air Coordinating Committee, International Civil Aviation Committee.

Attorney at Law, New York City.

Harvard Law School, LL.B., 1939; New York City College, Bachelor of Social Sciences (with special honors in History and Government), 1936.

Publications include: Supervising editor (current edition), *The Constitution of the United States of America—Analysis and Interpretation; Handling Federal Tort Claims,* New York, Matthew Bender & Co.

WILLIAM T. KNOX

Vice President, McGraw-Hill, Inc.

Consultant, Office of Science and Technology, Executive Offices of the President, and several other government agencies.

Staff, Office of Science and Technology, Executive Office of the President, 1964–66.

Manager, Corporate Planning, Esso Research and Engineering Company; Technical Information Division; Research Chemist, 1938–64.

Virginia Polytechnic Institute, M.S.; Mercer University, A.B.

Publications include: "The New Look in Information Systems, Prospective Changes in Society by 1980," *Designing Education for the Future,* The First Area Conference, Denver, Colorado, July 1966; "The Government Makes Plans," Towards National Information Networks, *Physics Today,* Vol. 20, No. 1, January 1966; "Guidelines for a Technical Information Service," *Research Management,* Vol. 7, No. 4, July 1964.

THE HONORABLE ROBERT McCLORY

Member of Congress, 12th Illinois District.

Republican, of Lake Bluff, Illinois; elected to the 88th Congress in 1962, re-elected to the 89th and 90th Congresses.

Member, House Committee on the Judiciary, 89th and 90th Congresses (Ranking Minority Member, Subcommittee No. 4, 90th Congress); Member, House Committee on Government Operations, 88th Congress.

United States Delegate, Inter-Parliamentary Union, 88th, 89th, and 90th Congresses.

Sponsor, 89th and 90th Congresses, H.R. 18428 and H.R. 21 (bills to authorize the Legislative Reference Service of the Library of Congress to acquire and make use of automatic data processing equipment and services in the performance of its functions in support of the Congress) ; also, sponsor, 90th Congress, amendments to the Judicial Center Act to direct that the proposed Federal Judicial Center of the Administrative Office of the United States Courts study and determine the ways in which automatic data processing and systems procedures may be used in Federal judicial administration.

Member of Illinois House of Representatives, 1950–52; Illinois Senate, 1952–62.

Attorney at Law, Illinois; Senior partner (inactive) of the law firm of McClory, Bairstow, Lonchar and Nordigian, Waukegan, Illinois.

Member, Illinois State and American Bar Associations, Law Club of Chicago.

Chicago-Kent College of Law, LL.B., 1932; Dartmouth College and L'Institut Sillig, Vevey, Switzerland.

Publication: "Reforming the Fiscal and Budgetary Machinery of Congress," *We Propose: A Modern Congress,* New York, McGraw-Hill, 1966.

THOMAS STUART McFEE

Director of Systems Development, Office of the Assistant Secretary for Program Coordination, Department of Health, Education, and Welfare.

Technical Assistant to the Director, Office of Science and Technology, Executive Office of the President; Executive Secretary of White House Panel operated under guidance of the Foreign Intelligence Advisory Board and the Special Assistant for Science and Technology, 1965–66.

Project Leader, Weapons Systems Evaluation Group, DOD, 1962–65.

Head, Systems Analysis Branch, Operations Research Division, David Taylor Model Basin, 1958–62.

Mathematician, Mathematical Computation Division, David Taylor Model Basin, 1956–58.

Education Officer, U.S. Air Force, 1954–56.

Mathematics Teacher, 1948–54.

Member, American Mathematical Association; Association for Computing Machinery.

University of Maryland, B.S., Mathematics, 1953; graduate study in Mathematics, 1956–59.

CHARLES T. MEADOW

Manager, Information Sciences, Federal
Systems Division, IBM Corporation.

Specialist in information retrieval and man-machine communications with IBM since 1960.

Consulting Analyst, General Electric Company.

Assistant Mathematician, RAND Corporation.

Mathematician, Bureau of Ships, U.S. Navy.

Member, Association for Computing Machinery; Operations Research Society of America.

Rutgers University, M.S., Mathematics, 1954; University of Rochester, B.A., Mathematics, 1951.

Publications include: *The Analysis of Information Systems,* New York, John Wiley & Sons, 1967.

JOHN S. SALOMA III

Assistant Professor of Political Science,
Department of Political Science, Massa-
chusetts Institute of Technology.

Participant, The Study of Congress Project, American Political Science Association, 1965 (Grant by Carnegie Corporation).

Director of Research, Brooke for United States Senator Committee, 1966.

President, Ripon Society, 1963–67.

Fulbright Scholar, London School of Economics.

Congressional Fellow, American Political Science Association, 1961–62.

Member, American Political Science Association.

Harvard University, Ph.D., M.A., Political Economy and Government, 1962, 1959; M.I.T., B.S., Business and Engineering Administration, 1956.

Publications include: *Evaluation of Congressional Performance, The Study of Congress*, Boston, Little, Brown, 1968; *The Job of a Congressman: Some Perspectives on Time and Information* (to be published); *The Responsible Use of Power*, Washington, American Enterprise Institute, 1965.

FRED SCHWENGEL

Member of Congress, 1st Iowa District.

Republican, of Davenport, Iowa; elected in 1954 and re-elected in 1956, 1958, 1960, 1962, and 1966.

Member, Public Works Committee and the House Administration Committee; Vice Chairman, Civil War Centennial Commission, 1961–65; President, United States Capitol Historical Society.

Member, Iowa Legislature, elected in 1944 and served 5 consecutive terms.

PETER L. SZANTON

Staff Member, The RAND Corporation.

Deputy Director, Program Evaluation Staff, Bureau of the Budget, 1965–67.

Policy Planning Staff, International Security Affairs, Office of Secretary of Defense, 1962–65.

Attorney at Law, New York City.

Consultant, Office of Secretary of Defense, Bureau of Budget, President's National Crime Commission, President's Task Force on Government Organization, and others.

Foreword

Students of political systems have long recognized direct relationships between legislative organization and substantive questions of public policy. In the past few years the organization of the United States Congress has itself become an important policy issue, involving direct challenges to the ability of Congress, as presently organized, to fulfill its constitutional responsibilities. Of all the facets of congressional organization which have come under scrutiny, perhaps none is so fundamental as the complex of formal and informal procedures which permit the flow of information to and within Congress.

Although scholars disagree as to whether the present balance of power between Congress and the executive branch represents a desirable state of affairs, there is considerable agreement that the executive branch maintains the initiative in the policy process and that a major factor in this initiative is the access to and use of information by the executive. Program budgeting and cost effectiveness, which involve increasingly sophisticated techniques of information management and evaluation, promise to strengthen further the relative position of the executive branch.

The purpose of the seminar, whose proceedings are set forth in this book, was to provide Congress and the public with a series of expert assessments of the problems and payoffs which would probably result from an attempt to improve the quality of information support available to the Congress. Members of the seminar were drawn from Congress, the executive, academic life, and private industry. The importance of such deliberations was perhaps best expressed by one of our distinguished participants, Colonel Andrew Aines, Executive Secretary of the President's Commission on Science and Technology, who remarked: "This is the first meeting I have ever attended where people in both branches have talked about mutual information problems." These proceedings should constitute a significant addition to the recent literature on the organization of Congress.

WILLIAM J. BAROODY, *President*
American Enterprise Institute
for Public Policy Research

May 1, 1968

Part One

Problems and Prospects
in Information Support
for Congress

ROBERT L. CHARTRAND

The Congressional Milieu—Information
Requirements and Current Capabilities

THE COMPLEXITY and dynamism of contemporary America is nowhere more accurately reflected than in the Congress of the United States. This elective body of men and women, representing an average constituency of 450,000 persons, works hard to serve the needs of an ever-increasing, heterogeneous, highly mobile population. Dr. Ernest S. Griffith brings the dilemma of the national legislator into sharp focus:

> Congressmen necessarily and properly reflect the attitudes and needs of their individual districts, and many, if not most, of these are economic. It is perhaps the supreme task of Congress on the domestic front to create out of these individual, often very limited, local outlooks an amalgam that shall in some measure represent their fusion into the more general national interest and welfare.[1]

If the monumental task of governing the most powerful nation in the history of the world is to be performed successfully, it is imperative that every instrumentality be laid hold of, and used to the utmost. This is an age of innovation. Dur-

---

[1] Ernest S. Griffith, *Congress, Its Contemporary Role* (New York: New York University Press, 1961), pp. 2–3.

ing the past 25 years our technological achievements have had an impact of major proportions on all sectors of society. The leadership of the United States, charged with maintaining national security and promoting a continually rising level of living, recognizes that the national goals, programs, and governmental procedures must be responsive to *current* conditions. The crux of this interaction is brought into focus by Professor Alfred de Grazia who states: "It is in the matching of the institutions to the changing issues of the times that the genius of each generation is tested." [2]

The congressman is called upon to function in three distinct, yet often intermeshing, ways:

1. As a legislator, responsible for examining, debating, and formulating decisions regarding issues of international and national scope;
2. As a representative of his district or state, with primary concern and responsibility for its well being, progress, and relationship to other governmental elements, and for the necessary legislative action involved; and
3. As an *ombudsman* of sorts, accessible to each individual constituent and responsible for providing assistance in a thousand ways.[3]

The purpose of the Seminar on Information Support for the Congress, sponsored by the American Enterprise Institute for Public Policy Research, is to examine in a candid and thorough fashion the problems faced by the members of the Federal Congress in obtaining that information that will allow them to make the best possible judgments on a broad range of issues, great and small.

Congressional Information Requirements

It is difficult, if not impossible, to identify the boundaries within which the Congress' needs for information are contained. The criticality of the situation, which continues to worsen, is well known to most members. An often-quoted sur-

[2] Alfred de Grazia, "Toward a New Model of Congress," in *Congress: the First Branch of Government* (Washington, American Enterprise Institute for Public Policy Research, 1966), pp. 8–9.

[3] Robert L. Chartrand, "The Systems Approach: a Tool for the Congress," in Extension of Remarks of Honorable Hugh Scott, *Congressional Record* (daily ed., Washington, March 20, 1967), Vol. 113, p. S4052.

vey [4] conducted among 80 members of the House of Representatives, which asked them to identify general categories of problems encountered in their job, resulted in 78 percent citing "complexity of decision making; lack of information" as the single, most important concern. If one were to characterize the information desired, these four classical elements would appear: completeness, accuracy, timeliness, and *relevance*.

In recent commentary regarding the "information explosion" and its effect on the Congress, Representative Robert McClory of Illinois described the unflagging need of himself and his colleagues for "information on current legislation, future legislation, national issues, local issues, world problems—almost anything and everything imaginable." [5]

Among the information needs of the Congress are certain types which may be identified. First, the Congress as a whole may express a definitive requirement through statutory action; an example of this is the directive to the Legislative Reference Service (LRS) of the Library of Congress to publish periodically a *Digest of Public General Bills*. A second category of recurring inquiry for information, usually directed to a committee staff, outside consultants, or LRS, is that for "intensive background studies on subjects within their jurisdiction"; an example is *A Case Study of the Utilization of Federal Laboratory Resources*.[6] The third category of information asked for by the Congress is that initiated by the members themselves; it could range from hemp production statistics to a speech on the reaction of African nations to the Peace Corps to an explanation of what is meant by a "model city." The fourth type of request, which has no known limits, is that encyclopedic range of constituent needs.

---

[4] Kenneth Janda, "Information Systems for Congress," in *Congress: the First Branch of Government* (Washington, American Enterprise Institute for Public Policy Research, 1966), Table 1, p. 421.

[5] Robert McClory, "Congress needs ADP," in Extension of remarks in the House, *Congressional Record.* (Washington, January 10, 1967), Vol. 113, p. A20.

[6] Library of Congress, Legislative Reference Service, Science Policy Research Division, *A Case Study of the Utilization of Federal Laboratory Resources. A Study Submitted to the Research and Technical Programs Subcommittee of the House Committee on Government Operations* (89th Cong., 2d sess., November 1966), (Washington, U.S. Govt. Print. Off., 1966), 141 pp.

This brief recital of exemplary information needs of the Congress becomes more meaningful when placed within the context that in the 89th Congress a total of 26,566 bills and resolutions were introduced in the two chambers; of these, 4,016 were passed.[7] There has been a significant amount of debate and commentary in leading journals regarding the mounting demands upon the time and energies of the members of Congress. Some believe that the legislative loads, plus the handling of constituent correspondence and delegations, are impairing the balance between the executive and legislative branches. The ability of the member to function effectively is predicated on receiving the correct information, as reflected in one study of congressional operations which stated bluntly that "Congress often does not get the kind of information needed for sound evaluation of proposed legislation or adequate examination of alternatives." [8]

Several proposals for congressional reform have been proffered by groups in business, not-for-profit institutions, universities, and political task forces. Professor Kenneth Janda, a member of this seminar, astutely points out that:

> Despite the variety of these proposals, they are all curiously restricted in range. Basically, they can be divided into two types: those which offer the congressman more *time* and those which offer more *help*. Few offer him more information.[9]

Thus, we face a situation where every possible tool and technique should be placed at the disposal of the congressman and his staff so that they may better function in a decision-making role. Improved handling of this information—its collection, indexing, storage, correlation, retrieval—is vital to the member of Congress. With the advent of the electronic computer and its associated techniques and man-machine procedures, an awareness is developing within the Congress that perhaps this technological innovation can assist the legislator in his multiple roles.

---

[7] *Congressional Record* (Washington, November 21, 1966), Vol. 112, p. D1045.

[8] A. D. Little Company, Inc., "Management Study of the U.S. Congress," Report to NBC News (November 24, 1965), p. 11. Reprinted with permission.

[9] Kenneth Janda, "Features of an Information System for Congress," in *Proceedings of the A. C. M. National Meeting* (1966), p. 363.

Information Resources for the Congress

Two problems often facing the congressman, not having enough information or, conversely, having too much (i.e., irrelevant) information, remain unsolved. Senator A. S. Mike Monroney, writing in the *Political Science Quarterly*, comments:

> Much thoughtful analysis should be given to the relative role played by such informational sources as personal staff, committee and subcommittee staff, common research organs such as the Legislative Reference Service, use of outside consultants, "borrowed" experts from the executive branch, and lobbyists for interested organizations.[10]

Many congressmen, either for personal or committee work, may prefer to use only persons of unquestioned loyalty to them. When outsiders are added to the team—for example, during the preparation of a subcommittee report—it is felt that the degree of member control over the activity is lessened. In addition to the need to identify, locate, acquire, select, and utilize information which is germane to a given problem, there may be a need for maximum objectivity. In some instances, there also is a requirement for the confidential analysis of selected subject matter. The role of the Legislative Reference Service in providing this type of support and an increasingly broad range of services warrants mention at this juncture. Representative Fred Schwengel, in the book entitled *We Propose: A Modern Congress*, indicates the importance of LRS developing an ADP-oriented capability:

> Automated information retrieval is a *must* for the Service. Congress has been inexcusably slow in exploring the possibilities of electronic information systems to aid it in the legislative process. The functions of the Legislative Reference Service present a tantalizing number of opportunities for utilizing such devices.[11]

Today the Congress not only is striving to avail itself of all requisite information, but it has demonstrated a willingness to consider the utilization of modern technology in enhancing its day-to-day operations.

---

[10] Reprinted with permission from the *Political Science Quarterly*, Vol. LXXX, No. 42 (December 1965), p. 608.

[11] From "Information Handling: 'For a Vast Future Also,'" in *We Propose: A Modern Congress* by Mary McInnis (ed.), Copyright 1966 by McGraw-Hill, p. 309. Used by permission of McGraw-Hill Book Company.

Congress Views the Systems Approach

During the past several years, there has been a rising chorus in the Congress calling for the use of systems analysis and automatic data processing (ADP) by that body. Among the first to commit himself to the concept that the Congress should utilize every conceivable means of helping the member perform was Vice President Humphrey:

When Congress has better access to the answers it needs, it will be in a position to ask still better—more useful questions. . . . There are many questions about emerging trends—in population, health, industry—which no one has even thought to ask. The computer could help immeasurably to open up new vistas for Congress to explore —in our people's behalf.[12]

In the 90th Congress, a number of bills (H.R. 21, *et al.*) have been introduced in the House of Representatives by a bipartisan group of members calling for the creation of an automatic data processing (ADP) facility for the Congress. The importance of using ADP and modern program evaluation techniques in support of congressional budgetary review, thereby providing the members a logical way to comprehend and respond to the Planning-Programming-Budgeting System (PPBS) mode of operation within the executive branch, has been stressed. Other priority applications would include the preparation of legislative histories of bills, presentation of status information on committee action and pending legislation, and the establishment and maintenance of selected research data in machine-readable form. In his speech on the floor of the House of Representatives, Representative McClory closed with these thought-provoking words:

It has been said that the future of the United States resides in the efficacy of its decision makers, whose judgments are rendered with perspective and knowledge. Let us take that first, critical step forward by providing ourselves with the capability that is possible through the great achievements of American creativity and industry.[13]

[12] Hubert H. Humphrey, The Computer Revolution—Address by Senator Humphrey before the Eastern Spring Computer Conference. Remarks in the Senate. *Congressional Record* (Washington, April 25, 1964), Vol. 110, p. 9075.

[13] Robert McClory, "An Automatic Data Processing Facility to Support the Congress," in Remarks in the House. *Congressional Record* (Washington, October 19, 1966), Vol. 112, p. 26788.

While supporting the need for such an ADP facility for the Congress, Representative John G. Dow of New York has introduced a separate bill (H.R. 7874) emphasizing the importance of the selection of the statistical data and narrative information which would be placed in a congressional computer-oriented facility.[14]

Another effort to give impetus to the establishment of a congressional-support facility was made by Senator Hugh Scott of Pennsylvania, who prepared an amendment (No. 63) which was incorporated by the Senate in the Legislative Reorganization bill passed in 1967 (S. 355). Underscoring the fact that "the broad spectrum of issues facing the Congress . . . can be coped with only by the utilization of all available human and technological resources," [15] Senator Scott went on to note many applications of the computer to the tasks of the member. His concluding words set in proper perspective the role of the systems approach, including automatic data processing in the legislative environment:

> The electronic computer and the systems techniques connected with its use are simply tools for use by the decision maker. They are designed to help provide that information which is necessary to make balanced, accurate decisions.[16]

Summary: Objective of This Seminar

All too seldom do persons qualified by virtue of experience, training, and motivation gather to explore a subject such as the question of information support for the Congress. Speeches may be delivered and monographs inscribed which treat sundry aspects of the central problem, but upon this occasion, information scientists from business, the academic world, and government have been brought together to comprise a peer group with a single objective in mind. That is to discuss openly and in the presence of selected observers, including members

[14] John G. Dow, "Data for Congressmen," in Remarks in the House, *Congressional Record* (Daily ed., Washington, April 4, 1967), Vol. 113, p. H3507.

[15] Hugh Scott, Remarks in the Senate during Debate on the Legislative Reorganization Act of 1967, *Congressional Record* (Washington, February 16, 1967), Vol. 113, p. S2124.

[16] *Ibid.*

of the Congress, the various ramifications of providing information which is essential to legislative decision making. Although the projected role of the electronic computer in the congressional milieu of the near future will be considered, this subject will in no way pre-empt the central seminar theme.

Of particular importance will be the establishment of a perspective, which allows the discussants to view congressional information needs in the light of executive branch information activities, and related efforts in the private sector. How vital has become the question of the selection and communication of information! New bases for interdisciplinary solutions to problems are being formed and the so-called "cybernetic revolution" even now is with us. Dr. Glenn T. Seaborg struck the proper note when he stated that:

> ... computers amplify the collective intelligence of men—the intelligence of society—and while the effect of the sum of men's physical energies may be calculated, a totally different and compounded effect results from combining facts and ideas.[17]

At this juncture in the development of our nation, those who govern must have at their disposal maximum resources to define objectives, formulate programs, allocate manpower and moneys, and identify alternative courses of action. The ability to perform these functions is dependent, in large part, upon the information by which decisions must be made. The moment of truth is at hand for the Congress as it strives to adapt the advances of technology to serve the needs of the lawmaker responding to the needs of society.

---

[17] Glenn T. Seaborg, Time, Leisure and the Computer: the Crisis of Modern Technology. Remarks at a Conference on "the University in a Changing Society," (Howard University, Washington, D.C., March 1, 1967), p. 3.

WILLIAM T. KNOX

External Sources of Information for Congress: The Executive Branch and the Private Sector

T HE CONGRESSIONAL FOCUS of our attention today is, in my mind, appropriate, desirable, indeed absolutely necessary. However, it is not a unique situation because there are other groups in our society that require complex information brought to them in an easy-to-assimilate form just as the Congress requires it.

The Congress requires a set of information which is different in quality, in the depth to which the subject material is treated, in the timeliness with which it has to be assembled and brought to the lawmakers' attention, as well as in the amount that must be available. Congressmen are people. They will be able to handle information, we hope, at a level of ability considerably above that of the average person, but I don't think any of us expects our congressmen to be superhuman when it comes to handling information. Their information requirements, I believe, are different in some respects but certainly not unique.

It is interesting to note that the expressions by numerous congressmen about their needs for better information support are markedly different from some of the understandings and motivations of their counterparts across the Atlantic. One of

9

the parliamentarians from a national parliament, which is a member of the Council of Europe, told me that he wanted the scientists on tap but not on top, with respect to information support. He also said that if he knows more about certain topics than his electorate then he should cease to be their representative. In the case of our congressmen we do find a more broad-minded and, I think, a more desirable approach to this problem.

We are reflecting here the vector sum of several major forces acting in our society. We have the increased volume of information, more people who want to use information, the increased complexity and sophistication of its use, the increased demands, which are purely humanistically derived, another set of demands for faster and more complete utilization of this information and, finally, we have new technology for information transfer. These six forces at work in our society have focused attention on information transfer and its role in furthering our progress. As we all know, information transfer really is the basic process by which civilizations get built. It is nothing new in kind in our world, but the factors that I just mentioned mean that information transfer, as a function today, requires considerably more attention than societies in the past have given it.

Each one of these factors that I have mentioned differs in degree from anything that has happened in the past. Bringing together all of them or, as I said earlier, calculating the vector sum of them, is going to result and is resulting in a forced-draft change in our attitude toward the handling of information in all sectors of our society. It will be reflected sooner or later in the congressional handling of information. It is my hope, because of the important role of the Congress in our society, that it is reflected there sooner rather than later.

Now, I would spend just a few moments dwelling on scientific and technical information because I am more familiar with it and more comfortable in talking about it. I recognize that it is only an illustration of information flow. It happens to be very important both for our society and to the Congress. I could also mention education, as an example, which is not science and technology. But it happens that in the field of education the information system has been neglected. It has hardly existed as a matter of fact, until very recently.

10

Compare this to a very long-standing tradition in the field of science and technology for organized information systems. Scientists and engineers have recognized from the beginning that their work was dependent on organized information systems. I think it's not unnatural, therefore, that we find in science and technology the best examples of information systems.

The Congress over the years has recognized the importance of information flow in technology and in science. It was recognized by Thomas Jefferson and the Congress of almost 200 years ago when they established the Agricultural Information Services that we have used so effectively in this country. It was recognized again when the Atomic Energy Commission was set up and told to see to it that the results of its research were distributed widely, not only in this nation but throughout the world. It was recognized again 15 years later when the Congress set up the National Aeronautics and Space Agency (NASA), and NASA was told to insure that the results of the work it financed were distributed widely throughout the world.

The Congress has also been quite interested in the effectiveness with which the executive branch has done the things that it was told to do. With the leadership of the then-Senator Humphrey, the Department of Defense was almost mercilessly criticized for its inattention to the information system serving its needs. As a result of some specific prodding by Senator Humphrey, the Department of Defense established a Director of Technical Information about 1962. Senator Humphrey also made quite an examination of the information services in the medical and health areas and, as a result of that, the executive departments in those areas also put much more top-level attention on their information services.

A matter of specific concern to the Congress has been its control over the total research program funded by executive agencies. This concern led to the establishment of the Science Information Exchange. I believe this is a very healthy organization at this point. When the National Defense Education Act was passed in 1958, the National Science Foundation was specifically directed to become much more active in providing, in this country, a very effective and efficient system for handling all scientific and technical information.

11

The executive branch responded in the manner I mentioned earlier. In the Office of the President, the Office of Science and Technology brought on board several people to exercise leadership and coordination among the executive agencies. Today there exists a staff office in the Office of the President concerned with information systems broadly, not just in science and technology. There exists a Federal Council Committee, the Committee on Scientific and Technical Information (COSATI), which coordinates federal programs in this area. On the outside, we have the Committee on Scientific and Technical Communications of the National Academy of Sciences and the National Academy of Engineering, which represents the professional community of scientists. The President established a National Advisory Commission on Libraries to recommend by the end of this year a coordinated national program for strengthening the role of libraries in our society.

COSATI established a National Systems Task Force, which has stirred the waters rather vigorously in the last two years. Perhaps the most interesting result has been its report, prepared by the Systems Development Corporation, leading toward the establishment of a national network of information systems. This report and the efforts behind it have been widely misinterpreted as a call for a monolithic, concentrated, centralized information bank to be controlled and operated by the Federal Government, supplying information to all who want it through laser beams and other advanced technologies. I would like to take this opportunity to make sure this group understands that the National Systems Task Force was primarily trying to conceive, in the very broadest terms, the structures and mechanisms required to bring about more effective information utilization in our society. We were not attempting to say that the Federal Government should embark on a centralized program trying to bring all of the information processes in our society under its control. It would be doomed to failure, to begin with. It would be an act of extreme folly, I think, for the Federal Government even to attempt that. Fortunately, I believe the word is finally getting around.

I think it is appropriate that we consider substantive information today. I note that later this group will be talking more about administrative information systems so I will not dwell on these. Permit me merely to mention that it seems to me that as the executive agencies increase their capabilities to handle information for their own means, their own program needs, inevitably the Congress will be able to make greater use of these same systems for substantive information. I would not presume to specify the form in which the information connection will take place. Undoubtedly people will still talk to people. Books will still be printed. Abstracts and indexes will be prepared. We can evolve from where we are today into, hopefully, a more effective and efficient system.

Three major problem areas seem to be involved in congressional use of information. First, Congress' information requirements, not only for carrying out its own traditional responsibilities, but also for playing a very central and important role in the evolution of our national network of information systems. It seems to me that the Congress, in order to legislate wisely in this area, is going to be called upon to understand a great deal about our information-transfer systems and about people's use of information. There are two current examples of pending legislation specifically related to the information transfer process: One is the copyright revision bill; the other is the bill for a revision of the patent system. Both of these are mechanisms related to the information transfer process.

Throughout most legislation, however, you will find various information-systems problems. One that recently came to our attention was a request from the Census Bureau to enlarge its staff in order to undertake a continuing program to provide a certain type of construction statistics to state and local governments, a purely informational problem on behalf of the construction industry in this country. I can put on my private McGraw-Hill hat at this point and mention that it devolved upon us to point out to the Congress that there was private activity already providing this identical service. The Congress has to be informed about the informational resources existing in the private sector. All too often it is unaware of them. All too often it is not told about them. I want to see to it that Congress is told about them more often in the future.

Another problem area is the user and his influence on the design of these information systems. We don't know very much about people's real requirements for information. People

13

seem to use whatever information systems they have and, once they get familiar with using them, they become uncomfortable when they are asked to change their systems. But still, confronted with a new system and no alternative, they will use the new system.

As we add new information technology to the existing means for getting information, we are likely to force users to use the new technology without really understanding its optimal use. In this period of rapid change in information technology it seems to me we are required to maintain a tremendous amount of systems flexibility, so that what the human user really wants and can use will influence the system design in an optimal way. The user should be allowed to express his true needs, not just as they exist today but as they can be developed. Too often we have, in the case of federal agencies, administrative and political mechanisms by which the user tries to influence the development of systems. This is an awkward mechanism. I am concerned that we are not creating better mechanisms in which the user can make his influence directly and quickly felt on these new systems.

I have had personal experience trying to influence the American Chemical Society to provide a better system to serve the people who wanted their information. It took ten years before a group of users was able to get the ACS to do a simple thing such as splitting the complete volume of abstracts into sections. I submit, and they now agree, that this is an intolerable system response. This is the kind of system response that is all too frequent when administrative and political mechanisms are the only way in which users can make their influence felt and their needs known.

This leads me to the next problem: the mechanisms for resources allocation. These presumably should reflect what the users want and need, but there are different categories of users, of course. We have astronomers in the physical sciences. Very few of them can find commercial applications for their findings. There are relatively few of them. Yet it is just as important to the development of astronomy, and to our total cultural experience, that these people have an effective information system as it is, say, to somebody working in another field of more direct application to people's down-to-earth needs. At this point we still have relatively poor mechanisms

14

for allocating information systems resources among these various needs. Most of the resources are still administrative and political, or both. I believe we have to develop better mechanisms.

This brings me, in conclusion, to the problem of the new definition or the redefinition of the most appropriate and effective roles of the various sectors in our society with respect to information systems. We have the Federal Government; we have state and local governments; we have universities, which Joe Becker will talk about at greater length; we have the nonprofit institutes, and there are a good many of them in existence concerned with information. In the days when our demands for information utilization were not as forceful as they are today, when we didn't have the technological alternatives for information transfer that we have today, the definition of sector roles was arrived at slowly, over the course of many decades.

Under the influence of the factors I mentioned earlier, though, it is obvious to me that we are going to have to re-think very carefully the most appropriate roles of these various sectors in our society. We have passed from a condition where information was hard to come by and where, therefore, all kinds of devices and mechanisms were required to make information easily accessible. This was the principle on which we first started out in this Republic of ours: that it was going to be helpful to our economy for the government to undertake a large role in the dissemination of information.

I submit that we are rapidly passing, if we have not already passed that point. The Federal Government no longer has to bear the major burden for disseminating information to those who really can make use of it.

We have the development, in many cases, of what amounts to business enterprises by universities. I can mention, for example, the University of Wisconsin, which runs a selective dissemination service for a fee, providing businessmen with abstracts and digests of articles that have appeared. Universities, as they relate more and more to our current social requirements, are finding that the field of information dissemination is a very easy one for them to get into. Using the wage scales that are prevalent among graduate students in universities, they can frequently afford to perform very

15

useful services at very low prices. The net effect of this increasing activity in the universities is, of course, to weaken the profit-making sector.

The profit-making sector, therefore, has a rough job on its hands: to understand what it is that is required in the future, to supply it, and to convince not only the users but the Congress and the other people in our society that it is beneficial to our society to have the profit-making sector play an important role here. It must not sit back and, by default, let the role of information dissemination pass more completely into the hands of federal agencies, universities, and the nonprofit organizations such as professional societies and research institutes.

I think that the private sector probably understands the user better than most of the other administrative and organizational sectors. I think that the private sector has mechanisms for penalizing poor efforts and rewarding good efforts faster and more completely than these other sectors do. It either makes a go of it from a profit standpoint or it doesn't; in the latter case it gets out of the business. Simply from these two intrinsically desirable facets it appears to me that the private sector can take a much more active role in the transfer of all kinds of information, not only to the Congress but to all sectors of our society. As these mechanisms get built up for other users, it will be even easier to supply the information to the Congress as the lawmakers require it.

COMMENT ON KNOX PAPER

Dr. Kenneth Janda, Northwestern University: I am very much interested in Mr. Knox's last problem, the redefinition of the most appropriate role of organizations in our society concerning information transfer. I focus on this in the light of your review of the various kinds of information processing services that have been sparked or sponsored by the executive branch. When information requests come into the Legislative Reference Service, for instance, how much use is made of these external information-gathering bodies for congressional requests?

Lester S. Jayson, Library of Congress: Only on insignificant occasions, very insignificant occasions, do we go outside the government. The Library has extensive resources of its own. We do go to the executive agencies to locate information, which may be available only in their offices, such as statistics from the Commerce Department about oil imports or exports, or things of that kind.

It is relatively rare, however, that Congress wants something that would send us off to the medical library or to one of the highly specialized data banks.

Mr. Knox mentioned the need to know what information resources there are in the nongovernmental area. Here is an example: In the legal field, the University of Pittsburgh has various statutes and codes on tapes in computers. We have a great many occasions where this quick-retrieval device would be very helpful to us, but the facility is not available to us on a day-to-day basis as yet. We made a test of it on one or two occasions because we were anxious to see how it operates, but we are not a paying customer of theirs on a regular subscriber basis.

The information needs of the Congress are broad and they are of different types.

There are situations in which Congress concentrates on particular issues for one or two or maybe three years. As an example let me point to the issue of auto safety. Last year it was a very hot issue. This year it's still a big issue, but next year it's going to be an issue that is pretty much resolved from a legislative point of view. Congress last year, and to some extent this year, needed a lot of technical information in order to understand what was involved. Now, however, that issue is substantially behind us. But, for one very brief period in history, the Congress had to be expert—in the aggregate sense —on the subject of automotive safety and engineering.

Contrast that with the field of agriculture, where the need for information was sustained for decades. This country was a rural country for so many years that members of Congress had to have a continuing knowledge about all aspects of agriculture and its related programs, what the farmers' needs were and the like.

There is always a broad conglomeration of issues facing Congress. There are many small aspects of these broad issues in which Congress must become expert from time to time. It must get the information it needs quickly if it is to become expert enough to provide effective solutions of the issues before the country.

Mr. Chartrand: Given the existence of some information centers within the executive branch and also outside the executive branch and recognizing that Congress really doesn't make very much use of these information centers, we might cite two reasons to account for this.

Mr. Jayson: I know we don't make much use of such centers today at the Library.

Mr. Chartrand: There are reasons for this. One is that the information that outside centers have in their banks is not really very relevant to many congressional requests. Another reason you have alluded to: We have not established a real rapport with the information centers as they exist, or perhaps we aren't able to operate with them yet, using the University of Pittsburgh as an example.

Is it that these outside centers are not inventorying information that is relevant to most of the requests that you get? Or is it that the interface between these centers and—not just the Library of Congress but also Congress more generally—isn't very good?

Mr. Jayson: If I were to give an answer off the top of my head it would be simply that the congressional needs are so varied, and the information systems available today are so narrow compared to the broad spectrum of all knowledge that there isn't much opportunity yet for cooperation. But a beginning will have to be made.

There are areas, for example, in which Congress feels very frustrated by the lack of seemingly available information. In the budgetary area they are trying, as you know, to give the General Accounting Office an automated connection into the executive agencies to enable GAO to meet the constant requests it gets from members concerning the amount of money that is being spent by the entire Federal Government in one particular state or in one particular community.

This information will be readily available at some future time when data about each agency's spending is put into some central machine unit on a routine basis. Then it could be pulled out very quickly. I don't know whether I can answer the question beyond that.

Mr. Chartrand: Among the things we are always looking for in the Legislative Reference Service are sources of available information, particularly statistical types of data, in machine-readable form. I can think of one or two minor achievements we have witnessed in the last 12 or 15 months. One concerned obtaining from the National Science Foundation, on punch cards, information on federal grants to state universities. I remember actually getting hold of a set of punch cards, and this we considered to be an absolute triumph!

More recently there has been increased interest expressed in the federal use of automatic data processing, which is certainly not a totally new area since the Brooks Bill was passed. Here again we were able to discover that there is available, in machine-readable form, certain information on this subject from such places as GSA. But these are only very fragmentary efforts on our part and I think Mr. Jayson reflected the situation very accurately.

Joseph Becker, Inter-University Communications Council: These discoveries are not only fragmentary but also accidental, aren't they?

Mr. Jayson: We often act as a broker of information; if we don't have the information readily available to us, we try to find out where it is. In case we find a data bank of some kind, why that's wonderful.

There is another element to this that I think ought to be injected. You are all aware that the legislature is very jealous of is own role in the Government. It is very frustrated by the fact that a lot of the information that it has to rely upon comes from the executive department. It is very frustrated by the fact that very often it doesn't itself have the means behind it to test the accuracy of that information in some independent way.

It is one thing to deal with statistics that the executive branch can very readily provide. It may be the only place where one can get the information. But it's another thing when Congress has to rely on the accuracy of those statistics and still come up with a different analysis, or with alternatives to

19

a presidential program or an administration proposal for solving a social problem or what-have-you. In the science field it gets to be a lot easier, I suppose, than in the social sciences.

Mr. Knox: I think it is perhaps only because the physical sciences and the natural sciences understood that organized information systems were necessary for their progress before the social scientists and others did.

Mr. Jayson: It is easier, I think, for a member of Congress, once he gets the basic facts, to make a decision whether Congress ought to spend a billion dollars for development of a supersonic transport plane than it is to determine whether a particular program is going to aid the farmer.

Mr. Knox: I call that technology too, unless it is simply a problem of economics.

Mr. Jayson: Well, I'm talking about the economics field also. You see, congressmen can visualize something much more concretely when it comes to the supersonic transport; they can estimate how much money will be involved, and they can recognize many of the problems of the sonic boom and so forth.

Dr. John S. Saloma, Massachusetts Institute of Technology: This question gets back to Ken Janda's comment about why some of this data isn't used. We have at MIT an experimental project Ithiel de Sola Pool is working on called the ADMINS system. The MIT group is setting up a comprehensive file of social science survey research data and attempting to look at this problem. How do you take a wide range of surveys and make them interchangeable, or usable, so you can ask comparable questions? Can you design a computer-based system that enables you to reorganize completely the original data files according to your requirements?

They have found, at least in the early phases, that most of the surveys to date include a good deal of data that do not meet quality standards. This deficiency suggests that as you begin to ask questions across the board of a number of agencies, which are using or surveying social science data, you will begin to develop quality controls that will make information more useful. The current discussion on social indicators also points in this direction.

Also, once you begin developing a central data system, or standards for social science data, you should be able to tie in the various pieces of surveys and statistics that already exist in governmental agencies. I think the knowledge of the existence of such a central system will in turn begin to attract other private and public data resources that aren't being tapped by the federal government today.

Comprehensive, random-access, social-data files are still in the developmental stage. It probably will be several years before a system like ADMINS is perfected at the university level and then transferred to the use of the government or private industry.

Mr. Chartrand: As you are going along, are you defining the evaluation criteria? In other words, do you plan to engage in a running assessment of the efficacy of this activity? This is something I always look for, because so very often, as I think everyone around this table has seen, well-thought-out or grandiose endeavors have been undertaken without the criteria for assessment being formulated and agreed upon in advance.

Dr. Saloma: I am not sure of the administrative background of the project but I know there are people from Harvard and other areas who are working with comparable data that have used the ADMINS system and worked on its development. So it is being reviewed and criticized by some of the top people in the field.

Mr. Chartrand: Mr. Jayson, you recently attended a meeting involving social scientists. Some of the discussion centered on the integration into the Scientific Information Exchange of certain information that heretofore had not been included. I think the meeting was the National Conference of the Legislative Research Services for the states. You were quite impressed because at that meeting, perhaps for the first time, there were some discussions along this line.

Mr. Jayson: One of the things they are working on, through automation, is bringing together all research activities going on in the state legislative bureaus. Thus, a state, if it has to undertake some research with reference to highways or taxes or what-have-you, instead of immediately embarking upon a research task of its own, would be able to find out what research is currently being undertaken by others, or what re-

21

search has already been done, by searching a central bank of information.

Mr. Knox: In this connection, I presume you were trying to be all-inclusive because there are centralized groups in various sectors. For example, in the case of highways, which you mentioned, the Highway Research Board, which is operated by the National Research Council, does that very thing. Its information is made available to the Science Information Exchange. This is one of the deals I helped work out while I was in the executive offices.

As a matter of fact, they operate a computer-based system there that uses the same indexing technology as a counterpart operation (but manual) in Western Europe. So there is quite a bit of free flow.

I don't know what the plans are for tying into outside organizations. I would assume that they would want to do this as they move along. I used highways because they represent, if not the most funds the states spend, at least the second largest amount. Some of the states probably spend more on highways than on education. I think the state of Georgia, for example, when I grew up, was spending more on highways than on education. That's why I am what I am.

Mr. Becker: How do you keep track of new data banks that might be of interest to the Congress?

Mr. Jayson: This is done largely through our own specialists. Our researchers know that they are responsible for their particular fields, whether it is taxes or what-have-you. We would expect them to know what is available in their fields and where to look for it. We, ourselves, as an organization, don't maintain any central index of that kind.

Mr. Becker: As far as I know, there is no mechanism of that kind in existence. Even Mudge and Winchell, the two subject-reference books used most frequently by librarians, do not include any references to the existence or location of magnetic-tape files.

Mr. Jayson: I think this is one of the areas which in years to come will be centralized.

Dr. Janda: Along this very line, I had an encouraging experience with the Library of Congress National Referral Center. I had made a pretty exhaustive search of tertiary sources like

Europa Yearbook and Mallory's *Handbook of the World* to gather election data for countries around the world. Ironically, I had no trouble in finding such information as cinema attendance per capita in Gabon for 1955 or 1966, but often I had great difficulty learning if a given country had an *election* in a given year—much less learning the distribution of seats among the parties in the legislature. That was the problem I presented to the National Referral Center over the telephone, after outlining the various sources I had already examined. My contact at NRC asked if I preferred a letter or telephone call in response to my inquiry. I requested a letter. About a week later, he wrote informing me of material that really wasn't relevant to my interest. Nevertheless, I was very pleased to find out that these information sources were in their files. For instance, he told me about the Yale Political Data Program, which collects and distributes cross-national data in punch card form. He also told me about the cross-national holdings available from the International Data Library in the University of California at Berkeley.

While neither of these information sources contained the data I sought, I was pleased to learn that the National Referral Center included them in its information base. The letter also suggested contacting the Department of State, which I had on my list but had not yet checked out.

But I was pleased to learn that an inquiry to the National Referral Center would direct the requestor to such "unconventional" sources of information as the Yale Political Data Program and the Berkeley International Data Library.

Mr. Jayson: You were dealing with the National Referral Center which is not in LRS but in a different branch of the Library of Congress. LRS itself is the department working exclusively for Congress, but those referral services would be available to us to assist our researchers who might go to them, just as you doing research, would go to them.

Mr. Knox: I'm surprised that they would handle your question, because they were set up to handle science and technology. It seems to me your question wasn't exactly under the umbrella of science and technology, as then conceived. Now, if we are going to spread science and technology to cover everything—technology, after all, is considered by some to be the application of knowledge to the useful benefits of mankind—

23

that subsumes a great deal. I think the NRC still is confined to science and technology, but they may have gone beyond that.

Mr. Chartrand: It is worth noting that the National Referral Center does many things on a reimbursible basis. I know that it is conducting at the present time for the Air Force an exhaustive bibliography on unidentified flying objects (UFOs). This is going to be something that will take many months, for which they will receive a fixed fee.

Colonel Andrew A. Aines, Committee on Scientific and Technical Information, Executive Office of The President: Some of the things that I would like to talk about later are being brought up now. Let me mention one of the difficulties in trying to get at the question of what relationships exist for Congress to exploit the information resources of the executive branch more readily and more efficiently. There is really no organization in Congress primarily concerned with the overall problem of communications, the application of communications to better management of congressional activities. Legislative liaison, I think, is the nearest to this. But I am not sure its charter permits it to negotiate with the executive branch to determine how best to work more closely to improve both information systems and programs. I suspect we will be doing more of this. I call to your attention that this is the first meeting I have ever attended where people in both branches have talked about mutual information problems.

Bill Knox, in the past, has initiated meetings with the top officials of the Library of Congress and we have talked about some of their requirements and some of ours. But I am talking about the development of systems. I suspect that there will be a payoff, a spin-off, if you will, from this kind of a meeting, wherein the need for this will become more obvious, and we will be doing more of it in the future. It is true we have impermeable membranes surrounding our activities to some extent. I would like to see some of these membranes removed so we can work in unison in developing information systems.

Mr. Chartrand: The need for increased education and orientation of the various parties concerned is a key to the future. Obviously, we are talking about both the leaders, the program directors, and those who are the actual participants at the working level. This need is very much with us and is one of the essential things that is going to have to take place in order for us to cope with this so-called "cybernetic revolution."

ROBERT McCLORY*

Automatic Data Processing as a Major
Information Tool

THE FACT that Congress needs additional information support comes as no surprise to the distinguished members of this seminar. Indeed, this seminar itself—the first to be devoted exclusively to the information requirements of Congress—testifies to the growing awareness of Congress' need for the best and most selective information possible with which to carry out its constitutional and public responsibilities. I wish to commend the American Enterprise Institute for its efforts in convening this forum, and I am certain that the discussions developed in these meetings will elicit an even greater concern from the public and from the Congress, regarding the information problems of the legislative branch of government.

It is no secret, least of all to members of the House and Senate, that Congress is a heavily burdened organization. According to a recent study by the American Political Science Association, the "average" Congressman works a 59½ hour week, dividing his time among the myriad duties of committee work, constituent business, legislative study, and party functions, in addition to time spent on the House floor. As national and international problems grow more difficult and the legisla-

---

* Mr. McClory's paper was presented by Mr. Bill Casselman, Assistant to Congressman McClory.

tive process becomes more complex, it is increasingly important that the individual congressman be supplied with timely, accurate, complete, and relevant information with which to make his legislative decisions.

Few members of Congress are qualified by experience to discuss in detail the applications of automatic data processing or the fine points of systems-analysis procedures. However, it takes no technical expertise to realize that Congress does not possess the information-handling capability to make the legislative decisions expected of it in the face of the "information explosion" now taking place in the private and public sectors of the economy.

The daily flow of information to the members and committees of Congress is truly staggering. The growing dilemma of the congressman and his staff centers about the voluminous written information—reports, books, periodicals, specifications, memoranda—which must be screened, reduced to a usable length, and filed for later reference. When one considers that more than 13,000 bills and resolutions have been introduced in only five months of the 90th Congress, the need of members and committees for up-to-date information, regarding pending legislation, becomes alarmingly apparent. Yet, despite these tremendous information requirements, Congress possesses virtually no automatic data processing capabilities. As a recent management study of the Congress by Arthur D. Little, Inc. revealed, "the use of high-speed computers to facilitate the work of Congress and its committees is almost non-existent."

By contrast, the executive branch of government has long recognized the merits of ADP in dealing with its own information-handling problems. The number of electronic computers in use by the departments and agencies of government has risen from 90 in 1956 to a projected 2,252 for fiscal 1967. Judging by the outlay of funds for ADP equipment and services in the executive branch, an estimated $1,292,000,000 for fiscal 1967, the electronic computer has taken its place alongside the typewriter and dictaphone as a standard capability used in dozens of ways by the executive branch. At a time when the legislative branch is particularly concerned with inroads by the other branches of government into its traditional prerogatives, it is ironic that Congress equipped itself so meagerly to meet the information requirements of space-age government.

To give Congress the kind of information-handling capability which a modern legislature requires I introduced a bill late in the second session of the 89th Congress to authorize the Legislative Reference Service of the Library of Congress to acquire and make use of automatic data-processing equipment and techniques in the performance of its functions. This was the first bill applying ADP techniques directly to the work of the Congress to be introduced in either the House or the Senate. In the 90th Congress I re-introduced this bill and was joined by 13 other members, representing both parties, who introduced identical bills.

During Senate consideration of S. 355, the Legislative Reorganization Act of 1967, the substantive language of my bill, H.R. 21, was offered as an amendment by Senator Hugh Scott, Republican of Pennsylvania. This language was adopted by a voice vote, and without opposition from the Senate floor, becoming part of the Reorganization Act finally approved by the Senate on March 7. S. 355 is now pending before the House Rules Committee.

The Scott amendment does not provide for specific applications of ADP to the work of Congress. There are, however, several such applications which would appear to be of particular value to the legislative process. These are, for example:

—The collection, formation, and maintenance of key information relating to each public bill before the Congress, including the legislative history of such bills.

—The automated compilation of the *Digest of Public General Bills*, published by the Legislative Reference Service.

—The creation of a general repository of vital governmental data—including current information on issues before the House or Senate, an index of congressional documents, or perhaps the entire U.S. code stored on magnetic tape.

Automatic data processing is a tool for the storage and processing of information that is useful to the Congress. There is no doubt in my mind that the creation of a computer-oriented information system for use by the Congress will have immeasurable beneficial effect upon this branch of government. The prerogatives as to how it is used, where and when it is applied—in other words, the judgmental decision-making functions that are the essence of Congress' existence—these remain with the members of Congress.

It is of the utmost importance that Congress become educated in the general applications of ADP to the legislative process, that it begin to take advantage of the information-handling capabilities made possible through ADP. Certainly, the American Enterprise Institute—through its publications and through seminars such as this one—has gone a long way toward meeting this goal. However, much remains to be done, and I am hopeful that—through seminars for members and staff, through debate, and by the enactment of appropriate legislation—the Congress will come to understand and cope with its information problem.

COMMENT ON McCLORY PAPER

Dr. Saloma: With the politics of the Reorganization Act such as they are, is there a good prospect that a reform like the one proposed in Congressman McClory's bill could get through by itself, or are you really depending on the general reorganization bill to get action this session?

Mr. Casselman: Leaving political commentary aside, I think the fact that H.R. 21, which Senator Scott incorporated in the Legislative Reorganization Act, was adopted without opposition in the Senate should certainly give it some precedent for favorable action by the House without being a part of a general reorganization act. H.R. 21 is truly a bipartisan or a nonpartisan bill. For this reason it's somewhat difficult to envision any real opposition to it. We haven't seen any yet.

We are hopeful that this bill will come out of committee as part of the Reorganization Act because it should be an integral part of any comprehensive congressional reform measure. There are other data processing provisions in Title II of the Reorganization Act, which direct the Comptroller General to prepare data summaries and things of that nature, but these provisions do not overlap the language of our bill.

Mr. Chartrand: I might add one point of fact. Also contained within the Legislative Reorganization Act (S. 355) is a section discussing the possible future role of a Joint Committee on Congressional Operations, which would be responsible for oversight of the development of automatic data processing for the Congress.

Mr. Jayson: I think this is one of the prime considerations in setting up that committee. I think it would be looking into use of ADP for the Congress and, as a matter of fact, I have heard that it may threaten the McClory proposal's chances.

Mr. Casselman: We are not sure of this yet. What we are sure of is Congress' present need for a data-processing facility and the logic of establishing such a facility via the Reorganization Act.

Paul Armer, The RAND Corp.: I wonder if we are over-emphasizing ADP when dealing with the information needs of the Congress. ADP is certainly an enormously important tool and will become more important in the future, but I wonder if the discussion has concentrated too much on ADP. I am very pleased to see someone here from a congressional office who can tell us first hand about its information needs.

Mr. Casselman: The information needs are quite diverse, I find. As I mentioned, what we emphasize is the sheer volume of material that comes into a congressional office, perhaps half of which is useful and half of which never gets read. If you read the wrong half, you may have troubles. I just can't stress enough, particularly with regard to committee work and the decisions which a member must make on the floor, the need for some type of concise information summary regarding issues under consideration. The problem is that there is always too much information. There is also a need to give Congress, through the Legislative Reference Service, an information-handling capability that would permit analytical evaluation of budgetary information submitted on a P-P-B basis by executive departments and agencies. This should be particularly helpful to the appropriations committees. Finally, there are the "housekeeping" needs that I previously mentioned.

Dr. Janda: In the committee report there is a statement of several recommendations. One of the recommendations is a very general one saying that a Joint Committee on Government

Operations should be concerned with the application of data processing to the activities of the Congress. That can be looked at in two ways. One way, it's so vague that it may never get implemented. On the other hand, it's so broad that it would encompass everything.

So there is a real question, even if the Act were to pass, how the recommendations would be implemented. It could be so vague that nothing really gets done. It depends on who happens to be on the committee and who would like to try to push that kind of activity. It certainly had a broad enough charge, given the wording of that particular provision, and assuming it's pretty much the same as it was in the report.

William M. Capron, The Brookings Institution: I think that there is a real cautionary flag, we call it the yellow flag out at Indianapolis, that should be waved about focusing too much on ADP.

The statement was made, which surprised me, that half of the stuff that comes into a congressman's office is useful. I would have said it's probably more like 10 percent. But, ADP itself doesn't help sift information. This requires people. While the result of the sifting can be efficiently recorded and made accessible on a timely basis through ADP, the machine is not really able to do this, of course, by itself. And I don't know of any program that has been developed yet which reads a document and decides whether it's worth anything. This requires a human input, and I think that the results of the work, for example, of the Legislative Reference Service, can be made much more efficient by the use of the ADP. But the prime thing is getting good people there and in the congressmen's offices who can be intelligent about the data and the machine as a tool.

Now, Paul Armer is here and he is probably going to tell me that he can write a program which will read documents and report and tell me whether they are good or bad. That will be indeed a marvelous thing, but I don't think we have it yet. So I think the people part of ADP, and the fact that this is a tool for intelligence and not a substitute for intelligence, is extremely important and ought to be emphasized.

JOSEPH BECKER

Role of National Information Networks

THE SUBJECT that I am to cover this morning is information networks. Networking has long been with us. We are familiar with an old network, the telephone, which has existed now for 30 or 40 years in the United States; it is a very effective, very reliable, two-way communications system with some 90 million phones in the United States now. These are not connected to one another but to switching stations that have evolved through sampling techniques the telephone company uses to determine the traffic distribution of telephone conversations in the United States. This has led to a series of central offices, secondary stations, primary stations, regional stations, with interconnecting trunklines.

When we speak of networking in terms of information systems, we are talking about moving printed information, digital information, graphic information through arteries of communication now having the capability to carry these different forms. These arteries can handle not only voice information but also the digital information which the computer speaks. This opens up quite an opportunity for sharing information resources that couldn't previously be shared.

For example, in the library world it has been traditional for copies of the same books to exist in different libraries. Each locality has concentrated on the notion of local self-sufficiency, essentially duplicating the other institution's collections and efforts in order to satisfy the local community. This has been as it should be, because the population has, up to now at least, been required to come to a central building, a library, in order to make use of its catalogue information as well as of its resources.

But with the opportunity to transmit information, we suddenly can think in terms of broadcasting information from a library rather than having the library serve only as a passive receiver of information. The library can now be thought of as an institution which can also be an active transmitter of information.

Technological developments suggest that, in addition to being able to transmit digital information over these telephone lines, we are upgrading our facilities in the country so that we can accept what the communications specialist calls "wider band transmission." This, then, will give us the additional capability of scanning film and sheets of paper, regardless of what is on the film or paper. Essentially, video techniques can be transmitted with the same ease to which we have grown accustomed in oral communications.

Research is going on in the country today which suggests that, with satellite communications broadcasting and TV broadcasting capacity, it will be possible not only to send out TV programs on a continuous basis—because we have already become accustomed to receiving them in our homes on this basis —but incrementally, in response to a specific inquiry on the part of an individual. In other words, short bursts of messages will be sent out over a television facility that will wind up at a specific monitor, just as our conversations now wind up at a specific telephone.

Moreover, this monitor can have associated with it a video recorder that will receive, unattended, the information you have requested from some remote location. That conversation can take place over standard telephone lines but only your set will receive those frames, recorded on a video recorder not unlike the AMPEX and SONY recorders that are now available. In addition, Westinghouse is building a video disc that will fit in between this video recorder and the TV monitor. This will give you the opportunity to replay information on your own TV screen at home or in the office at your pace and according to your own schedule of interests.

These are exciting ideas because they suggest that we will in the future have communication arteries in this country that will be moving information at a rate and with an ease that do not exist today. Although we do not have information networks, strictly speaking, in existence today, there are certainly trends toward the development of such networks. For example, in the library community, the Library of Congress has a project which it calls MARC—machine readable catalogue. It is recording on magnetic tape the same information which it customarily puts on three-by-five catalogue cards. I was in the state of Washington recently and I watched them process one of those tapes, submit it to a computer program there, which came along with the tapes from the Library of Congress, and produce a wide variety of products to serve the state. This capability means that the cataloging, the intellectual effort which was expended at the Library of Congress in cataloging this book, no longer has to be done at 16 institutions in the state. In Washington, librarians have formed a small local network of their own to utilize the same system. Even the little labels on the spines of the books are prepared by machines for each of the participating libraries, thus conserving a good deal of clerical time throughout the state, time that can be released to provide professional help in other areas of library interest.

This is one indication of the way in which the functional, mechanical side of library operations can be improved by communications. The same information can then become available in a centrally or regionally distributed data bank. It can then be *accessed* by teletype much like Dr. M. Kessler's project at M.I.T. General Electric has a comparable project that is commercially available. Once the data are in machine-readable form, they have the additional value of being available for retrospective as well as for current use.

The library community is not the only one that is thinking in such terms. The engineering community is very much interested. The very fact that you can now time-share computers utilizing programs that have been developed by other people throughout the country for their own purposes, while using your own data, means that we are beginning to see a sharing of computer programs and resources on a scale that was not heretofore possible. Here is another way in which communications can help.

In the financial and banking area all we have at the moment is the ability to get a stock quotation from an exchange, but there are plans under way to record transactions, individual transactions, and to derive from them a whole series of statistical data that can be used to analyze the economy of the country.

As for medicine and law, we have talked briefly this morning about our desire to provide the individual, in the first instance the family physician, and, in the second instance, the attorney, an opportunity to gain access to information in a more uniform and consistent manner than exists at the present time.

If you look at the distribution of physicians in the United States, you will notice that most of them are physically close to big cities and to printed resources, to information resources that can support them, but quite a number of them elsewhere in the country lack access to such information. With communications, however, it becomes quite possible to equalize the distribution of information to all parts of the country, giving each individual physician, for example, an opportunity to obtain access to the same kind of data in the time-frame of his need.

The world of education, with which I am now associated, is much aware of this problem. It thinks not only of sharing information resources and files that exist in different locations, such as the one at M.I.T. that was described earlier this morning, but also of ways to use networks to support teaching. For instance, the greatest human talent, the most eminent specialist in a given field at Harvard, can make his lectures available to Alabama and to other schools in the country where, at the moment, such resources do not exist.

So I see networking as an adjunct to ADP. I think the wedding of the computer to communications already has taken place. What we are seeing now are the early stages of the marriage. I predict that this is going to be a very close and continuing relationship. It suggests that, if we have in the Congress files of data which are machine processable, then we should start building systems now which will support the information needs of the Congress. In addition, however, I recommend that Congress' ADP center also develop into a communications center of a sort that has the capability of reaching out to other information networks, such as the few that I have described, in order to take full advantage of the detailed information of interest to the Congress, which exists elsewhere.

COMMENT ON BECKER PAPER

Mr. Chartrand: I think that we have reflected here, in several different ways this morning, the fact that the use of any tool or any technique is a function of the education of the users. This is such a cliché I almost hesitate to repeat it.

But, I think that this question of meaningful interaction between elements—whether it be the Congress and, let's say, lobbyist organizations that provide information, on one hand; whether it be between universities and state governments; or whether it be between a regional development commission and federal agencies back in Washington—deserves our closest attention. It is the age-old question: How willing are the people involved in any system to depart from the printed circuitry of human behavior? It is a fact that all of us follow certain well-known patterns, and we don't like to depart from these. How can necessary change, such as we have identified here today, be expedited? In what ways can we urge people to use these new techniques, whether it be a dataphone or a computer?

To handle the traffic between the members and committees of the Congress and the Legislative Reference Service, for a number of years we used six telephone lines to receive the majority of inquiries through the central point. Recently, additional telephone lines were installed, and it was only a matter—I'll exaggerate—of hours before the additional capacity was saturated.

This question, then, might arise in many persons' minds: What unrecognized need still exists, not necessarily on the part of Legislative Reference Service serving the Congress, but in terms of the channels that need to be opened by the Congress to those other areas of information support that were identified earlier this morning?

Bill Casselman, would you care to comment about the difficulty of simply identifying where to go to get the key information that is asked for either by the member in his legislative role, in his congressional office operations, or in trying to support a constituent? I know this is something you face every day.

Mr. Casselman: This is true, and I do want to touch on this as a collateral point. I think you said it when you mentioned the need to educate users, and I think Bill Capron touched on it, too, in stressing that: "idiot input yields idiot output," as Congressman Curtis has said on occasion.

I think, until you can—or perhaps it is a question of can you—educate the congressional staff member to the point where he knows what information can be asked for from networks or from data banks, we will be in trouble. I think this is crucial. Indeed, it is one reason why, in the McClory bill, we located our data processing center in the Library of Congress, in order to allow a screening of user requests. I think there is a tendency on the part of most congressional offices to ask for anything and everything, without any discretion as to what is available or what can be made available through the service of LRS.

In this respect I think there is a tremendous need for educating the congressmen and for educating his staff as to what information handling is, its functions and its limitations.

Mr. Chartrand: I know that there are at least a few hundred liaison personnel that are specifically assigned by various executive branch agencies and departments to work with the Congress. Would you care, Bill, to make a comment regarding their usefulness and the way in which your office or other offices that you know about utilize these? From time to time the question arises: What is the best way to humanize the relationship between the members of Congress and these resource agencies in the executive branch?

Mr. Casselman: Again it's a problem of not knowing what to ask for. Perhaps it's a nonrecognition of roles by the Congress and the agencies themselves, as to what information can be given, what information can be received, what's available, and what's relevant. It is hard to characterize. In working with various agencies, one finds that they are all different—they all have different methods and approaches to handling various problems.

Dealing with a military service case is very different from attempting to service funds for a sewer-development project. I think the relationships between the Congress and departments and agencies of government can't be stereotyped at all but can be improved upon by more effective communication. A greater understanding of one another's work requirements and information needs is essential for both the legislative and executive branches of government.

Dr. Janda: I wanted to comment on Mr. Capron's remark that ADP doesn't analyze information. On the one hand, you might point to some content analysis programs that are working on this, but I think we have a long way to go. So I would agree at the present, the computer doesn't really help you analyze information to the extent that you can find out whether a document is good or bad. But you can use the computer to retrieve information that may be more relevant to your purpose, and this can help analysis considerably.

If we use our imagination in thinking about information networks, moreover, all sorts of potentialities emerge for facilitating analysis. When Joe Becker was suggesting video tape for transmitting pages of books, I wondered why one couldn't provide a running audio commentary on the text. The commentator might tell what the author talks about on a given page and how he develops the idea. If you are not interested in the content, you don't have to read that page. There can be very expert criticism and commentary on the text, helping you find the pages you wish to read in their entirety.

Mr. Becker: Paul heard me mention the other day in New York that the University of Wisconsin has a dial-access, medical tape recording library which does pretty much what you say, but it is strictly audio. The audio library contains recordings on about 100 medical topics and surgical procedures, each of which is discussed by an eminent physician in a four- to five-minute statement. A physician, anywhere in the country, can dial Wisconsin at a certain number and hear that discussion, just as we call the weather or get the time.

The interesting thing is, however, that each one of these physicians is working according to a schedule and that he is

37

required to change his tape periodically, based on his new knowledge that he gets through conversations with his colleagues and through interaction with the literature.

You get some kind of a synthesis and some kind of a distillation of the information prepared by an expert in the field. This is then made widely available over the telephone network.

Mr. Armer: I would like to refer back to what Bill Capron said earlier about the dependence of ADP on human input. I am not about to disagree and, in fact, I would make the statement stronger. It is also relevant to what Joe Becker just said.

The political arena is more controversial than medicine, even though medicine does have its controversy. I think rather than "sift" the word is "filter." You are going to have different filters passing different information. We don't want to lose sight of the fact that it is really more complicated than just sifting. Different people with different axes to grind will want to sift their information in different ways.

Mr. Becker: In the case of the medical tape recording library, he signs off. That is, a speaker gives his name, his affiliation, and his telephone number, so that you, if you are willing to pay the cost of another call, can call the speaker directly and discuss any aspect of his remark.

Mr. Knox: Do you consider this something that is a proven pattern of behavior that people will exhibit in large areas, or are you really looking at this as just an interesting experiment?

Mr. Becker: I guess I am looking at it as an experiment at the present time, because it hasn't been tried often enough, but I think the idea will, in time, prove itself worthwhile. To me, the trend is unmistakable toward greater reliance on oral communication rather than on the printed word.

Mr. Chartrand: I might add, Bill, that a number of people on Capitol Hill, members and staff people, have from time to time asked whether or not status information on major bills and resolutions could be put into audio form. Another question is whether or not committee scheduling, involving the activity of the 150-plus congressional committees and subcommittees, might not be put into a form where you would have a short statement that the committee is meeting today in executive session, or open session, or similar basic information.

The Florida Legislature is actually printing out the schedule of its approximately 80 committees on a daily basis, so that each legislator knows each morning precisely what each committee is going to do that particular day.

Michael Hugo, American Enterprise Institute: There is a publication that tries to provide coverage like that for Congress.

Mr. Chartrand: Yes, the *Congressional Monitor*. Again, I hear mixed reactions on the accuracy of the information, but I cannot comment personally. I have heard a few people say they have found, in checking, that some of the information is outdated. Here again is this question, I think, primarily of acquisition of information on a very timely basis, because these committee hearings, for example, change very quickly sometimes.

Mr. Knox: I would like to raise a question of technology here, Joe. Communication of information via the ear channels is a lot slower than through the eye. Do you think this is desirable when we are faced with a need for a desire to use more information, and use it more completely? Do you think it's desirable to encourage oral communication?

Mr. Becker: I don't think that one is a replacement for the other or should ever be thought of as a substitute, but I do believe that there are undoubtedly areas in the information world in which the oral form of communication would be superior to the written. Maybe it's timeliness which is the . . .

Mr. Knox: Can't you have written information just as timely as oral? That is, if it's in the computer in a form such that you can reproduce it through a speaker, it is in a form that you can also reproduce it on a cathode ray tube display.

Mr. Becker: Technically you certainly can do that, but I don't know whether you would want to incorporate into a computer all information—

Mr. Knox: Couldn't you get technologically to a point where the user could receive either an optical projection, print out, or audio response at his option?

Mr. Becker: Probably so. There are some companies now working on techniques for taping essentially a Xerox copy of what you see on the cathode ray tube (CRT).

Mr. Knox: You know, this is an interesting philosophical point and it goes back to this question I raised earlier, about making sure the user is in control of the system design. People probably would, given their choice, rather have no information. That's their first choice: Ignorance is bliss. The second choice then, if they have to have information to carry out what it is they have to carry out due to external pressures on them, would be to get it slowly and in an oral mode. Thirdly, I guess, we would face up to the technical point that, with all of this information to distribute and to gather in, we should use the most effective way we have of putting it into the human brain, and that happens to be through the visual, optic-nerve channel. Should our technology really be encouraging people to use something that is at a lower level of intrinsic value in this process, namely, the oral mode?

Dr. Saloma: Some of the M.I.T. experimentation in information transfer is quite sophisticated, like Project INTREX, which is developing a model computer-based library. But you already have a wide range of information services available by telephone today—time, weather, dial-a-prayer, recorded information on theater schedules. This is a mechanical extension of the telephone network.

I think what you are talking about is the marriage of computers with communication networks where you are able to have on-line interaction between the user and the system—such as where the student or the doctor or the congressman can ask the computer a series of questions from remote locations tension of the telephone network.

Mr. Becker: I saw this recently in a commercial setting in Chicago at Carson-Pirie-Scott. It has its credit information on a computer downtown, and uses the touchtone telephone with·dial card slot. The dial card, in this instance, is the customer's credit card, and it has punched into it the computer's telephone number and the individual's account number. This is depressed into the touchtone telephone and communication is made with the computer. The computer becomes alert to that particular account. At that point the saleslady enters the amount of the purchase by depressing the pertinent push-buttons on the touchtone phone. The new touchtone telephone differs from the rotary dial because it permits you to transmit additional data after the connection has been made.

Here we have an oral device being used for conveying digital information. When that information is received by the computer, it does some logical processing, determines whether credit thresholds have been exceeded, and then composes an appropriate audio response from an audio drum, which has a series of phrases and numbers. The response comes back over the telephone. This is an example of a hybrid arrangement being used operationally in the commercial world. I expect that the medical tape recording system at Wisconsin will eventually use an automatic response mode too.

Col. Aines: It appears to me, Bill, that you are really posing a philosophical question in a sense that I don't think it's possible to solve with legislation.

I would like to go back to some of your earlier words in talking about the marketplace mechanism. It appears to me that if the marketplace prevails, and I hope it will, then the user will determine what it is he wants and what it is he is going to buy.

If it turns out he wants it in the oral mode, I don't think we can quarrel with him. I am sure that protection can, in some way, be extended for the printed word, and I venture to say that McGraw-Hill, Inc., and other publishers will be searching for a way to sell data and information in the oral as well as other modes. Are you trying to tell us that somehow or other there ought to be some retention of what appears to be a totemic arrangement of various media of information?

Mr. Knox: If I gave that impression, I regret it. I wasn't trying to imply anything in my statement except a questioning spirit of what it really is that we ought to be trying to do.

Although I respect their individuality, personality, and humanity, people *can* be educated to do things differently. We try it all the time. They can be educated also to use different alternatives, alternative processes and devices, to accomplish the same end. You and I can be persuaded, and we are persuaded every day, by advertising, to do a certain thing instead of something else.

41

We should encourage experiment. We know so little about this that we've got a long way to go before we run out of good experiments. But I question whether we should be looking toward the continuing allocation of resources to support an information-transfer mechanism that I think operates at a lower level of efficiency than another one; that other mechanism is not printed, but uses the eye to scan material. We still have a long way to go before we beat that as a means of getting information.

Dr. Janda: Your remarks now cause me to change what I was going to say. I was going to say that it's an empirical problem as to which method of information transmission is most effective. We are not interested in the transmission of information per se but in the kind of impact that it will make upon the person. If information makes a greater impact by means of oral communication rather than visual, then we should employ this consequence in our planning.

Ingrained habits, like reading, have been changed by Evelyn Wood's Institute, which demonstrates that we can change people's behavior with some of these devices.

Dr. Saloma: Isn't this really where the experimentation with computer systems in education is leading—to help determine what educational approaches are the most effective? Already we are seeing generations coming into college that speak and think in quite different terms than their professors.

Mr. Knox: I just can't help but believe that if New York City proceeds as it hopes to do and plans to do, with having all six-year-olds at the present time—and it may go down before long to the four-year-olds—learn typewriter manipulation, we are going to have a different response on the part of that generation or that group of people to information-transfer devices. They will be so accustomed to using typewriters that perhaps their willingness to use the traditional information devices that we are familiar with might be different. I don't know whether it would be more or less, but it will be different, because I certainly didn't grow up learning to read by using a typewriter, and they are teaching three-year-olds, you know, to do that today.

Col. Aines: Bill was my colleague for two years at the Office of Science and Technology where we have had many discussions of all kinds, and today we are simply resuming the same conversational procedure, just to understand what thoughts we are trying to convey. The point I want to add is that I hope this doesn't become a problem for us. Perhaps we can accept what Professor Janda was saying a moment ago about experimentation, and agree that we are talking mostly experimentation here.

I know that Dr. Orr, of the American Institute of Research, has been working on the possibility of word compression. That is, he has methods of putting words through mechanical systems and increasing the number of words spoken per minute; say he starts with 100 or 200 words a minute and he keeps increasing the rate to see how much a person can learn to comprehend out of this torrent of words. I think we all favor seeing this sort of experimentation continue. I don't feel at this stage of the game—and I don't think Bill was trying to imply this—that we should consider one method superior to the other, no matter how we are attached to it.

Mr. Capron: Allow me to bring the discussion back more directly to needs of congressmen. Actually this goes for lots of other potential users of all of this technology we are talking about. The point I think we're hung up on now, which is evident in many applications, is the development of an efficient indexing system. The primary need of a congressman, as I see it, is not so much for transmittal of information, but acquiring it for his own use. He wants to go into the library—and I'm using this in the broadest sense—and be able to pull out the information he needs on the question he has. This means we need an abstract indexing system. It's a very tough job because you have to develop a vocabulary lots of people can use. Then a very few words or phrases can be efficiently used by the retriever to go into the memory and pull out just the bits and pieces he wants. As far as research or experimentation goes, one of the things we are not putting enough resources into, at least as far as the Federal Government is concerned, is just a lot of hard work in developing a working indexing system.

I don't know; I'm an economist and we have recently produced—our profession has—an abstracting indexing system of economic service. It's got an awfully long way to go before

43

it's really useful. You still spend a lot of time finding what you really want because the indexers have their own definition of terms. It's going to be a long time before we can make really effective use of information retrieval in a congressman's office, just because it is so hard to ask the question in a way that the system can respond to efficiently.

Dr. Saloma: As information systems become more complicated, at the same time they will become simpler for the individual user, much the way that automobiles have developed. Today there is a generation of Americans who really don't understand a thing about the mechanics of an automobile. I think the same thing will come in time with automatic data systems. Congressmen and staffs which now couldn't begin to cope with programming will be able to in a matter of time. Considerable progress has been made over the past decade in developing new and simpler computer languages.

KENNETH JANDA

Future Improvements in Congressional Information Support

I WOULD LIKE to begin by stating my indebtedness to the American Enterprise Institute for getting me interested in the topic of information support for Congress. My active interest dates back to June 1965, when Professor Alfred de Grazia was responsible for assembling the group of scholars, which produced the book *Congress: The First Branch of Government*. He phoned at that time, asking me if I would contribute an essay on the general topic of automation of the Congress.

The group met at AEI in the latter part of June to discuss the focus of the project and to allocate writing responsibilities. We then retired to our respective universities to write our essays during the summer. So my interest in information systems for Congress really developed in the summer of 1965. While I had experience in information retrieval generally, and its application to political research in particular, I had not tried to focus upon the information-processing problems of Congress.

The paper I prepared at that time appeared first in November 1965, in monograph form. In June 1966, it was published in *Congress: The First Branch of Government* along with 12 other essays on congressional reorganization and reform. As a result of this paper, I found myself appointed to the Illinois Commission on the Organization of the General Assembly in Illinois. That was the start of my interest in information-retrieval systems at the state level.

Before examining the congressional situation, I would like to discuss data processing in state legislatures for its relevance to our concern. I think the state which first used information-processing capabilities was Iowa, when in about 1963, it automated the preparation of its daily calendar of activities. Shortly thereafter data processing was adopted selectively by the Florida Legislature. Iowa and Florida today probably have the two best developed computer systems for disseminating information about daily legislative activities. Interestingly enough, they have developed their systems on different kinds of equipment, involving hardware from IBM, General Electric, and RCA.

Oregon has also used data processing equipment, but in a little different way. It has used a system of remote terminal—actually, IBM's administrative terminal system, ATS—to help draft legislation. They type the legislation on a terminal connected to a computer—without the use of punch cards. Through computer programming, the typist is able to revise, delete, or otherwise alter individual words, lines, or whole paragraphs. Legislation can be amended and typed-out copy can be made quickly ready for reproduction and distribution to the legislators.

New York State also has had a pretty successful application of data processing, but in more of a research capacity than in an administrative capacity. In New York the statutes are stored on tape for rapid search and retrieval of laws relevant to a given inquiry. Perhaps a score of states have contracted for a similar computerization of their statutes, using the methods developed by John Horty and his associates at the Health Law Center at the University of Pittsburgh. These successful applications of computers to legislative activities at the state level are meant to establish the *practicality* of my suggestions concerning "information systems for Congress." These suggestions were set forth in my essay of the same title, reprinted below.

After that essay was published, I talked with people at AEI about implementing my suggestions. I focused upon the relationship of the congressman to his constituency as the easiest level to implement. We might provide a Democratic and a Republican congressman with data processing facilities for the purpose of improving their relationships with their own constituencies. The way a congressman would use the facility would depend upon the political situation in his district. I made several suggestions to guide our choice of congressmen: That they should not be committee chairmen; they should be more or less average members of the legislature; they should come from districts that were neither too competitive nor too safe; and that they should have committee assignments which might lend themselves to computer assistance. We identified several congressmen and prepared to invite their cooperation in our experiment, provided it could attract financial support.

But in our discussion about how to secure funds for our experimental project a major problem developed. If the system really operates to improve the congressman's relationship with his constituency, will it entrench the incumbent in the legislature? As most of you know, congressional politics across the United States produce few "competitive" districts. If one regards a victory of 55 percent or more of the vote as "reflective" of a "safe" seat, about 80 percent of the districts are safe and only about 20 percent competitive.

Many people, including me, do not believe that a situation of noncompetitive politics is especially healthy. If the proposed computer system actually works as planned it might reduce competition even more. Consequently, I countered with a suggestion to secure support for a similar data processing facility for the opposition party organization in the same congressional district.

You see that this leads to all sorts of important ramifications for electoral politics. A proposal to equip the party organization in the congressional districts with information-system capabilities would probably have the important consequence of strengthening the party organizations in these areas. The party organization within a congressional district perhaps would no longer be a captive of the successful candidate, as it often is. Nor would it be an empty structure for the opposing party, as it often is.

47

Needless to say, I am merely speculating about very weighty possible outcomes of an information system for Congress. In view of difficulties in anticipating these outcomes, we decided not to implement any part of the proposed system at that time. In part, this conference today has been arranged to help identify and cope with such problems of implementation.

Information Systems for Congress*

S TUDENTS of government generally agree that the legislative branches of modern governments have gradually lost power relative to the power of executive authorities. This phenomenon has been referred to variously as the "parliamentary crisis," [1] the "atrophy of the legislature," [2] and the "decline of the legislature." [3] Although some students hold that Congress constitutes an exception to this generalization,[4] most detect the same trend in the United States. Indeed this very symposium of recommendations for revitalizing Congress is an acknowledgement of it.

Congress' loss of power is manifested in three important governmental functions traditionally reserved to the legislature: initiating legislation, evaluating legislative proposals, and overseeing the execution of legislation. In recent decades, Congress has abdicated to the President its initiative in preparing a legislative program, has faltered in thoroughly evaluating proposals submitted by the President, and has been unable to exercise effective direction and control over the administration of legislation in which Congress has aquiesced.

Some students of government are not alarmed by the diminution of congressional power.[5] They favor what has been termed

---

* Originally published by the American Enterprise Institute, Washington, D.C., 1965. Reprinted with permission.

[1] David B. Truman (ed.), *The Congress and America's Future* (Englewood Cliffs, N.J.: Prentice-Hall, 1965), p. 1.

[2] William J. Keefe and Morris S. Ogul, *The American Legislative Process: Congress and the States* (Englewood Cliffs, N.J.: Prentice-Hall, 1965), p. 483.

[3] K. C. Wheare, *Legislatures* (New York: Oxford University Press, 1963), p. 221.

[4] *Ibid.*, p. 223; Ernest S. Griffith, *Congress: Its Contemporary Role* (New York: New York University Press, 1961), p. 88.

[5] See, for example, James MacGregor Burns, *The Deadlock of Democracy* (Englewood Cliffs, N.J.: Prentice-Hall, 1963).

an "executive force" model of government, which would ascribe even greater power to the President and relegate Congress to the role of notarizing the President's legislative demands. Other students, including the authors of these essays, do not favor a governmental system in which Congress sits as a corporate notary public and are consequently alarmed by the present imbalance of power between the two branches. Their position is inspired by the belief that democratic government functions neither long nor well in the absence of a strong and independent representative legislature.[6]

As an alternative to government by executive force, this symposium creates a model of government by legislative force wherein Congress functions as a vital, independent authority which boldly initiates legislative proposals, thoroughly evaluates proposals presented to it, and effectively oversees the administration of enacted legislation. The recommendations in these papers are calculated to redirect the flow of power away from the presidency and back toward Congress. They do this by identifying the major obstacles to government by legislative force and by suggesting ways to remove or circumvent those obstacles.

Most of these recommendations are of two types: proposals for reform and proposals for reorganization. Broadly speaking, proposals for reform are designed to make Congress more representative of popular demands within the country and to facilitate expression of majority sentiment within Congress. Proposals for reorganization concentrate on improving the structural and procedural aspects of the legislative process.

The symposium contains many far-reaching proposals for reform and reorganization designed to strengthen Congress. The recommendations in this paper, however, cannot strictly be classified either under "reform" or "reorganization." They are better described as proposals for *retooling* Congress. This paper advocates the development of automated information processing systems to help Congress surmount one of the biggest obstacles to government by legislative force—the lack of information and knowledge by legislators faced with increasingly complex problems and decisions. My concern and recom-

---

[6] This philosophy forms the central theme of Charles S. Hyneman, *Bureaucracy in a Democracy* (New York: Harper, 1950), especially pp. 10–17 and 77–79.

49

mendations focus exclusively upon the information problem confronting Congress.

The Information Problem for Congress

Students of the legislative process have identified the information problem as a major factor in the decline of modern legislatures. Griffith, for example, fixes the need for information in "problems inherent in the complexity and magnitude of the legislative output itself." [7] Woll also notes that "legislation today, in regulatory and nonregulatory fields alike, requires specialized information on the part of policy makers before it can be conceptualized, drafted, and implemented." [8] The legislature's need for information to conduct the business of modern government has not gone completely unfulfilled; it has been satisfied largely by the executive. As Keefe and Ogul have observed, "The problems of modern government now have become so technical and complex that the legislature has found it increasingly necessary to defer to the executive for answers and recommendations." [9]

The concentration of information resources in the executive branch has had several consequences for legislative-executive relations. One of these, Robinson concludes, "is an increasing inclination to rely on the executive for the presentation of proposals to deal with problems. Congress' role, then, becomes less and less one of the initiation of policy alternatives and more and more the modifier, negator, or legitimator of proposals which originate in the executive." [10] Not only does Congress lose initiative in creating a legislative program, but lack of information also prevents Congress from adequately evaluating the proposals it receives from the executive. As Woll states, "To a considerable extent, when the administrative branch can control the channels of information to Congress it can control the policies supported by that body." [11]

[7] Griffiith, *op. cit.*, p. 72.
[8] Peter Woll, *American Bureaucracy* (New York: W. W. Norton, 1963), p. 130.
[9] Keefe and Ogul, *op cit.*, p. 483.
[10] James A. Robinson, *Congress and Foreign Policy-Making* (Homewood, Ill.: Dorsey Press, 1962), p. 8.
[11] Woll, *op cit.*, p. 131.

As a consequence of these developments in legislative-executive relations, the very function of legislatures in the total governmental structure has altered over time. Harris' recent book, *Congressional Control of Administration,* begins, "Control of administration is one of the most important functions of legislative bodies in all modern democracies." [12] A recent survey of the structures and functions of parliamentary institutions in 41 countries concludes with an even starker recognition:

> . . . the legislative function is no longer the preserve of Parliament. The initiative in legislative and financial matters has to some extent slipped out of its grasp; the practice of delegating powers has made for the curtailment of its role in the realm of law. But concurrently, the prerogatives of Parliament have shifted in the direction of control of government activity. The Government initiates and directs; Parliament controls, approves, disapproves and, now and then, inspires. [13]

But how well equipped are legislatures to play this new role? Again the information problem is present—this time frustrating the legislature's direction and control of the executive.

The executive branch is perhaps the legislature's main source of information. [14] As Robinson reports:

> For reasons which are not altogether clear, bureaucracies associated with executive offices have more efficiently collected and processed information than have legislatures. Not only is Congress unprepared to obtain independent information about the world through its own resources, but it must rely on data collected by the executive. [15]

Dahl and Lindblom state in general terms the consequence of a situation which finds the governed possessing more information than the governors:

> Because the hierarchy originates much of the information its nominal superiors require in order to act intelligently, and because the superiors are usually less expert on any particular subject than some of their nominal subordi-

---

[12] Joseph P. Harris, *Congressional Control of Administration* (Washington: The Brookings Institution, 1964), p. 1.

[13] Inter-Parliamentary Union, *Parliaments* (London: Cassell and Company, 1961), p. 298.

[14] Charles L. Clapp, *The Congressman* (Washington: The Brookings Institution, 1963), pp. 115–18.

[15] Robinson, *op cit.,* p. 192.

nates, it is often possible for the hierarchy to manipulate communications in order to control their nominal superiors.[16]

Later on the same page, they continue:

In these situations the saving element is the existence of a plurality of competing and conflicting hierarchies that provide alternative sources of information to those who need to make decisions.

What "alternative sources" of information are available to Congress, and are they adequate to support a vital, independent legislative force in government? Some authors have implied that they are adequate by singling out Congress as one of the few legislatures in the world that has held its own with the executive.[17] Griffith, in fact, asserts: "Congress has mastered, or has provided itself with the tools to master, the problem of assuring itself of an unbiased, competent source of expert information and analysis which is its very own." [18] The tools of which Griffith speaks are Congress' professional staffs:

. . . the enlargement and strengthening of the staffs of Congress have in fact been a major factor in arresting and probably reversing a trend that had set in in the United States as well as in every other industrialized nation. This is the trend in the direction of the ascendancy or even the virtually complete dominance of the bureaucracy over the legislative branch through the former's near-monopoly of the facts and the technical and specialized competence on the basis of which decisions are ultimately made.[19]

Notwithstanding the fact that staff aids have helped Congress considerably with its information problem, few writers are as sanguine as Griffith in evaluating their contribution. The collective judgment seems closer to that of Woll, who writes:

Although Congress has made strenuous efforts to fulfill its constitutional responsibilities, neither its committees nor its staff aids are any match for the administrative branch with respect to knowledge and information in particular areas of legislation. Much of the staff employed by Congress comes directly from the administrative branch,

---

[16] Robert A. Dahl and Charles E. Lindblom, *Politics, Economics, and Welfare* (New York: Harper and Row, 1953), pp. 260–61.

[17] See footnote 4.

[18] Griffith, *op. cit.*, p. 88.

[19] *Ibid.*

in which initial competence was acquired in an atmosphere where the points of view of the agencies predominated.[20]

Keefe and Ogul concur: "No matter how hard the legislature tries to inform itself (and Congress tries very hard indeed), its store of information and its access to necessary knowledge are rarely if ever as developed as that of the executive authority." [21]

One test to determine whether Congress has adequate access to information for fulfilling its governmental function is to examine congressmen's attitudes toward obstacles confronting them in performing their job. Unfortunately there has been little reliable data available on this point. But a recent study by Dartmouth's Public Affairs Center has provided the answer at least for the House of Representatives.[22]

Findings for a random sample of 80 representatives interviewed during the summer and fall of 1963 indicate that congressmen do not feel that they have adequate control of information. Each respondent was asked to "name any problems which prevented him from carrying out the role he would like to play in the House and all problems which he saw as preventing the House from operating as he thought it should." [23] The responses were grouped into 14 categories; the percentages of all respondents mentioning something in each category are given in Table 1.

As Table 1 clearly shows, by far the largest number of responses (78 percent) came under the category of "complexity of decision-making; lack of information." The same evaluation of the importance of this problem was expressed publicly by congressmen attending a conference held early in 1964 on

---

[20] Woll, *op cit.*, p. 131.

[21] Keefe and Ogul, *op. cit.*, p. 483.

[22] This study is reported in Michael O'Leary (ed.), *Congressional Reorganization: Problems and Prospects—A Conference Report* (Hanover, N.H.: Public Affairs Center, Dartmouth College, 1964).

[23] *Ibid.*, p. 22. According to personal communication from Roger Davidson, one of the researchers, the exact wording of the questions was as follows:

"Now, what are the most pressing problems you face in trying to do your job as Congressman—what are the things that hinder you in your tasks?" and "What are the most pressing problems which prevent Congress from doing what you think it ought to do?"

Answers given to both these individual and institutional foci were lumped together in Table 1.

TABLE 1: General Categories of "Problems" Articulated by
Eighty Members of the House of Representatives [a]

Type of problem	Percent mentioning
1. Committee system, seniority system and Rules Committee	27
2. Scheduling and general procedure	43
3. Member pay, office allowance, staffing	26
4. Diffusion of leadership and "failure" of incumbent leadership	23
5. Caliber of individual members	29
6. Problems arising from present operation of separation of powers	50
7. Problems of House-Senate comity	12
8. Public lack of understanding of Congress and failure in communicating with constituents	45
9. Service for constituents	58
10. Electoral system and electoral vulnerability of Members; campaigning	30
11. Complexity of decision-making; lack of information	78
12. Criticisms of present power distribution and policy output of the House	38
13. Lack of time [b]	39
14. Other	9

[a] Source: Table V in Michael O'Leary (ed.), *Congressional Reorganization: Problems and Prospects—A Conference Report* (Hanover, New Hampshire: Public Affairs Center, Dartmouth College, 1964, pp. 22–23).

[b] "Because 'lack of time' is such an obvious and commonplace problem, we excluded it from analysis whenever a Member mentioned his quota of ten other problems. It is therefore underrepresented in this table." *Ibid.*

the role of Congress in the American democratic process.[24] The summary of conference proceedings states:

Many members stressed that the quality and quantity of legislative output is jeopardized by the problems of gathering information. One Congressman expressed the conviction of most conferees when he stated that a high-priority goal should be to improve the gathering and analysis of information and the detailed consideration of alternative policies by Congress. It is in these areas, he felt, that Congress is most deficient.[25]

Thus, lack of adequate information for developing knowledge and making decisions is recognized by scholars and legis-

[24] This was the first annual Orvil E. Dryfoos Conference on Public Affairs, held on the Dartmouth College campus, March 7–8, 1964.
[25] O'Leary, *op. cit.*, p. 45.

lators alike as one of the major problems confronting Congress. Various recommendations have been made to cope with this problem in one way or another. Recommendations for home rule for the District of Columbia would, for example, reduce Congress' work load and provide members with more time to become informed about other legislation. Suggestions for electric voting machines to record roll call votes would also save time and presumably free congressmen for reading and otherwise informing themselves. And, of course, all proposals for increasing Congress' professional staffs are directed toward the information problem.

Despite the variety of these proposals, they are all curiously restricted in range. Basically, they can be divided into two types: those which offer the congressman more *time* and those which offer more *help*. Few offer him more *information*. Although these various recommendations impinge upon congressmen's lack of information, they do not attack it *directly* as an information problem. They are restricted in failing to propose information processing solutions to an information problem.

Many scholars and legislators have apparently resigned themselves to the inevitability of inadequate information. This thinking is revealed in the Dartmouth Center analysis of congressmen's own opinions about their problems:

> . . . an examination of [Table 1] leads to the important conclusion that most of the problems perceived by Congressmen relate to conditions which are only marginally, if at all, susceptible to reform. The most frequently mentioned set of responses relates to the complexity of decision-making—the problem of obtaining adequate information and of selecting the proper alternative from among many conflicting courses of action. This group of problems —about one-fifth of all those mentioned—is probably a concomitant of policy-making under any set of rules or organizational form, rather than a manageable, "reformable" situation.[26]

Dahl and Lindblom display a similar fatalism in conceding, "Probably the problem of the modern legislature cannot be solved. But it can be reduced by changing and simplifying the agenda of legislators."[27]

---

[26] *Ibid.*, p. 23.
[27] Dahl and Lindblom, *op. cit.*, pp. 322–23.

By failing to view the lack of information as an information problem, one is led to recommend oblique rather than direct solutions. In this era, however, direct solutions to information problems are available through the use of automated information processing systems.

Present Use of Information Systems in Government

The relatively recent development of methods and equipment for information processing may account in part for the failure to propose information processing systems as a solution for Congress' problem. Real advances in mechanical means of information processing did not come until the advent of electronic computers, which were not marketed until the early 1950's. Then there is always a lag between technological innovation and its application to practical problems.

Nevertheless, the paucity of recommendations for introducing information systems within Congress is still hard to understand, for automated information systems have been used in business and industry since the late 1950's. Moreover, as we will see, executive agencies of the government have long been engaged in programs of research and development of information systems to meet their own needs. Yet, the idea of information systems for Congress has still not caught on.

Consider the recommendations recently published in the *Interim Report* of the Joint Committee on the Organization of the Congress.[28] This document summarizes results of hearings conducted from May 10 through June 25, 1965. During this period, testimony and statements were received from 12 senators, 51 members of the House of Representatives, 17 political scientists, and representatives of 13 different voluntary associations. The recommendations advanced by congressmen, political scientists, and organizational representatives are summarized, respectively, in Appendices A, B, and C to the *Interim Report*. Within each Appendix, the recommendations are classified into categories of proposed reforms. Table 2 summarizes the total distribution of recommendations within each category.

---

[28] U. S. Congress, Joint Committee on the Organization of the Congress, *Interim Report* (Senate Report No. 426, 89th Congress, 1st Session, 1965).

From hundreds of recommendations [29] summarized in the *Interim Report,* only three can be classified even liberally as proposals for providing Congress with integrated information processing systems. Under the category "electronic aids and television," the *Report* listed Representative Edmunson's suggestion for establishing "a public information center in the Capitol with an electronic board providing information on matters under consideration on the floor, name and location of committee hearings, etc." [30] The same category contained the Council of State Governments' proposal to use "automatic data processing for bill indexing, statutory search, budget preparation, etc." [31] (Most of the other recommendations under this category dealt with such items as television, filming, and recording floor proceedings and installing electric voting machines.) The third and most comprehensive recommendation for an information system was listed under "research services," where Professor Alfred de Grazia referred to the use of computers and information processing methods for developing "an adequate intelligence and research system." [32] (Other recommendations for "research services" dealt with expanding the Legislative Reference Service and forming a scientific advisory commission for Congress, among other things.)

The *Report* contained other recommendations intended to increase the information flow to Congress, but these neglected to include means for *processing* the information before use. In one sense, Congress has quite enough information available in the form of bills, reports, speeches, testimony, regulations, decisions, and so on. Congressmen are swamped with documents produced by Congress itself, and they are deluged with publications of executive agencies. On the one hand, not all this information is needed by Congress, while, on the other hand, Congress still needs much information it does not get. Speaking more properly, Congress' problem is one of obtaining *relevant* information. What Congress really requires is a procedure for acquiring the information it needs and a method for processing that information in order to learn what it wants to know. This conception of the problem suggests that far

---

[29] See footnote b in Table 2.

[30] *Interim Report, op. cit.,* p. 18.

[31] *Ibid.,* p. 28.

[32] *Ibid.,* p. 23.

TABLE 2: Distribution of Recommendations for Suggested Reforms of Congress Made in Hearings of the Joint Committee on the Organization of the Congress,[a] May-June 1965

Category of Reform	Number of Recommendations [b]
Committee Chairmen	18
Committee Jurisdiction	25
Committee Meetings	21
Committee Staffing	16
Office Staffing and Workload	17
Housekeeping Functions	23
Research Services	14
Fiscal Controls	45
Scheduling	14
Floor Procedures	26
Electronic Aids and Television	13
Oversight	14
Elections and Campaigns	10
Ethics	13
Foreign Policy	8
Leadership Policy	10
Total	287 [b]

[a] These data are compiled from the enumeration of suggested reforms in Appendices A, B, and C to the *Interim Report* (Senate Report No. 426, 89th Congress, 1st Session, 1965) of the U.S. Congress Joint Committee on the Organization of the Congress.

[b] Recommendations by congressmen, political scientists, and voluntary associations in each category have been summed without regard to duplication. Because some recommendations by the three groups may be substantially the same, the amounts in the Table do not necessarily represent numbers of *different* reforms. Some overlap exists, but the effort required to eliminate duplicates was judged greater than the gain in accuracy to be achieved.

more is required than just increasing the information flow to Congress. It suggests information processing systems that are integrated with congressional tasks, functions, and activities.

Although the hearings did not produce many recommendations for automated information systems, some members of the Joint Committee on Organization expressed a personal appreciation of their possibilities. The statement of Representative Brooks is particularly relevant:

My experience as sponsor of legislation dealing with the streamlining and centralization of the Government's automated data processing equipment and procedures leads me to believe that the committee should explore the services of modern technology as it can assist the legislative process, especially in the areas of ADP [automatic data processing] and other electronic devices. Such innovation is not to be shunned if it would help the individual legislator to better fulfill his role as an informed representative.[33]

Representative Brooks' statement refers to the successful use of data processing techniques within the executive branch. The branch of government with the lion's share of informational resources has been increasing its information processing capacity while Congress, which sorely needs to develop these muscles, has been virtually inactive. This situation clearly emerges from a review of executive and legislative activities in research and development of information systems during the last eight years.

Widespread interest in information processing systems and their applications in business, industry, government, and academic research has developed only within the last decade. In July 1957, the National Science Foundation inaugurated its periodic survey of activities in information processing with the publication of issue No. 1 in its continuing series *Current Research and Development in Scientific Documentation.*[34] Each issue in the series not only discloses new projects underway but also updates earlier reports—providing a statement of work in progress at the time. The continuous expansion of information processing activities during the period from July 1959 to November 1964 is reflected in the steady increase in the number of pages in each issue. This trend is graphed in Figure 1, which shows an increase from 55 pages for issue No. 1 to 486 pages for issue No. 13.

Some indication of governmental activities in information processing can be obtained by reviewing the projects reported

---

[33] U. S. Congress, Joint Committee on the Organization of the Congress. *Hearings*, Part 1 (89th Congress, 1st Session, 1965), p. 12.

[34] Issues in this series were published semi-annually through issue No. 11 dated November 1962. Publication had fallen behind schedule, however, and the eleventh issue did not appear until 1963. The series was resumed with issue No. 13, which was dated November 1964. That issue carried a notice stating, "No. 12 will consist of an indexed bibliography of all reports and publications cited as references in Issues Nos. 1–11. This report is scheduled for publication in early 1965."

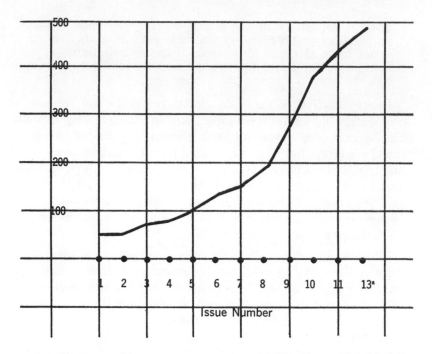

FIGURE 1: Increase in Number of Pages with Each Issue of Current Research and Development in Scientific Documentation, No. 1–13

[a] See Footnote 34 for an explanation of the absence of Issue No. 12.

in these surveys.[35] Most of the projects reported on were undertaken by universities and private corporations. From the beginning, however, some research work was conducted directly by the government—and almost exclusively by agen-

---

[35] Perhaps a better source of information for such a review would have been the National Science Foundation publication series *Nonconventional Technical Information Systems in Current Use*, which reported on systems that embodied new principles for the organization of subject matter or employed automatic equipment for storage and search. But according to my inquiries and my examination of the *Monthly Catalog of U.S. Government Publications*, this series terminated in October 1962, with issue No. 3. For the sake of continuity in reporting, I decided to use *Current Research and Development in Scientific Documentation* exclusively in this paper. Furthermore, it deserves to be noted that the term "scientific documentation" has been interpreted very broadly in the CRDSD series, which reported projects under such headings as "organization of information," "information needs and uses," "mechanical translation," and "equipment development."

cies in the executive branch.[36] Three of the 43 projects (7 percent) reported in July 1957 were conducted by executive agencies: two by the National Bureau of Standards and one by the U. S. Patent Office. By November 1964, 22 of 496 projects (4 percent) were reported by executive agencies. My compilation of the projects reported by all government agencies during this period is given in Table 3. Format inconsistencies from issue to issue and mistakes in tallying entries

TABLE 3: Projects Undertaken by Government Agencies as Reported in "Current Research and Developments in Scientific Documentation," Issues No. 1-13 [a]

Agency Issue No.:	1	2	3	4	5	6	7	8	9	10	11	13 [a]
National Bureau of Standards	2	2	3	6	6	6	4	4	7	7	8	7
U.S. Patent Office	1	1	1	1	1	1	1	1	1	1	1	
Rome Air Development Center	1										1	1
National Library of Medicine			1	1	1		1		1	1	1	1
U.S. Atomic Energy Commission						1	1	1	1	1	1	1
Armed Services Tech. Info. Agency						1	1	1	1	1	1	
U.S. Army Chemical Corps Res. & Dev.						1	1	1	1			
National Institutes of Health						1			1	1	1	1
Air Force Cambridge Research Lab.							2	3	3	3	3	1
Post Office Department								1	1	1	1	1
Department of Defense									1	1	1	
Library of Congress									1	1	2	2
U.S. Forest Service									1	1	1	
U.S. Naval Ordnance Test Station									1			
Walter Reed Army Medical Center									1	1		
U.S. Army Biological Laboratories									1	1	1	
Department of Agriculture									1	1	2	
Bureau of Ships										1	1	
U.S. Naval Postgraduate School										1	1	
National Agricultural Library												1
U.S. Public Health Service												1
Totals per issue: [b]	4	3	5	8	8	12	10	13	20	23	27	22

[a] See footnote 34 for an explanation of the issue sequence in this publication series.

[b] Some agencies reported progress on the same projects in each issue. Amounts at the bottom of the columns, therefore, cannot be summed so as to give the total number of different information processing projects undertaken by governmental agencies.

[36] It is not always easy to decide what is and what is not an executive agency. Some of my decisions might be challenged. For example, the Rome Air Development Center was classified as an executive agency; the RAND Corporation was not. Disagreement with some of my classifications should not, however, be great enough to produce different interpretations of the data.

from tables of contents may have produced some errors in my tabulation, but the inaccuracy cannot be great.

A word is in order about the nature of these government projects. Some of them—like the Post Office's attempt to devise an optical scanner that will read addresses and sort mail, and the Air Force Cambridge Research Laboratories' work on pattern recognition and speech analysis—cannot easily be construed as giving the executive an edge over Congress in managing information and knowledge. But in general, experience in any type of automated information processing begets other applications, and such projects provide the requisite experience. Moreover, some of them clearly do contribute to the executive's ability to manage information. A case in point is the Defense Department's project "to design an all-computer document retrieval system which can find documents related to a request even though they may not be indexed by the exact terms of the request, and can present these documents in their appropriate order of their relevance to the request." [37]

The question may arise as to why Congress cannot be content with using the information systems developed within the executive. Why must Congress develop its own systems? This question deserves several answers. The first, of course, is that Congress' information needs are somewhat different from those of the executive and are unlikely to be fulfilled by any combination of systems prepared within the executive branch. Secondly, even granting that congressmen might use the executive's information systems upon occasion, they would not use them with the proficiency that comes from familiarity. And congressmen cannot be expected to familiarize themselves with every agency's particular system. Lastly, there is some doubt as to whether executive agencies would in fact grant congressmen unlimited access to their information systems. A staff report prepared by the Senate Committee on Government Operations in 1960 revealed such reluctance by an executive department to share its information resources with Congress:

> .The staff was informed by officials of the Department of Defense that the Library of Congress was not being fully utilized as a scientific and technological storage

[37] Statement provided for the National Science Foundation report *Current Research and Development in Scientific Documentation*, No. 9 (Washington: U.S. Government Printing Office, 1961), p. 48.

center by the Department of Defense because much of the Department's material is classified, and that it is the Department's position that a documentation storage center of this nature should be a part of the executive branch, and not under the jurisdiction of the legislative branch of the Government as is the Library of Congress. Further, it was pointed out that it is the practice of the Department of Defense and other agencies to withhold from the Library classified and certain other information which is now being withheld from committees of the Congress under executive policy. This position is based upon the premise that such information should not be made generally available to any agency of the legislative branch, since it would then be available to committees of the Congress, and be inconsistent with Presidential policy. The executive branch of the Government has consistently held that officials thereof should not provide information to the legislative committees when it is considered to be in the national interest to deny such information, or when it is related to so-called internal affairs of the executive branch and not a legislative concern of the Congress.[38]

All these considerations argue strongly for the development of information systems *by* Congress for use *within* Congress.

In 1965 the same Senate Committee on Government Operations reported on interagency coordination of information systems and commented on the relevance of all this activity to Congress' responsibilities:

> It may be observed that, as the executive agencies better organize their intra-agency information systems and hopefully, interagency systems, they may thereby facilitate the studies of expert committees of the Congress.
> It may also be noted that for the fulfillment of its many duties, the Congress may wish to have the latest technological systems directly at its own command.[39]

What has Congress actually done so far to place such systems at its own command? In contrast to the work in progress by the executive branch, the National Science Foundation surveys disclosed only two projects conducted under authority of the legislative branch. The earlier project, first reported in 1961, was to survey

---

[38] U.S. Congress, Senate Committee on Government Operations, *Documentation, Indexing, and Retrieval of Scientific Information* (86th Congress, 2d Session, Senate Document No. 113, 1960), pp. 18–19.

[39] U.S. Congress, Senate Committee on Government Operations, *Summary of Activities toward Interagency Coordination* (89th Congress, 1st Session, Senate Report No. 369), p. 27.

. . . the possibilities for automating large research libraries, with the Library of Congress as primary focus of the survey. The emphasis of the survey is on the information organization, storage, and retrieval functions of libraries whose collections number in the millions and which serve research through the availability of both current and retrospective literature.[40]

The later project, first reported in 1963, was designed to determine user reactions to the Library of Congress' *Monthly Index of Russian Accessions*. While the second project does not pretend to improve Congress' position relative to the executive in the struggle for information and knowledge, the suggestion for automating the Library of Congress, which resulted from the first project, may have real strategic consequences.[41] Notwithstanding this effort, Congress has hardly distinguished itself by exploring the applications of automated techniques to its information problems.

If Congress itself is not undertaking these explorations, perhaps it is contracting them out to other organizations? How does Congress come out on this standard? Beginning with issue No. 6 in May 1960, *Current Research and Development in Scientific Documentation* has indexed projects according to their sponsoring organizations. The index to issue No. 6, for example, discloses that executive agencies (mainly the armed services) sponsored a total of 36 projects, although they themselves conducted only 12.[42] Figure 2 graphs the total number of projects sponsored and undertaken by government agencies, as reported in each issue of *CRDSD* since 1960.

Although the armed services sponsor most of the government's information processing projects by far, many civilian

---

[40] Statement provided for the National Science Foundation report, *op. cit.*, p. 64.

[41] A report on this project is published in The Council on Library Resources, *Automation and the Library of Congress* (Washington: Library of Congress, 1963). Also relevant are the proceedings of a conference reported in Barbara Evans Markuson (ed.), *Libraries and Automation* (Washington: Library of Congress, 1964).

[42] The organization of the index in *CRDSD* did not facilitate checking for duplicate sponsorship. Because two or more agencies could sponsor the same project (and sometimes did), this does not mean 36 different projects. Moreover, there may be some additional overlap because of agencies mentioned both as sponsors and as conductors of a project. But my examination of these possibilities suggests that these occurrences would not significantly alter the pattern of data if taken into account.

The tally of projects supported by executive agencies does not include grants awarded by the National Science Foundation.

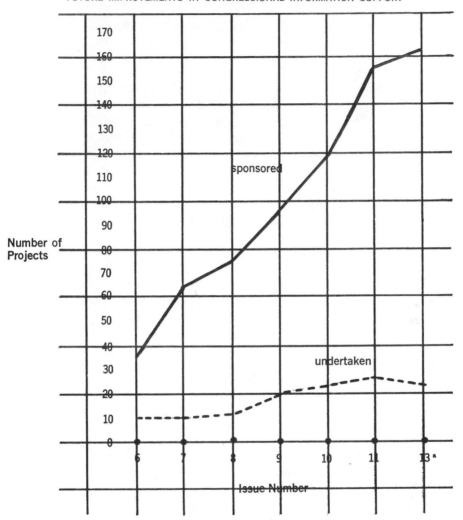

FIGURE 2: Growth in Number of Projects Sponsored and Undertaken by Governmental Agencies as Reported in Issues No. 6–13 of Current Research and Development in Scientific Documentation.

ᵃ See footnote 34 for an explanation of the omission of Issue No. 12.

agencies have also been listed as sponsors—including the Office of Technical Services in the Department of Commerce, Food and Drug Administration, Office of Education, Fish and Wildlife Service, and the Peace Corps—to mention some that have not reported their own propects. In contrast to the support given by executive agencies for research and development in information systems, the National Science Foundation surveys disclosed *no* projects that were financed by Congress or its agencies. The projects undertaken by the Library of Congress mentioned earlier were *not* financed by Congress. The study of user reactions to the *Monthly Index of Russian Accessions* was supported by the National Science Foundation, and the more relevant investigation into automating large research libraries was supported by the Council on Library Resources, Inc.

The foregoing analysis of projects reported in *Current Research and Development in Scientific Documentation* was intended to illustrate Congress' lethargy in exploring the application of information processing systems to its information handling problems. By any standard, its activities in this area lag far behind those of the executive branch, which is already far ahead in informational resources. An extrapolation of present trends indicates a broadening, rather than a narrowing of the "information gap" that now exists between Congress and the executive.

The thesis of this paper is that this gap can be reduced substantially by retooling Congress with modern equipment and techniques for information processing. Before suggesting in some detail how this might be done, a few words are in order about some technical aspects of information processing systems.

Technology of an Information System [43]

It is perhaps most important to point out initially what automated information systems are *not*. They are not devices

---

[43] This paper will not discuss technology of information processing in any detail, but there is a growing literature on the subject. On computers in general, see Bert F. Green, Jr., *Digital Computers in Research: An Introduction for Behavioral and Social Scientists* (New York: McGraw Hill, 1963). Information processing is treated in Charles P. Bourne, *Methods of Information Handling* (New York: Wiley, 1963); Allen Kent, *Textbook on Mechanized Information Retrieval* (New York: Wiley, 1962); Joseph P. Spiegel and Donald Walker (eds.), *Information System Sciences* (Washington: Spartan Books, 1965); and Allen Kent (ed.), *Specialized Information Centers* (Washington: Spartan Books, 1965). Kenneth Janda, *Data Processing: Applications to Political Research* (Evanston: Northwestern University Press, 1965) may be helpful to the beginner.

for grinding out policy decisions, and they are not designed to replace human judgment. Rather they are intended to provide the human decision maker—here, the congressman—with knowledge for making informed choices. Automated systems for information processing, therefore, should not be confused with electronic schemes for solving complex social and political problems by putting them on a computer.

Dahl and Lindblom caution against sophomoric thinking that machines can replace man in decision making:

> Techniques regarded by some people as of great importance are mathematics and electronic calculators. Crudely stated, if there are too many variables for the human mind to handle at once in policy judgments, the problem is to reduce the variables to mathematical equations that can be fed into electronic calculators for a solution. Thereby, it might be suggested, an entirely new level of rationality in policy decisions would be possible, a leap forward roughly equivalent to the invention of language, writing, printing, or mathematics itself.
>
> It is not really open to doubt that mathematics and electronic calculators can be of enormous aid in a number of specialized situations where quantification in comparable values is possible. . . .
>
> Yet it would be easy to exaggerate what mathematics and electronic calculators are capable of. For as a substitute for decisions by human beings through social organizations the electronic computer suffers from several basic limitations.[44]

The limitations that Dahl and Lindblom recount deal with inabilities to reduce all variables to numbers, difficulties in assigning values to alternatives, uncertainties about consequences of actions, and problems in controlling those who control the machines. All of these limitations, and others, attest to the absurdity of substituting computers for congressmen.

When Dahl and Lindblom published their book in 1953, computers were used almost exclusively for solving mathematical problems. Now, however, computers deal with words as well as numbers, with sentences as well as equations. They can therefore accept questions and provide answers. Computerized information processing systems are not designed to solve problems by means of mathematical equations but to provide infor-

---

[44] Dahl and Lindblom, p. 76. *Congress: The First Branch of Government.*

mation upon request. They propose not to eliminate the congressman as a decision maker but to increase his capabilities for making decisions by telling him what he wants to know.

A computer's ability to do arithmetic in a hurry is well known, but a computer can do other things as well. It can make logical decisions: if value A is larger than value B, do X; otherwise, do Y. It can also manipulate symbols, reading data in one way and printing them out in another. These capabilities enable computers to do more than just "compute." Speaking more broadly, they *process* data. The term "data" is usually associated with numerical values, and, strictly speaking, computers recognize and deal only with numerical values. But numbers can be made to stand for letters of the alphabet, which enables computers to process alphabetical as well as numerical data.

The term "information processing," in its broadest sense, applies to computer handling of either alphabetical or numerical information. "Information retrieval" is a somewhat more restricted term, frequently reserved only for computer processing of alphabetical information. In an even narrower sense, "information retrieval" is sometimes applied only to computerized systems that store alphabetical information in memory, search the memory according to a set of instructions, and then retrieve items of information which satisfy the instructions. This paper will employ "information retrieval" in its narrower sense—meaning storage and retrieval—and "information processing" in its broader sense—including data processing and information retrieval.

Interest in computer processing of textual material first began with problems of information retrieval. Although librarians have always been engaged in storing and retrieving information, applying computers to these tasks seemed to breathe new life and interest into the methodology. Information retrieval technology now involves more than just computers, and considerable progress has been made with the use of microfilm and even purely mechanical devices. However, while product development in non-computer techniques of information retrieval seems promising, computers will clearly be the dominant force in information processing systems of the future.

Until recently, non-computer information systems had the great advantage over computers of being immediately accessible to the user: the system (e.g., a file of key-sort cards) could be at his side, available for use whenever he wanted an item of stored information. But few people could afford to maintain an electronic computer stationed alongside their desk at their beck and call. Economical use of the computer required that it be placed in a central location and fed a series of "jobs" assembled in "batches." The answers to a specific job, even a short one, could not be obtained until the entire batch had been processed and all the results printed out. The period of time required between submitting a job for processing and picking up the results—called the "turn-around time"—depended on the nature of the equipment and its work load. Even now, it is not at all uncommon for turn-around time to average about six hours, which is hardly quick enough to satisfy demands for immediate information. Recent technological developments in the computing industry, however, have brought the processing power of computers much closer to the user and his needs.

The development of "time sharing" and "remote terminals" has produced the first feasible desk-side information processing systems. "Time sharing," as its name implies, enables many different users to tap into the same computers at the same time. In actuality, the computer processes only a small part of one person's job at a time while rotating from user to user. But it returns so quickly that the wait is unnoticeable to the user, who feels he has sole use of the machine to answer his inquiry —thereby eliminating turn-around time completely. "Remote terminals" are input-output devices located in the user's office and connected to a central computer (usually on a time-sharing basis). These devices enable the user to communicate his inquiry to the computer (input) and provide for the computer to express its answer (output) without requiring a trip to the computing center.

Important advances in input-output devices themselves have also increased the value of computerized information processing systems. Typewriter keyboards now allow the user to type out his inquiry to the computer as if he were preparing a memo to his assistant. In due time, the user will even be able to communicate his request orally to the computer. And the perfection of optical scanning devices will empower the computer

69

to "read" instructions typed, printed, or even handwritten on paper. Still more flexibility appears in types of computer *output*. The computer can answer by typewriting (for short replies) or through a high-speed printer. It can also display information on a cathode ray screen for viewing or photographing. If desired, standard oral messages can be recorded on tape and selected for response.

Not all of these devices have been fully developed, but perfection is close at hand. Time sharing and versatile remote terminals should certainly be incorporated in planning information systems for Congress.

Features of an Information System for Congress

The information processing system sketched out below is meant to illustrate ways in which electronic equipment and computers can help congressmen perform their job. Its various features presuppose a sophisticated level of technology. Although some features incorporate devices that have not yet been perfected, the system in its broad outlines can be put into operation with present capabilities. In any event, the task of recommending an information processing system for Congress should not be limited by the capabilities of today's equipment. Not only can we count on continuing progress within the industry to increase the performance and improve the flexibility of computing hardware in general, but we should also be aware that manufacturers are often able to design and build machines to meet customers' individual needs and specifications. This is already routinely done for agencies in the executive branch, most notably for the armed services. Preserving the strength and integrity of our national legislature—and thereby preserving the virtue of our government—is worth the price of some research and development to deliver the system that Congress needs.

The system outlined here is not necessarily the ideal one for Congress. It is suggested as a starting point for future thinking. Of necessity, the suggestions are not very specific, for specific suggestion would involve specific equipment, which is certainly premature. Instead the features of the system advanced here are primarily designed to illustrate how information processing can be tied directly to congressmen's daily activities.

Information systems for Congress probably should be organized on four different levels, serving Congress as a whole, each chamber separately, committees within Congress, and individual congressmen. The levels of organization are not irrelevant to type and amount of computing equipment needed. It is hardly conceivable that a single computer, however gigantic, can service the combined needs of Congress, each chamber, scores of committees (standing, select, special, and joint), plus 535 individual members and their staffs. Some configuration of computers would probably be required to handle this load. Be that as it may, this discussion will largely ignore physical requirements and assume simply that each congressman and each committee will be served by a remote input-output terminal connected on a time-sharing basis to some central computing facility.

The proposed features of an information system for Congress will be grouped and discussed according to different levels of organization.

Congress as a whole: Certain kinds of information can best be collected and processed centrally for the use of both houses of Congress. Individual congressmen would tap into this centralized service.

1. *Informing congressmen of relevant bills:* Every congressman develops interests in particular legislative measures. These interests may develop from committee work, personal attitudes, or constituency requests; they may be permanent in nature, or merely temporary. At present, congressmen seek to locate bills affecting their interests by searching the "Daily Digest" of the *Congressional Record* and other publications about Congress, such as *Congressional Quarterly*. Sometimes the congressman finds what he wants; sometimes not. In any event, his search always requires time, and he seldom can be confident that he did not miss something relevant to his interests that was indexed under a different heading. Moreover, the congressman never has the information come after him; he must go after it.

An information retrieval technique called "selective dissemination of information" (SDI) has a very definite application here. SDI originally was developed to notify scientists as their

71

library received new publications relevant to their research interests. In brief, SDI operates as follows.[45] The scientist personally prepares a list of the key terms describing his research interests. This list, which constitutes his "interest profile," is stored on magnetic tape, along with interest profiles from many other scientists. Meanwhile, as each new publication comes into the library, a group of abstractors examines the document, describes its contents with a set of key terms, and prepares an abstract summarizing the research. Periodically this information is also recorded on magnetic tape. The computer then compares the scientists' interest profiles with the key terms describing each publication. When a document is found that deals with a term in a scientist's interest profile, the computer prints on a special form the name of the scientist and the abstract of the document. This form is then mailed to the scientist, notifying him that such-and-such a publication has been received in the library. If, upon reading the abstract, he decides he would like to see the whole document, he can return the card by mail to receive a copy of the original publication.

Much the same idea can be used for notifying congressmen of bills relevant to their interests that have been introduced in either house of Congress. Congressmen could establish their own "interest profiles," which could be changed or updated at any time, to be matched against abstracts of bills prepared soon after they have been introduced. Through a remote terminal in his office, the congressman could be notified of the bill, its sponsor, and the committee to which it was referred. He could then send for copies of the bills that especially interest him simply by typing the appropriate request on a keyboard input to the computer. At somewhat greater expense, the computer could actually print out complete bills upon his request.

If a congressman were to change his interest profile during the session, the system should be able to search the entire file of bills previously introduced. In fact, the system should be able to search all the bills for specific key terms by any congressman upon request. The main advantage of using interest profiles in an SDI system is to disseminate information of interest to con-

---

45 SDI is described in detail in *IBM, Selective Dissemination of Information* (White Plains, N.Y.: IBM Technical Publications Department, No. E20–8092, dated 1962).

gressmen *selectively* and *automatically.* Relevant information is literally brought to their attention without their having to go after it.

2. *Disseminating information about lobbyists:* At present, lobbyists are required to register either with the Clerk of the House or the Secretary of the Senate. These registrations are required by law to be published quarterly in the *Congressional Record.* However, there is some question about how useful this reporting procedure is to congressmen.[46] For this reason, it is proposed that registration data on lobbyists could be stored on magnetic tape and made available for computer search and retrieval. Congressmen could then instruct the computer to search the lobbyist file for the name of any individual who has approached him with respect to legislation before Congress. Through its remote terminal, the computer could reply immediately whether or not the person is a registered lobbyist, whom he represents, with what particular piece of legislation he is concerned, what organizations he has represented in the past, his address, etc.

There is no doubt about the importance of the role in the governmental structure played by lobbyists, who constitute one of the most valuable sources of independent information available to Congress. The purpose of this recommendation is not to hamstring lobbyists' operations but to place congressmen in a more knowledgeable, and therefore more advantageous, position from which to interact with lobbyists. This proposal reflects the familiar thesis that "knowledge is power." Whatever increases the knowledge of individual congressmen increases their power, and thereby strengthens the position of Congress as an institution. Increments to knowledge can come from many quarters, and this proposal to keep congressmen informed about lobbyists is simply one possibility.

3. *Communicating with the Legislative Reference Service:* The Library of Congress and its Legislative Reference Service are already engaged in automating their information handling procedures. Congressmen's terminals could tap into these systems for routine interrogations of their information files. Specialized inquiries, however, might better be communicated

---

[46] Lester W. Milbrath, *The Washington Lobbyists* (Chicago: Rand, McNally, 1963), pp. 318–19.

through the terminals to a reference person in the Library of Congress or LRS, who would translate them into technical requests for computer searching. Results of the search could be routed directly back to the congressman through the terminals. This direct connection would again increase the amount of knowledge available at the congressman's fingertips.

4. *Searching the U.S. Code:* The entire U.S. Code of Laws has already been recorded on magnetic tape by the Health Law Center of the University of Pittsburgh and is available for computer processing.[47] The tape can be searched for laws affecting any given subject. The computer can retrieve all laws under that subject in the Code and also find laws dealing with one subject but entered under a different heading. It should be noted that at least one state legislature already has such a "legal retrieval" facility at its command. State Senator Earl W. Brydges reports on New York's system:

"Give me all the laws affecting banking that are not in the banking law," New York Senator Jeremiah B. Bloom recently asked the computer. The machine spewed forth 1,604 of them that this experienced lawmaker never knew existed. "This means," he said, "we have to bring sense out of this disorder. How can any bank possibly know its duties and obligations with so many laws scattered all over the legal lot?" And when Senator Bloom starts to modernize the law, the computer will point out duplications, obsolete sections and reorganize the laws into a logical order on command.[48]

Congress should provide itself with at least the same capability for conducting its lawmaking business that state legislatures have seen fit to develop.

Each Chamber of Congress: Some activities of Congress, particularly those of a scheduling and housekeeping nature, are best handled on the basis of each chamber. Applications of information processing techniques to a few such activities are illustrated below.

1. *Locating bills in the legislative process:* Congressmen should be able to learn immediately upon request the location

---

[47] John C. Lyons, "Computers in Legislative Drafting," *American Bar Association Journal*, June 1965. See also Earl W. Brydges, "The Electronic Solon," *National Civic Review*, July 1965, p. 351. I want to thank John S. Appel for calling this citation to my attention.

[48] *Ibid.*, p. 350.

of any bill in Congress, its status in the chamber, and its history of action to date, including amendments, committee votes, floor votes, and scheduling for future action. This information could be gathered within each chamber and immediately stored in the computer. It could then be recalled by the congressman simply upon keying the bill number into the remote terminal typewriter. The response should appear at the terminal in one of two forms: a printed message—if hard copy is desired—or visual display on a cathode ray tube—if the information is to be used immediately. In general, the use of visual display units in input-output terminals would substantially reduce the amount of paper messages generated by the computer, and would thereby result in savings on material and filing of documents with transient value.

2. *Providing information about votes:* One of congressmen's main complaints is that they find it difficult to obtain information about measures on which they must vote.[49] Summoned by sound of the voting bell, congressmen sometimes rush into the chamber with little or no knowledge of what the vote is all about. Often the only information available is that supplied by a colleague on the floor or even by the doorkeeper. A chamber-based information system can substantially increase the congressman's knowledge of the vote as it is announced.

With the announcement of the vote, his office terminal can reveal the issue involved along with the bill number, sponsorship, legislative history—all of which could be taken from the information files proposed above. It would also be possible to build into the system, if desired, voting positions favored by the President and adopted by party leaders, including also perhaps the positions of individual congressmen volunteered in advance of the vote. At somewhat greater expense, announcement of the vote could include a summary of the issue and consequence of the vote for passage of the bill. The net result of these proposals would be to arm individual congressmen with relevant information in order to make more rational voting decisions.

3. *Providing for automated voting:* Voting itself can be viewed as an information process, with individual congressmen originating information instead of receiving it. But replacing

---

[49] Clapp, *op. cit.*, pp. 145–49.

traditional roll call voting in Congress with electronic voting machines is a controversial proposal—notwithstanding the fact that these machines have been used for varying lengths of time in 30 states legislatures.[50] The Dartmouth survey of congressmen's attitudes toward this innovation reveals 62 percent opposed to it and 35 percent in favor, with 3 percent undecided.[51] On the other hand, the *Interim Report* of the Joint Committee on the Organization of the Congress shows electronic voting advocated by five congressmen, two political scientists, and one organizational representative—while opposed by only one congressman.

The main advantage claimed for electronic voting machines, of course, is the saving of time. Galloway has calculated that recording votes electronically would have saved the 78th Congress as much as two calendar months.[52] While virtually everyone concedes the time-saving advantages of automated voting, opposition to this innovation is sometimes rooted in the fear of what *else* it will do besides save time. The authors of the Dartmouth study of congressmen's attitudes toward reforms detected this apprehension:

> Some efficiency-minded respondents looked to electronic voting as a method of saving at least an hour of their time each day of a session; other Members, equally concerned with the demands on their time, explained their opposition to automatic voting by suggesting a "horror show" of unanticipated consequences of such an innovation.[53]

Probably the most vocal opposition to electronic voting stems from concern that installation of voting machines would limit congressmen's freedom to attend to business outside the chamber. This is the position taken by Representative Matthews,

---

[50] Council of State Governments, *Book of the States: 1962–1963*, Vol. XIV (Chicago: Council of State Governments, 1962), p. 54.

[51] O'Leary, *op. cit.*, p. 58. The representatives were asked to state if they agreed or disagreed with this proposal: "Use electronic voting devices on the floor of the House, which would record a Member's vote on any measure on which one-fifth of the Members present request such a vote (that is, the present requirement for a roll call vote)." Conceivably, some congressmen might be in favor of electronic voting based on some other criterion or perhaps on all votes. Therefore these figures may understate support for electronic voting in general.

[52] George Galloway, *Congress at the Crossroads* (New York: Thomas Y. Crowell Co., 1946), p. 80.

[53] O'Leary, *op. cit.*, p. 25.

the single opponent of the innovation listed in the *Interim Report*.

> I think the fact that we have 20 or 30 minutes in the House—and I don't know, sir, what the time is in the Senate—to leave from attending to those myriad responsibilities at other places and yet get to the House to answer the roll is more of an advantage than the electronic voting device. . . .
> . . . it would seem to me that we have our committee responsibilities and can't always be right on the floor. We are over in our offices, or meeting with a delegation, for example. And the electronic system may not necessarily work here in our setup as well as it would work and as it does work in some of the State legislatures.[54]

The same attitude is revealed in the remark addressed to an advocate of electronic voting by Representative Griffin, a member of the Joint Committee:

> . . . when you suggest that we have electronic voting and electronic devices for taking quorum calls, are you saying that committees should never sit while the House is in session?
> I raise that question because I think in order for it to be effective, all the Members would have to be on the floor in order to press their electronic button or whatever it is.[55]

It is true that voting machines in state legislatures require members to be present on the floor in order to cast their votes. But this condition can be eliminated through proper technology and, in itself, constitutes no real obstacle to automated voting in Congress. At the very least, congressmen could be empowered to cast their votes by direct connection from their offices.[56] Various electronic safeguards might be employed to insure that this power is not usurped by imposters voting in the congressmen's stead. One obvious protection against this would be closed-circuit television showing the congressman casting his vote. The action could be recorded on video tape

---

[54] Joint Committee on the Organization of the Congress, *Hearings, op. cit.*, p. 130.

[55] *Ibid.*, p. 37.

[56] There seems to be no constitutional requirement for congressmen to be present when casting their votes. The relevant passage states, "and the Yeas and Nays of the Members of either House on any question shall, at the Desire of one fifth of those Present, be entered on the Journal" (Article I, Section 5).

and preserved to prove the legality of each vote. An even more ambitious step toward freeing congressmen to move about Washington without missing out on roll call votes would be to establish congressional "polling booths" in government buildings throughout Washington for their use while visiting executive agencies. These too could be equipped with closed circuit television and devices to protect against usurpation.

The point is that proposals to install electric voting machines should not be defeated merely by arguments that this would restrict congressmen's freedom. Under proper planning, it could very well increase their mobility while saving their time. On the other hand, electronic voting might deserve to be rejected for the reason that it would impair Congress' vitality rather than improve it. Other authors in this symposium, for example, fear the loss of personal contact and communication that now occurs when congressmen congregate for roll call votes.

The introduction of electronic voting would undoubtedly have many unknown consequences for congressional behavior. Perhaps additional assessment is required in order to predict its net effect upon Congress. But vague fears of unanticipated consequences alone should not kill this innovation. Virtually all change brings some unforseen results. The task is to calculate carefully according to best available knowledge, and choose the means best designed to achieve a given goal. To do more is impossible; to do less, irrational.

Individual congressmen: Congressmen vary in their legislative interests, constituency relationships, and styles of operation. Any information system for Congress should be adjustable to fit their individual needs. Here are a few suggestions of ways in which each congressman might use his own information processing facilities.

1. *Deciding how to vote:* Many pieces of information are important for congressmen's voting decisions. Some of this information can be furnished automatically by computer announcement of every vote, as described above. Yet there are many political factors, personally important to the congressman, that would not be included in the announcement but which he might like to review before voting. For this purpose, each congressman should be equipped with computing facilities to

handle his personal file of information and his own retrieval system.

When a roll call vote is announced, the congressman could use this system to review his voting record on the subject; past votes can be stored in memory and recalled for study. He could also examine the attitudes of various groups in his constituency toward the issue; the computer could retrieve whatever constituency data he had read into storage beforehand. Exactly what he would put into storage would depend on what information he has collected and how his system has been organized. He might, for example, want to recall his own speeches and public statements on various issues. In the last analysis, the shape taken by the system would be determined largely by the imagination and resourcefulness of individual congressmen.

2. *Maintaining relations with his constituency:* Congressmen could use their computing facility for performing a variety of constituency-oriented activities. Constituents' names and addresses could be stored in memory along with other relevant data for automatic preparation of specialized mailings, e.g., to campaign contributors, labor leaders, businessmen, supporters of the congressman's party, supporters of the opposition party, and so on. Constituency mail might even be answered with the computer. Some printing devices now have both upper and lower case characters, which would give each computerized reply the appearance of an original letter, with the printing done at the rate of hundreds of *lines*—not words—per minute.

Obviously, this computing capability might also be used to analyze polling data and elections returns, thus helping the congressman in his continuous campaign for re-election. Here again, input to the computer would depend largely on the politics of the congressman's constituency and the ingenuity of individual congressmen. A man from a safe district might not bother with such analysis; one from a competitive district might cultivate it to a high degree.

3. *Reading and analyzing written material:* Modern congressmen are expected to devour daily an astounding stack of reading matter. In addition to the massive *Congressional Record* there are bills, committee reports, House and Senate documents, agency reports, constituency mail, newspapers, and

so on. Much of this material need only be quickly scanned for occurrences of terms of interest before thoughtful reading begins. Other material has to be analyzed thoroughly, sentence by sentence. Automated equipment definitely can be used to scan documents for relevant passages marked by certain terms and—perhaps surprisingly—can also be employed for careful content analysis, sentence by sentence.

Some progress remains to be made in optical scanning equipment before computers are ready to assist congressmen with their reading load. Devices have already been built, however, that can read a variety of type fonts and enter the information into a computer for processing.[57] All the material to be read need not be stored in memory; this would soon exhaust the storage capacity of the largest computer. Instead, programs can be devised that would retain only material which satisfies search instructions that are given to the computer beforehand. In this way, the computer would not generate reel upon reel of magnetic tape for the thousands of pages it reads. It would analyze information in the process of reading it and be selective about what is communicated to the congressman.

Congressional committees: Most legislative work in Congress is conducted through committees, and at least the standing committees should serve as a basis for organizing a congressional information system. However, it is even harder to be specific about system features at the committee level, for the shape of the system will depend largely on the committee's jurisdiction and will have to be tailor-made to its workload. But a few general features readily suggest themselves.

1. *Compiling histories of committee action:* Over the years, each committee often considers many bills with identical or quite similar content. To a large extent, the combined memories of the senior committee members can recall important facts about similar bills that had been considered in the past. Upon occasion, however, their memories fail, and they forget results of previous hearings and actions on proposed legislation. More important, perhaps, is the inability of newer committee members to draw as extensively upon previous com-

---

[57] Work undertaken by the Post Office Department is quite relevant here, which underscores the fact that research and development in even purely "administrative" applications of technology can have broad consequences for information processing in general.

mittee experience, which prevents them from functioning to maximum capacity as lawmakers.

To make previous experience generally available, the full history of committee action could be compiled on magnetic tape and made available to any committee member for computer processing. Upon request, any member could find all bills on a given subject that the committee had considered in past Congresses, the bills' provisions, whether or not hearings were held, relevant documents reporting the hearings, action taken by the committee, action taken in the chamber, action by the other chamber, whether the bill became law, and so on. Most of this information is available now through traditional methods of research. This proposal, however, would make the search and retrieval operations automatic, swift, and routine —thus eliminating the need for laborious study in order to locate basic information.

2. *Processing data on subjects under committee jurisdiction:* This is a general proposal for strengthening research capacities of committee staffs by equipping them with computers. It is difficult to say exactly how the computers would be used, for that would depend on the research needs of the committee. One example might be to use a computer for analyzing questionnaire data collected on special groups affected by governmental programs. The data could be processed and analyzed by the committee staff using Congress' own computing facilities. At present, committees do conduct such surveys, but they usually process their data on computers in some executive agency—which is usually only too happy to oblige.[58] This method of operation, however, hardly promotes Congress' independence of the executive. Congressional committees should be given their own research tools so that they need not be beholden to the executive for information, expertise, or computing time.

---

[58] A good example of congressional use of executive computing facilities is provided by the Subcommittee on Domestic Finance of the House Committee on Banking and Currency, which used computers and computing time provided by the Federal Reserve Board and the Federal Deposit Insurance Corporation to analyze questionnaire data collected from some 3,000 commercial banks. This research is reported in several documents issued during the 2d Session of the 88th Congress, including *Correspondent Relations: A Survey of Banker Opinion* and *A Study of Selected Banking Services by Bank Size, Structure, and Location.*

81

3. *Controlling the administration:* One of the most needed areas of improvement for Congress lies in direction and control of the federal bureaucracy. In general, congressional committees are organized to parallel executive departments and to divide responsibilities accordingly for reviewing activities of given agencies. Committees can increase the effectiveness of their direction and control over the agencies through information processing techniques. One such application immediately suggests itself: analyzing past and projected budgetary expenditures for each agency.

Appropriating monies and authorizing expenditures are cited together as the main weapon in congressional control of the executive. But it is generally conceded that Congress is underpowered to review effectively the enormously long and complex budget set before it by the executive. As Wallace has written:

> Congress does not now have access to nearly as much analytical data about the budget as does the Executive. Although there is probably a point beyond which additional information does not help to predict consequences of action, Congress has not yet reached that point. The present disparity between its information resources and those of the Executive means that effective control . . . is held in the hands of those who possess detailed information with respect to the various administrative needs and the adequacy of this or that amount of money for carrying out a particular program.[59]

Committees could use the computer for exhaustive and comprehensive analyses of current estimates according to past estimates and subsequent expenditures. The sources of increase and decrease (if any) can be pin-pointed and subjected to closer scrutiny. Patterns of supplementary appropriations could be entered into the analysis. At the very least, the committee should be able to do fundamental arithmetic on a grand scale with executive budgets. This in itself would not insure economy and efficiency within the bureaucracy, but—coupled with other analytical procedures devised by the committees and executed on the computer—it should give Congress more punch to use in the battle of the budget.

[59] Robert Ash Wallace, "Congressional Control of the Budget," *Midwest Journal of Political Science*, May 1959, p. 152.

Issues in Automating Congress

It would be foolish to recommend an automated information system for Congress without considering some of the basic issues involved in this dramatic innovation. Four seem to be of paramount importance: cost of the system, smoothness of transition, mastery of the system, and effect upon the distribution of power. Each of these issues will be discussed in turn.

Cost of the System: I would not hazard a guess about the dollar cost of an automated information system for Congress, for this would be far beyond my competence. But I can roughly estimate the absolute outer limit of expense. Let us suppose that the physical and human facilities of a modern computing center at a major university were provided for exclusive use of *each* representative, *each* senator, *each* standing committee in both chambers, the House and Senate *separately*, and Congress as a whole. The total number of computing centers needed would be as follows:

Number of congressmen 535
Standing committees 36
Both chambers 2
Congress itself 1

Total 574

The annual operating budget of the computing center at Northwestern University can serve as a standard. Its budget for 1965-66 is $533,000. This amount covers rental cost of its basic machines, Control Data Corporation's new 3400 computer and its satellite, the CDC 8090; rental of a full complement of auxiliary equipment; salaries of 17 staff members and wages of many hourly workers; and all associated supplies, cards, paper, magnetic tape, etc. Utilization of Northwestern's computing facilities has steadily increased over time. At present, the center serves 35 separate departments and schools in the University and has on file more than 500 active projects ranging in scope from nuclear physics to classical Greek. Even with this tremendous use by hundreds of students and faculty members and even with projected increases for the future, the present equipment will probably be able to handle Northwestern's demands for computer time for the next two years.

Suppose a vast computing facility like Northwestern's was made available to each of the users listed above. The annual operating cost for 574 such computing centers would be slightly less than $306 million. Given the magnitude of annual expenditures for some projects within governmental agencies, this does not seem like an astronomical figure. And a more sensible configuration of equipment using several very large central computers and remote control stations would bring the cost down to bargain prices for this contribution to democratic government.

Smoothness of Transition: It would be folly to automate abruptly. Automation should proceed gradually, one step at a time, while maintaining traditional procedures to prevent bugs in the system from disrupting communications. Disseminating notifications of new bills might be tried first. This technique involves computer programs and procedures that are now almost routine in information processing. It could be introduced in Congress with relative ease and would give all congressmen a taste of innovation simultaneously. If their reaction is favorable, the next application might be in the committees. Some committee staffs already have had considerable experience in data processing with computers in the executive branch and thus can aid in the transition for Congress.

Authorization for establishing information systems at the committee level should, of course, be permissive—enabling committees to automate at their own initiative. The change would not be sweeping, but should provide for incremental expansion, committee by committee. Finally, similar arrangements should be made in establishing systems for individual congressmen. Those who want to automate their own information-handling activities should be enabled to do so. A gradual approach like this should allow the system to win acceptance on merits demonstrated through actual performance rather than promise. And if the system seems to be developing undesirable consequences, it could be altered or even scrapped—whatever the evidence indicates.

Mastery of the System: Further expansion of professional staffs is frequently recommended to cope with Congress' information problem. Congressmen are understandably reluctant to follow this advice out of fear that their own staffs would become bureaucracies and would, in turn, be difficult to control. They might also resist installation of automated information systems because of the same basic fear: losing control of their own tools. This fear may be all the more pronounced because the tools are space-age inventions unfamiliar to elected officials.

Installation of computing systems for Congress would clearly demand employment of persons trained in the technology. This means both computer operators and—even more important— computer programmers. Probably each chamber would have to maintain a small staff of programmers to develop and maintain its information processing systems. In addition, the standing committees would have to add programmers to their staffs, and eventually individual congressmen might themselves employ programmers on a part-time or job basis. These technicians will possess specialized knowledge. The question is: can congressmen make them work effectively and obtain the information they want and need?

Some people stand in awe of electronic computers, computer programmers, and men from IBM. The uninitiated imagine white-robed technicians communicating in a strange language and performing mysterious ceremonies around frightfully complex machinery. In short, computers and related things seem far beyond the ken of these ordinary mortals. Congressmen might find absurd the suggestion that they might learn how to use computers themselves. But it is not absurd; computers are tools that can be used, if not mastered, by intelligent and interested people.

I submit that congressmen can readily acquire a basic understanding of computers and computer programming for effective use of the system. A series of talks by capable instructors followed by equipment demonstrations should prove adequate for communicating this understanding. In time, this instruction could become part of the orientation for new members. My experience in teaching computer use and computer programming to college juniors and seniors in political science indicates that a working knowledge of the equipment is acquired very rapidly, once the initiation has occurred.

Effect upon the Distribution of Power: "Knowledge is power." Granting that premise, the question becomes, "Who gets the knowledge?" This is largely answered by disclosing the beneficiaries of the information system outlined above. Two groups will benefit: Congressmen individually and committees of congressmen. The fundamental belief underlying this whole proposal is that Congress can be strengthened as a legislative institution by improving the effectiveness of congressmen as individual lawmakers. Providing congressmen with more information and greater knowledge is a major way of doing this. Providing committees of congressmen with more information and greater knowledge also strengthens Congress, by promoting specialization and division of labor in lawmaking. As a consequence, Congress as a whole will become a far more effective force in our governmental structure.

This proposal studiously avoids concentrating remote terminals in the hands, say, of the elected leadership or perhaps party committees. Such concentration would produce no substantial increase in knowledge and information available to individual congressmen and would accelerate centralization of power within Congress. And centralization of power within Congress would have as *its* main beneficiary the party in control of the White House, which ultimately means the President. And we do not need recommendations which further strengthen the President's hand in his dealings with Congress.

The recommendations in this paper harbor no great or systematic alterations in the present distribution of power within Congress. Providing a quantum of knowledge to all congressmen across the board might hasten the effectiveness of newer members, but this effect, although welcome, is not likely to be substantial. Providing specialized information to standing committees simply recognizes and reinforces their current influence in the legislative process. Other things being equal, then, this proposal should benefit no political factions within Congress.

But other things are seldom equal, and some individuals may wring more knowledge, and therefore more power, out of the information system than others. I am certain this will happen, but I see no basis for alarm from any particular quarter—unless people in that quarter place little confidence in their abilities to compete successfully with others in using these tools. Some congressmen will work the system better than others, but it is difficult to forecast in advance who these will be—which means, again, no predictable change in the distribution of power.

Conclusion

Without doubt, establishing an automated information system within Congress will have many unanticipated consequences. Far-reaching changes have always accompanied the introduction of new technology into society. The automobile brought not only faster transportation but also giant shopping centers and drive-in movies. Television brought not only improved communications but also TV dinners and "family rooms." Technological innovation in society changes ways of living; in Congress, it will change ways of lawmaking.

It is impossible to predict in advance all concomitant outcomes of this proposal. No doubt, some changes will be evaluated negatively by congressmen and by students of the legislative process. But the final tally of pluses and minuses should find this innovation clearly moving Congress toward a more vital and independent role in our governmental system. The evaluation of a state senator who has experienced the application of computing techniques in New York's state legislature supports this estimate in full. Senator Brydges says:

> The computer places one of the greatest research tools in history in the hands of legislatures from coast to coast. Because it can do its work quickly, surely and extensively and print laws in quantity, it saves interim committees, research counsel and law revision agencies thousands of man-hours that would be consumed simply in trying to find all laws on a specific topic and reproducing them in quantities for scissoring, pasting and reshuffling. Its importance, however, lies beyond its ability to serve as a legal research assistant. The computer becomes a means of restoring the legislature to its proper equal status with the judicial and executive branches of government. Today and in the future, control over facts—the ability to research in depth and quickly—can gain for legislatures some of the capabilities for leadership they have lost over the years.[60]

If computers can do this for state legislatures, why not for Congress?

---

[60] Brydges, *op. cit.*, pp. 351–52.

87

COMMENT ON JANDA PAPER

Dr. Saloma: Are you proposing, instead of locating the facility in the member's office, that it would be located in the district for the two party organizations?

Dr. Janda: Both; there would be facilities within Congress and also facilities within the districts. This means four computing centers, two in Washington and two in the districts for the opposition parties.

Dr. Saloma: Perhaps the opposition party would even keep a machine in Washington.

Dr. Janda: That's conceivable, but not under the proposal that I was discussing. If I might say just one final thing on implementation, our last discussion shifted to implementing an information system for one committee, instead of trying to improve the relationship between any given legislator and his constituency.

Dr. Saloma: As you know, Ken's article is the first that is aimed at this, and it very nicely raises a whole array of problems which are more political than informational. I think I suggested earlier that if information is a form of power, the control of information is crucial in politics. I would suggest a couple of problems here.

First, there are the committees themselves. You assume that the committees are going to make information available internally, that it will be possible for junior members on the committee to get information from what is now the province of the senior members. Are the senior members going to allow that type of information to be processed and available?

The next issue is that of committee versus non-committee members. If you read (Professor) Dick Fenno's (University of Rochester) discussion of the Appropriations Committee in the House, part of the reason for committee unity is the fact that they have the budgetary-information background before them that most of the other members don't have. You've got that bridge to get across.

I think that is a central problem apart from the whole problem of locating information terminals in the individual member's office. This kind of computational facility, if you would allow the member to direct it in a way that he would be most inclined to, enables him to build electoral advantage rather than necessarily increase his legislative productivity. The question is: What are the consequences—intended and unintended—of a given system design? And that raises the question: Who designs the system for what values or what ends? I think you are being much too optimistic in saying that an information system can be implemented without changing the power balance among factions within the Congress. Just to do that would require a very sophisticated design.

Dr. Janda: Let me comment on your last point first. I once said that it would be *impossible* to predict the effects of an information system upon the power balance. I changed that later to say that some congressmen will work with the system better than others, but it is *difficult* to forecast in advance who these will be. I think we *can* make some predictions, however. In a statistical sense, we may say that the younger people will be more likely to use it than the older. Depending upon what kind of access that you have to the equipment, it is also possible that committee chairmen would be more apt to use it than the rank-and-file members of the committee. So, I do think that the proposed system *would* affect the power balance, although I am not sure how.

You also asked if senior committee members would allow information to be available to junior members. I assumed they would, but that might not be true. I see no reason why the committee IR (information retrieval) system couldn't be effectively insulated from the total information system so a committee could follow whatever kind of procedure a given committee chose. Some committees operate with a very strong chairman, the chairman having control of virtually all the staff resources. I should think he would be able to operate this kind of system in the same way. If the committee was more egalitarian in its operation, it should also be able to operate similarly.

With respect to other committees, once again you could get the same sort of mixed strategy. Some committees might be willing to make their information more generally available. On the other hand, maybe most of them would like to keep the information they generate within their own province, so they could still present themselves as the experts on the legislation. These issues could be resolved within whatever political calculus is being used now. They wouldn't necessarily be resolved that way, but I think they could.

Mr. Chartrand: I know that in the case of some of the strong committee chairmen they take such a protective, personal interest in their position that many times the members of their own party on the committee may not be fully alerted to what is going on. This is a condition of life that needs to be faced up to.

I was particularly interested, Bill Casselman, in getting your comment here, because I know that Congressman McClory, in considering an automatic data processing facility for the Congress, has addressed himself on more than one occasion to the question of what kind of things a central facility, such as the one that he recommends in his legislation, should properly do. Would you care to comment on this?

Mr. Casselman: I think there is a vast difference between the installation envisioned by Ken and the one which we provide for in H.R. 21. H.R. 21 would simply place ADP equipment in the Library of Congress, to be used by the Legislative Reference Service in the performance of its nonpartisan research and counseling functions for the Congress. What Ken is talking about is obviously a much more sophisticated system, tailored to the individual needs of each member of Congress. It would have to take into account, as Jack said, many political factors. I am not sure they could all necessarily be accounted for or even foreseen.

There is a political tendency—returning to the idea that knowledge is power—to hoard information. I am not sure that you could get away from this no matter what sort of system you designed, and I am not sure it would be advisable to design such a tendency out of a system of the type described by Ken. The right kind of information, and the adroit use of that information, is the key to being a successful legislator.

Mr. Chartrand: There are tremendous problems connected with implementing either type of system. Consider the situation that already exists at the Democratic National Committee, for example, which attempts to provide certain politically oriented ADP functions, such as the mass mailings and so forth, for the senators and representatives that have chosen voluntarily to submit their mailing list. You find, of course, that you have a system totally saturated, that has already reached a point where everyone is crying for help. I think this is perhaps one of the factors that inspired Congressman Mc-Clory to take a strong and a realistic stand against allowing any type of even peripherally politically oriented activity to be placed in his proposed facility for legislative references.

Mr. Casselman: This is true. In the McClory Bill, political factors are minimized in the system by isolating the information user from the information-processing equipment. Requiring the congressional user to go to the Legislative Reference Service, which can in turn screen his request and which has the capability of knowing whether or not the desired information is available and available in the form that the user wants it, takes our system out of the political realm and puts it solely into the area of nonpartisan information-handling. I think you have to be more careful when you start putting these machines in a congressman's office, and when you start delving into the area of politics with respect to information handling.

Dr. Janda: My essay wasn't intended as a proposal for the present but as a view into a possible future. In fact, I talk about hardware that has not been developed.

Mr. Casselman: I have just one inquiry here. The systems you've discussed at the state level, I take it, are within the legislative body itself, either in a committee or legislative chamber. Do such systems perform primarily housekeeping functions? It was my understanding that they did. Obviously, maintaining either a bill print-out or an action calendar is a housekeeping function.

Dr. Janda: With the exception of the New York system and some of the states that are contracting with Horty's Health Law Center, they are housekeeping functions.

Mr. Casselman: How does the New York system differ from those other systems?

Dr. Janda: In the New York system the state statutes are actually on tape. Individual committees use the facility to search statutes with respect to any particular legislation they are working on. I quote one example here by Earl Brydges, majority leader in the New York Senate. He mentioned how one legislator wanted to do a revision of the state banking laws and asked the computer to give him legislation that had to do with banks. I would say that is *not* a housekeeping function. That is a research function. But, printing out action calendars and actually drafting bills all seem to me to be under the housekeeping area.

Mr. Capron: I am not quite clear on this Oregon system of the bill drafting. Can you, for an ignoramus, describe how this differs from the way we use the Government Printing Office in this town? I put my original draft in and I get it back like magic, practically in minutes, when I'm up on the Hill the next day. If I decide to change a line or a word, I get that back right away, and I have copies all over the place.

Dr. Janda: How fast is right away? Is this a day?

Mr. Capron: It's a 24-hour service.

Dr. Janda: The ATS (Administrative Terminal System) service would be instantaneous.

Mr. Capron: Can you get print-outs to all the other members automatically?

Dr. Janda: Not presently, but that could be accomplished, depending upon what kind of hardware one pays to develop. If you have cathode ray tube consoles for the individual congressmen, you could, for instance, display the amended bill for each one of the congressmen and then make copies off the screen by some type of photographic or Xerox process.

Mr. Capron: Since they don't do that, how does this really work?

Dr. Janda: They actually do it in Oregon. They have what is called an Administrative Terminal System, which is an IBM 1050 model typewriter hooked up to a cathode ray tube (CRT). The bill is typed once. It goes on tape. Then, if they want to amend any line, they just type in that line number and type in the new information they want. The computer will then replace what has already been there with the new information, or it can insert new information, automatically adjusting the text in storage so that it prints out in a form which is suitable for legislative action.

Mr. Chartrand: We do have a couple of commercial groups locally, including VIP Systems, Inc., which do this kind of thing on contract for such groups as the National Bureau of Standards and Lockheed Aircraft and so forth. It features a combined dial-a-phone and ATS system, and it has proven to be a useful, usable tool.

Dr. Saloma: As a postscript on the politics of this, Bill Knox this morning said that one of the problems he foresaw was providing a mechanism for resource allocation. Assuming this has to be funded through some central fund or appropriation, I could see that that would be one of the major problems in implementation, in getting the ground rules for who is to have access to or time on the central facility.

Once you introduce an information facility it seems to me that there will be built-in mechanisms that will expand its use. I could just suggest a few of these. Authorization versus appropriations. If the different committees can tie into the same system or some of the same systems there will likely be competition. Then there could be legislative-executive competition. If Congress discovers the facility and begins to learn how to use it, I think there is a possibility of competition there. Finally, we could see party competition and then "generational" competition between younger activists and senior members. So, I think there are plenty of dynamics in the congressional system, once you get over that threshold of acceptance. I could see a rapid expansion and adaptation.

Dr. Janda: Jack, this is one of our ideas, that perhaps AEI, as a private organization, would have more flexibility in getting over the initial hurdle, working with the system in an experimental way.

Dr. Saloma: In time probably you would get to a level of technology where individual members of Congress and the private sector or groups of congressmen working with the private sector could develop independent computer-based information and research facilities.

93

Dr. Janda: That wasn't quite what I had in mind. I had in mind more of a demonstration project for eventual support with congressional funds.

Mr. Capron: What are your cost estimates on your two congressmen?

Dr. Janda: My barebones cost estimate that I made up, including rental of an IBM 1401 system for a year, came to something like $50,000 for one year of operation, but this original estimate failed to provide for enough personnel, I'm afraid. Our later estimate more than doubled this figure.

Mr. Capron: This is not designed to include the investment in getting the original data either, I take it?

Dr. Janda: No. You know, we could have thought of this operating for senators instead of representatives. That may have in some way had more luster in terms of publicity value. But, on the basis of sheer numbers, senators have much larger constituencies, which means more input information to process. So there is some argument for working with congressmen who require a smaller amount of input data.

Mr. Capron: I wouldn't want to mention any names, since we are going on tape, but have you tried to sell a couple of members of the House or the Senate to do this on their own with private resources as an experiment?

Dr. Janda: No. Anyway, I would have felt that wouldn't have been a good test because some might attribute its success to the congressman's personal fortune.

However, there are some very serious problems in implementing the system at the individual level, and the more I come to think about them the more serious they seem to me. I am now persuaded that working at a higher level like that of the Congress as a whole, perhaps with the LRS, makes a lot more sense in terms of actual information support for the Congress, as does working with committees rather than the legislator and his constituency.

One of the presumed advantages in dealing with constituency relationships was that transfer of learning would occur, for every congressman shares the general problems of relationship with his constituency. They all have mailings; they all have this, that, and the other thing. So they could go to Congressman Jones' office to see his computer blink and buzz, while learning from him how it operates. I thought that if a system were implemented for just one committee, congressmen might not generalize its capacity to help other committees.

Mr. Capron: It seems to me, as an economist, that there are several natural places for the use of this kind of a system in the legislative process. For example, there are the Ways and Means, Finance Committees, or the Joint Committee on Taxation, where you have a highly professional staff which is much less political than many of the committee staffs. You have a need not only for looking at the existing tax code when you are thinking about amendments but also for looking at essentially an analytic use of the equipment, as proposals are made to vary rate schedules and so forth. You know, you could use this computer system when the committees were actually in session. This would be tremendously valuable.

It is done now by the executive branch and it takes 24 hours essentially. It seems to me a case where we already know a lot. There are computer programs and all the rest of it available to use. Now, this has the disadvantage which you just mentioned in that this would look very specialized. Oh, yes, I can see how it works when you are doing tax legislation, but I don't see how . . . .

Dr. Janda: If I could answer that: I favored working with individual congressmen, because the likely applications were really pretty routine from an information-processing standpoint. For example, information-retrieval programs are readily available to handle selective mailings.

One problem in working with committees is that you already have a professional staff that knows what it is doing. You must not only secure the complete cooperation of the staff, and you may not be able to get their cooperation in this kind of venture, but you also must have your system prove it's going to pay its way by providing information more rapidly. I am not that confident about the immediate benefits after installation, for it will take a long time to write proper computer programs and get them working. So, I think implementation in a committee requires a longer run before it begins to pay off. Working with the individual legislator promises a more immediate payoff.

FRED SCHWENGEL

Problems of Inadequate Information and Staff
Resources in Congress

I AM GLAD to come here to be with people like you, and I want to suggest, too, that the American Enterprise Institute should be commended for sponsoring a seminar such as this. Conferences like this stimulate the type of creative thinking needed to provide the help that Congress needs and the country needs from Congress. This seminar on information support is much more important, I think, than even you realize.

Every congressional office today is deluged with information and materials supplied by lobbyists, all kinds of government publications, plus innumerable publications from our own sources. In many cases, a congressman gets neither as much nor the specific kind of information he needs, but our problem, generally, is that we get too much information and have no efficient and effective means of thinking about what we need.

I have agreed to send everything I get from my office to the University of Iowa. They are making up a file called "Tensions File," and I'll tell you, that's quite a pile of information. If my office had kept all of the publications, documents, books, and reports we have received since January 1, there literally would be no room left in our office to work. I still have one of the old offices. The new offices might hold it.

As I see it, the problem of information handling is twofold: First, what information is needed? Second, how can it best be obtained and/or retrieved when needed? In Congress itself there is the committee system, which provides the bulk of the information on which both houses of Congress make their decision, but this source of information is not always adequate, especially when the White House and the Congress are controlled by the same party. It is interesting to note that about 80 percent of all legislation today is not only initiated but is drafted by the executive branch of government. I think this ought to give political scientists real concern as they ponder what this may mean over a period of years. This places a heavy responsibility on the committees of Congress, because the executive branch of government has immense resources at its disposal which it can use to push for its proposals. Congress must be in a position to consider legislation adequately and it is not now in a position to do that.

The minority party does not have sufficient professional staff on congressional committees to get the information it needs. One way Congress can make sure that it is getting needed information is to strengthen the ability of the minority party to constructively criticize and evaluate legislative proposals. The Legislative Reference Service provides another source of information, but today LRS is badly overworked, and it is most certainly understaffed. The people at the Legislative Reference Service, I can testify, are as good, if not better, than most congressmen. They do yeoman work for the Congress and especially for its members, but today the LRS simply doesn't have the resources or manpower needed to do an adequate job.

There is another source of information for the Congress which remains to be tapped. It is automatic data processing. Congressional committees, the Legislative Reference Service, and the individual members of Congress could put automatic data processing to work for them, and they should. Automatic data processing could be used for the storage and retrieval of the basic information on legislation. Automatic data processing could be used by members to call up specific information on bills when they are considered by the Congress. Hearings, reports, and testimony could all be abstracted and printed out daily, and made available for fast recall for members of Congress.

I have barely touched on specific applications of automatic data processing to the legislative process. Yet, I think it is clear that Congress is very far behind the times. It certainly is behind the executive branch. It is behind the state legislatures, behind educational institutions. It is behind business. It is behind industry and the professions in the handling of information.

Knowledge, it has been said, is power, and the uses to which that knowledge is put determine the fate of our nation and increasingly influence the destiny of others. Information is the key to wise decision-making. If people would retain a voice in their government, if Congress would regain its stature as a co-equal partner with the executive branch, Congress must look to the improvement of its methods of gathering, sorting, and analyzing data. The need is fundamental, and the case is very, very urgent. More realistic approaches to gathering information within the committees already referred to, plus some changes in the precedents and rules of the committees, plus a modernizing of the House itself by voting electronically, and other methods to save time, are very, very important for us to consider.

Now, if there is any time left, in the terms of the House, I yield back the balance of my time.

COMMENT ON SCHWENGEL PAPER

Mr. Capron: Congressman, I was fascinated by just one factual statement you made, and I would like you to spell it out; you said that 80 percent of the legislation is drafted at this end of Pennsylvania Avenue. I find that unbelievable. You mean public legislation that is passed?

Mr. Schwengel: Yes, that's passed.

Mr. Capron: I am not a political scientist so maybe I shouldn't respond. You said this should be pondered by political scientists. I'm an economist. If you are talking about major public legislation that is passed, it does not seem to me so shocking that as much as 80 percent of it originates and is drafted by the executive, because this is a sifting process on the Hill, a review process.

99

Mr. Schwengel: I am concerned about it because we ought to be initiating—we ought to be the ones that initiate the 80 percent. We are the legislative body, but we are not set up to do this and our time is taken away from us because of . . . . Well, this morning, for example, I've spent two hours taking people, students, around. Now, I like this. I love the history of the Capitol. It is good if I can do this, but it isn't part of my job, and it shouldn't be.

You could go through my mail this morning and see that probably 50 percent to 80 percent of it is to see about getting something for somebody or doing something. "I'm coming to Washington, what should I see?" "Send me some passes." "I haven't heard from my boy in Vietnam. See what you can do about finding out about him."

Mr. Jayson: To what extent do the parties themselves provide you with vital information concerning any major or quasimajor issue?

Mr. Schwengel: Up to now, practically none. Now, under Eisenhower we started something that was real good. First you became the chairman of a committee to make recommendations as we looked to the future, and that was in the publication of a book called *Programs for Progress*. Ray Bliss now has set up a coordinating committee, and out of that have come some things that are somewhat helpful.

Congressman Albert Quie, of Minnesota, in his "Quie Amendment," admitted that his approach didn't have anywhere near the kind of study that it should have had, but we wanted an alternative and so we presented it. Now, the coordinating committee did help some with this.

Mr. Jayson: Do the parties, for example, give you a pro and con on the major legislation?

Mr. Schwengel: No, they will more often tell you what they are against. Right now, on situs picketing, a lot of the financial interests are really excited about this and so, brother, the party is telling us how to vote on this, you see. That's an example of where they get involved. But, for the most part, parties do not give us any help and I think it's time that they should.

100

Mr. Chartrand: I have seen this series of booklets that is put out by the Republican coordinating committee on mass transportation, health, education, and welfare, and so forth. What is your opinion of the scholastic quality?

Mr. Schwengel: I applaud the effort, but the committee just doesn't have the facilities to do this right. I have talked to (Ray) Bliss (Chairman, Republican National Committee) about it. I said, "Bliss, the best thing you could do is to get a fund of a half a million dollars and put some real students to work on this." They can call on the Library of Congress through the congressional offices maybe and really get at the nub of these things.

For instance, take the Model Cities Program. I think the idea, the objective, is great; but I think, just from what I have seen, and I was a member of the Committee on Municipal Affairs when I was in the Iowa Legislature, that it is just woefully inadequate. It doesn't begin to harness all of the talents that could be harnessed from a number of different sources.

Some studies are done here, and I think political parties ought to spend some money for those studies. What would be the matter with them aligning themselves with political scientists? We want more political scientists allowed, and I think we should have them. I use them in my office.

I have college graduates on a research team doing basic research for me under Dr. Russell Ross at the University of Iowa. They are doing some pretty good research right now on watersheds, water conservation, and all of these programs that we have now in Johnson County and in Iowa County in Iowa. We are way ahead of the Department of Agriculture on watersheds, I think, in our practical approaches.

Mr. Chartrand: Then, would you take the results of their research and make this information available to your colleagues, for example?

Mr. Schwengel: In the past, we did this in the area of small business. My research team at the University of Iowa is responsible for five amendments to the Small Business Act and, as that research came in, we did several things with this. It was so good that I had asked this group of two college professors and a team of three graduate students to come in. They

101

testified before the Small Business Committee, and four of the propositions they worked on were accepted. Here is an indication that good, solid research can be done at the college level where there is talent, but it needs harnessing.

So, what I can do in a very small way with the limited money I have for my staff, and a large percent of this is volunteer, is just to open the doors and give them an opportunity. They just come gushing in there.

Mr. Jayson: Suppose you are faced with problems which are not within your own particular interest. You are from a rural community essentially, but if you are dealing with model cities or urban problems . . . .

Mr. Schwengel: This is where you would have to have a really topnotch, blue-ribbon committee, composed of people who have had experience. I think this is where you ought to invite the financial community in. All of the states, for instance, in this model cities question, think that the administration has not taken advantage of the studies and experiences that the municipal leagues have had. Every state has a municipal league. Now, many of them are like Iowa, they are very weak. In Iowa they have two levels: first, the smaller communities and secondly, those, I think, above 20,000. Some of the league's recommendations are fairly knowledgeable, particularly when they are dealing with some of their own experiences.

Mr. Jayson: The point I am getting at is that every member, as an individual, has a certain capacity or he is interested in certain things, or he *has* to be interested in certain other things. But, beyond that, there are national problems about which he has no direct interest. He has to rely on other sources of information. These are issues that face the nation or that face other parts of the country, and on this you need information.

Mr. Schwengel: Oh, my, my, yes.

Mr. Jayson: In what direction do you turn for information? What sort of information do you seek in this regard?

Mr. Schwengel: I think the record will show that I use LRS more than any other congressman; I don't know, but I use it a lot, and I am grateful that we have it available to us. But, I also know how understaffed LRS is and how incapable it is at times because we haven't equipped them. I think automatic data processing is an absolute must.

We in the Congress have appropriated money enough for the Federal Government to buy some 3,000 information data complexes, sets, or whatever you call it; more than a billion dollars is spent for new equipment and services in the executive branch. And we in Congress have not one—well, we have one automatic machine that's for writing checks, to take care that we get our salaries on time—to support our needs. That's about it, isn't it?

When you think of things like social security and Medicare, there are all kinds of known things that we could feed into the machine and get the answer in a matter of minutes. So, this is a must as I see it.

Dr. Janda: I wanted to expand upon your concern about the 80 percent of all passed legislation being drafted by the executive. What the congressman really is concerned about is the fact that this situation is continuing. The amount of legislation being drafted by the executive is increasing now over what it has been in the past. To my knowledge there is only one study that has been made of this trend. In 1946, Lawrence Chamberlain selected 90 significant pieces of legislation passed since the late 1800s.

About 20 percent of all of the major pieces of legislation— that is, of the 90 pieces he identified—came from the executive branch and about 40 percent from the Congress. Another 30 percent originated jointly by the President and Congress, and 10 percent appeared to stem from pressure groups. However, there is a real difference in the time periods he studied.

In the latter part of the 1800s and the early part of the 1900s most of the legislation was coming from the Congress. Beginning with the twenties and particularly into the thirties the major legislation originated with the executive. So there has been a definite change indicated by the comparative studies we have available. If the same kind of study were made now, it likely would show even a greater increase in legislation being initiated by the executive and even drafted by the executive branch.

Charles T. Meadow, International Business Machines Corporation: Is the main reason for this the lack of information available to the Congress?

103

Mr. Schwengel: Well, this is one of the reasons. The other reason is that the committees have not kept up to date. Every department of government requires job descriptions, and you've got to have qualifications to meet the job requirements, but there's no such thing for the House or the Senate employees.

Dr. Janda: I wouldn't think information availability would be the immediate cause, but I would probably identify it as the more fundamental, underlying cause. Congress itself has contributed a good deal to executive initiation of legislation. For instance, in passing the Budgeting and Accounting Act of 1921, which requires the President to submit a budgetary message, and the Employment Act of 1946, which requires him to present an annual economic report, Congress has thrust legislative leadership into the hands of the executive.

Mr. Jayson: Each year every executive department is asked by the top branch to make certain proposals which will be, of course, screened by the Budget Bureau and so on.

Dr. Janda: And, if they are not forthcoming, the Congress screams, which was the case in the Eisenhower Administration in 1953.

Mr. Schwengel: Yes, yes.

Mr. Jayson: One of the things provided in the proposed Legislative Reorganization Act of 1967 is to ask LRS to do some anticipatory type of work which, as I understand it at this moment, and this is quite preliminary, would be for LRS to talk to the committee chairmen and to the minority members and to staff directors in advance of the session and to ask: "What sort of things do you think your committee is going to be interested in next year?" Then LRS would try to do some preliminary background reports on these subjects.

Is this the sort of thing that might help you or would it not?

Mr. Schwengel: I think it would be of great help, but we also need to upgrade the committee staffing. Practically every major committee is understaffed, and the minority just has no chance at all. On the average the minority has one staff member out of ten on which it can call, and it doesn't even control that one, absolutely, because the majority can fire that one. We've seen times when that minority employee was fired because he went too far, and there was nothing the minority could do about it.

We've just got to do something to make some changes up there so that the minority has a chance, a fighting chance, at least, to be an intelligent and articulate opposition, which it cannot be now. We don't even have staff to write minority reports, the time to write the minority report, to say nothing about doing a *good* minority report.

Mr. Chartrand: If I remember correctly, even though we did not have specific direction by the Congress, there have been efforts made within the various divisions of the Legislative Reference Service, working with the committee chairmen, to attempt to anticipate in certain priority areas what should be done, let's say, in collecting vital information for a forthcoming session of Congress.

This has come to my attention in various division chiefs' activities. In fact, they attempted to anticipate, and this is not always easy. You certainly can't anticipate everything.

Mr. Jayson: There are two points to be made on that. One is a matter of history, and one is a matter of current circumstances. The matter of history: in years gone by LRS did attempt to anticipate, and didn't always guess right, so that a tremendous amount of effort was wasted.

At the present time, LRS staff members simply don't have the time, because of the pressure of their current assignments, to sit down and start thinking about next year. So, what Congressman Schwengel mentioned about a desperate need for greater staff resources, not only for the committees but for other organizations like LRS, is very true.

Mr. Schwengel: Let me point to something where the LRS couldn't help us very much. That was on the Appalachia problem. By accident I found out that some people at Princeton had been doing some studies on Appalachia. They had studied enough to find the problem. The problem they found was the same as the problem that we found in the testimony that was given, but some of the answers they pointed to suggested that they would be much different than the answers we proposed. Now, we have had Appalachia for two years or more, and that bill was before the committee, and we saw . . .

(Interruption—Quorum Call)

105

Mr. Schwengel: That means I've got to go right now. If I go right now I'll make it, if I don't I won't. It was good to see you. Good luck.

Mr. Hugo: Thank you very much for coming, sir.

Mr. Capron: I am sorry to make this comment after he has left, because I wanted discussion on it, but I think this 80 percent figure is really terribly misleading. In the first place, the major legislation may be initially drafted at this end of town, but it is carefully and heavily massaged at the other end of town and amended sometimes in a devastating fashion to the point that those who originally drafted . . .

Mr. Hugo: Even in the drafting stage, it's drafted often with the participation of the congressmen.

Mr. Capron: I think this is a distorted number because it sounds as if there has been a complete shift in the power. The other thing is this business of anticipating: Of all of the important legislation that I can think of, I can't think of one major piece of new legislation that has gone through in one year. All of the significant action has actually taken at least a year after its initial proposal and sometimes many years. So there is plenty of time. I think the real thing he is pointing to is that Congress has robbed itself of staff resources. The fact that the Library of Congress' Legislative Reference Service is understaffed is not the fault of the executive.

I felt there was a tone, particularly from the minority party, always, that there is a big power play on the part of the executive—and I don't mean the Johnson Administration—but the executive, whatever the executive. This, it seems to me, distorts it. There are really two points. One, Congress essentially is asking for what it gets, because it does control the budget of the Library of Congress unilaterally. Secondly, I think the significance of where the language is originally drafted is not really all that important.

Mr. Jayson: The Library of Congress and the Legislative Reference Service particularly are only one source of help to the Congress. Of course, what Congressman Schwengel is talking about when he talks about minority staffing is staffing which is designed to assist the minority in pointing out the weaknesses of the majority's proposals and coming up with alternatives. This, of course, has a political aspect, which is essential to our form of government.

The Legislative Reference Service, of course, has a non-partisan role; it serves both parties but, as Professor Saloma here knows, the situations in individual committees vary greatly. Some committees may have bipartisan staffs and some nonpartisan staffs and some very partisan staffs. I don't know the particular committees that Congressman Schwengel is on, but certainly what he is talking about is a very common situation. Too often they just don't have the facilities to develop and provide the minority point of view, which is a necessary element of our form of government.

Mr. Casselman: I think what you say is true with regard to the Legislative Reference Service. I do think there is a very grave problem with respect to minority staffing—given the way in which a minority staff functions and granted that it functions differently from committee to committee.

Some committees, such as Armed Services, are nonpartisan, requiring no minority staff. Most committees obviously are not. In the latter case, the minority staff member or members—and I can't think of any committee that has more than three minority staff members—are under the direction and control of the ranking minority member. Thus, you have a situation where younger congressmen, who may be the real legislative technicians or activists on a committee, sometimes have no effective voice because they cannot get minority staff assistance. The staff members' services are taken by the committee. Certainly ranking minority members have a tremendous work load, requiring a large staff. However, lack of a sufficient number of staff personnel in many cases takes away from the effectiveness of the less-senior members of a committee.

Dr. Saloma: We have some recent data on this from the study of Congress project of the American Political Science Association. We did a breakdown on the sources of information utilized by the congressman or his staff which showed that the problem is much broader than the need for minority staffing.

We found that there was a consistent pattern in *both* parties with information and staff resources being heavily utilized by senior members. This is in some ways the very problem that we are wrestling with here. How do you get a Congress dominated by the seniority system and by a committee system that in some ways puts constraints on information within the legislative body? How do you break this down to make it more receptive to automatic data processing or a more advanced information technology?

Congress won't accept the staff support that is available today, let alone seek a level of information processing that is far more advanced than the current system.

Mr. Chartrand: One other important point that might be made here, as we wrap up this staffing problem as related to needed information, is that the actual congressional sessions have lengthened year by year. The number of issues to be addressed obviously has gone up year by year. This has, of course, diluted the capability of many committees and of the members' staffs to cope with this.

Certainly this has been felt in the Legislative Reference Service. There used to be breathing periods. This is no longer true. The increased burden affects the type of information support that can be made available either by outside groups or those groups which support members or the committee staffs internally.

The sheer volume of activity has in many cases absolutely saturated the ability of existing groups to cope with it.

CHARLES T. MEADOW

Pros and Cons of Computer-Oriented Systems

IT APPEARS to me that the general tendency in this group is to assume that an automatic data processing system is the answer to congressional information needs, although we all recognize there are problems. My talk, then, is not so much on the issue of whether or not to adopt ADP but on consideration of some of the problems that we will encounter when we try to do it.

I would like, first, to review what I am sure is a standard list of pros and cons, and then I will consider some special aspects of these. The traditional factors for consideration are: *cost, speed, accuracy, control of information,* and the *capability for new accomplishments.* The first four of these are clearly two-sided.

Computers are neither always cheaper nor always more expensive than doing some job the other way. They ought to be faster, but there are occasional counter-examples. They ought to be more accurate, and they have the physical capability to be just about perfectly accurate, but they are not always used with perfect accuracy. Most of the errors that we find are human errors, but they are errors nevertheless. Anyone who has ever gotten a bill from a department store for zero dollars and zero cents or received somebody else's bill does not really care who made the error.

109

This introduces my next point which is "control over information." Again, the computer offers us the possibility of having tighter control of what goes in and how it comes out, of what is the official version of some fact and what is not. We have the capability; we don't always use it.

Finally, the fifth point, and the one most commonly used to justify a new computer installation, is "new accomplishments." The great advantage of using a computer is that you can do something with it that you could not do any other way, and while the better examples here are from the fields outside congressional applications, I will name one or two as examples.

There are differential equations that must be solved to build a nuclear reactor or to design an airplane that cannot be done by hand. If we want to build an SST, we must have a computer. In the area of non-numerical information processing, we find computers are able to search files and post changes to files at such speeds as to open entirely new paths for management control and library research. The business that always knows its exact, current inventory status and sales trends can reduce inventories, hence investment, with little risk. The scientist or intelligence analyst of today often has the majority of the published information in his field accessible through a mechanized search procedure. He can be more sure he is right, and take less time in his research.

Today, when we consider using the computer to handle documentary information for the Congress, we are on the verge of the day when this is the only way to do it. Soon, it will not be possible for any large organization to handle its information without a computer.

Now, I would like to spend the rest of my time discussing some points that have been brought up by other speakers this morning, either directly or by implication.

The first of these is the problem of *communication* between the builder, or designer, and the user of a data processing system. In my profession I represent the builder's side of this question. The second problem is that of *user skill*. This is a point we do not hear very much of, but, to my way of thinking, it is an absolute requirement. Third is the attention to *interface with the outside world*. How much attention do we pay, when we design a data processing system, to what effect it will have on the outside world, through communication with other systems or even modification of itself? Fourth, *what is the information that is really wanted or the function that is really to be performed?* Do we know this when we undertake to build an information system? In short, does the system do the right thing; is it under user control? I think it is quite clear from many points that have come up here today that this is, and probably always will be, one of the key questions in any data processing system. The final point I call the *management of the data base*. This is a bit of jargon. Included in this topic is the problem of invasion of privacy. Another aspect of the same problem is that somebody has to be responsible for making sure that the right data is in the computer, and that the data that is in there represents the view of the organization that uses it. Let us review these points, now, in greater detail.

Communication, I think, is the most significant problem and the most significant cause of failures of data-processing systems. I am sure that you are all aware of the frequent lack of communication between the user and the builder. Does the person who orders a data processing system know what he really wants? Does he convey this to the person he asks to build it? Does the person who undertakes the responsibility to build it understand what he is being asked to do? Definitely, this is a two-sided problem and the faults, in my experience, are equally divided.

When Frank Lloyd Wright designed a house, he spent a great deal of time with the owner, finding out about the family that would live in the house, making sure there could be a meeting of what was wanted with what could be provided. The builder of a data processing system has the obligation to say: Do we have available what you want? Can we solve your problem? Does the user or the buyer know what the problems are in building the system, what the costs are? Certainly, when we build a house, that seems to be the one item we never know for sure.

What are the various probabilities of success, and, of course, of failure? In data processing, particularly in something as complicated as congressional applications, we are almost always dealing with new techniques, new ideas, something that has not been done before, and there is always the problem of feasibility. Now, we cannot always give you a number, as the

Weather Bureau does today, that says the probability is 30 percent that we will do what you ask, but it must at least be understood whether or not there is any question of feasibility and, in some nonquantitative way perhaps, an assessment of what this problem is.

The second point, *user's skill*, I can divide into two parts: One, the user must understand the data he is working with. Two, the user must understand the logic of the processor, or program, which handles this data, to some extent. I believe he needs to understand this to a far greater extent than is normally assumed when we talk about management information systems or information-retrieval systems for decision makers. I do not believe that a two-week course in data processing fundamentals begins to scratch the surface. Certainly a person using a library wants to know immediately what kind of a library he is using. We do not ask the same question in the children's section of the public library that we might ask of a legislative reference service.

The inquirer must understand what data he is dealing with and how to "talk to this data," for example, in what language to express his requirements. How does he improve the response to his earlier request if he was unsatisfied with the results? The other, and probably less understood facet is the system logic. Do we understand what happens when, as Dr. Janda illustrated earlier, we ask for information on the cultural aspects of Gabon and retrieve only the theater attendance in Gabon? These are quite different topics, yet there is some commonality and there is a reason why a query for the one produces the other. The information-retrieval system user who would be successful must understand the difference. He must understand what would happen if he changed a single word in a request after the first tryout.

There is a great tendency, I think, in data processing systems to try to design them to be absolutely mistake-proof. The goal is to ask of the user almost nothing more than the physical ability to type the right key on a typewriter. I do not believe we design any other piece of machinery without demanding the highest skill on the part of the user. Certainly we expect quite a bit of airplane pilots. We don't try to make an airplane completely automatic, flyable by anyone. In doing so, I am sure we get better and cheaper airplanes and a better aviation history.

By demanding skill on the part of an ADP system user, I do not propose to take these systems out of the hands of the ultimate user, or to propose a special elite who are the only users. To me, the resolution of the dilemma of a need for skill and a need for direct user communication with his system lies in the explosive growth of data processing training in our schools and colleges. Tomorrow's leaders will come to the Congress and executive branch with a prior knowledge of ADP. For today's leaders, who recognize the need for ADP but lack the personal skill to make direct use of it, I recommend the addition of ADP-skilled people to congressional, Library of Congress, and executive staffs as the best solution.

Now, *interface with the outside world* or attention to universality essentially means investing money in something that has no immediate return to yourself. I can divide this, also, into two facets: changeability and interchangeability. Almost any data processing system that is new and is a first-time application is going to have something go wrong with it. Either it is not going to work as well as we hoped or we may discover that we must change the function it was originally designed to perform. The extent to which this system is designed to be able to be changed easily is perhaps a measure of its ultimate value. In other words, when we design a system, can we design into this system the capacity to cope with its own growth and its own changes without having to re-do it completely at enormous cost?

The second facet is interchangeability. Are we designing into our system the ability to talk to other systems, the ability to communicate through networks when there is no immediate and obvious gain to ourselves in doing this, although it seems culturally, in the long run, that this is the obvious thing to do? Here we have both a physical problem and what we call a software, or programming, problem. There are engineering problems of compatibility, such as the use of different codes to represent information, and there is also the programming problem of how to interpret information. Even with computers of the same manufacturer, where all of the engineering aspects are identical, very often we still cannot communicate between two ADP systems that perform nearly identical functions but were programmed differently.

To some extent, standardization will enable us to achieve this form of communication. In this way, each user, programmer, or manufacturer sacrifices some degree of independence, and probably adds some increment of cost, to work toward a universally desired objective. However, ADP is still a rapidly developing field, particularly the information retrieval, decision-making portions of the field. Overstandardization too early in our development cycle might stifle, rather than nurture progress. While I do not believe in trying to impose too many standards in the information retrieval field at this time, I believe it is possible to accomplish interchangeability without complete standardization. It is possible for us to develop programs, computers, and systems that can learn to understand each others' languages and to deal with each other without having to fall in line and accept an arbitrary standard.

User Control overlaps some of my other points, but there are three key questions here that the user must consider when building a system.

1. Can he control his input?
2. Does he retain a feel for his data?
3. Can he get the system to do what he wants?

Again, I think of the department store billing operations as a good example here. I had an experience with a department store in which what apparently happened was that a keypunch operator took a coffee break while punching out my application for a charge account. After putting down someone else's name and account number, she returned and punched my address on the rest of the card, and I soon began to receive the other man's bills. I, of course, wrote a letter about this, and got a partial change. After the first letter they changed the names and put my name on the other man's account, then started dunning me for failure to pay his bill, and I was put to some unpleasantness before the matter was settled. This is an example of lack of control over input. This is not the fault of the computer. This is the fault of the designer of the program and, even worse, the designer of the total information system into which this program fits. The biggest single failing was that no one read the mail like an *ombudsman*, who knows

114

there are going to be errors and understands the program and is able to do something about the inevitable errors.

On the output end, the analog of this is to consider how good a feel for our data we retain when we mechanize files. In intelligence and in politics, and politics is intelligence in many ways, it is very important to have a feel for what is available, who are the valid sources, who is merely copying other people's work, and who has got something really new to say. A good intelligence analyst, a good politician, and a good political scientist, I am sure, all develop this kind of feel for their data, and there is a great fear on the part of many people that bringing in a computer necessarily causes the loss of this feel for information.

I regret to say that very often they are probably right, but there is no need for them to be right. I recently talked with a gentleman in the executive branch who thought that he would not allow an automatic retrieval system in his agency just for this reason. He felt it was the obligation of his people to have this feel for the data and a computer must necessarily interfere. Therefore, no computer, and he was not listening to the advantages or the ways of getting both the advantages of the computer and retaining the feel for data.

The most important single point I would like to discuss about user control concerns being sure that the information we have and the information we can retrieve, or the function performed, is really what we want. For example, does the information we are searching for really exist in the way we think it exists when we ask a question of the system? Can it be produced? Can we compute this number we ask for? Can we, for example, compute the probability of a war starting in the Middle East? Certainly, the answer is no. We may have a feel for it, but we cannot have a computer calculate a number that means anything in this context.

What functions, then, should the ADP system play in getting the information that the decision maker or analyst wants? Here I would like to consider Mr. Capron's earlier point: Can the computer assess the importance or the value of a document in a retrieval system? My answer would be almost certainly no. I am sure almost all of us agree. But, on the other hand, do we want it to? We should design our system and so instruct its users that they clearly understand that we are not going to

115

do this, that it is still the user's prerogative to decide what to believe, what is important, and what he should read. The purpose of the ADP system is to bring information to the user and reduce the workload on him in acquiring data. The computer can also play a useful role in applying relevance measures that the user may care to invoke, but these measures are intended to supplement, not replace, the user's judgment.

Data base management is concerned both with entry and recovery of information. A term we hear very frequently these days in this connection is fingertip control of information, particularly for decision makers. I think this phrase was used by Vice President Humphrey in a paper quoted earlier. Here I would like to bring out my earlier point on user's skill. I do not believe we are going to see fingertip control of data by executives or congressmen in the very near future at all. One reason is that people at these levels want information that does not necessarily exist in the retrieval system, and the second reason is that most of these people are not themselves highly skilled in using ADP systems to acquire this data.

I had an experience at the Department of State a few years ago in which we set up a demonstration retrieval system using real and current data simply to prove the concepts. The objective was to take policy information and show what could be done with automatic information retrieval to provide the policy level of agency with the kind of information needed. We worked for about three months until one day someone asked, "Where is the policy information?" We finally agreed that there is no such thing, necessarily, as a document that says, "This is policy."

Policy results from a number of people reading a great deal of information, much of it extremely detailed; having conversations; making proposals; having those proposals accepted or rejected; sending a cable; receiving an answer back which might say, "Yes, I concur with your recommendation except paragraph four which should be changed to such and such." Out of this conglomerate of information evolves something called policy, which really exists only in the minds of the policy makers. We could not, therefore, directly retrieve policy. We could retrieve intelligence information and various forms of memoranda, but the difference between policy and intelligence in our project becomes quite vague at times.

The country about which we were storing data was then in turmoil, and the department, during our project, was re-evaluating its position toward some of the political parties in this country. There was some uncertainty about which of the parties had foreign support, if any. There was quite a division, quite a bit of heated debate and so, on this particular point, policy depended on some very, very minute and detailed bits of intelligence, such as where had thus and such a person gone to college. With whom was he seen when he was in Prague last? Such a fact as this is significant to judge whether or not he is a Communist. That entered into policy debates. There was no single piece of paper that said our attitude is such and such. Now, how then can the secretary of state or under secretary or a senator or a congressman make use of a system like this himself? In my opinion, in the present state of the art and of general knowledge about ADP he cannot and he will not.

The bureaucracy—and I don't mean that in the derogatory sense—in the executive branch of the government is a filter for this information. It comes in through a mailroom at the bottom and it filters its way up to the policy makers at the top. In Congress we have the same kind of arrangement, with committee staffs and administrative assistants. Apparently there is quite a shortage of qualified people, but nonetheless the filtering organization is there. If we do away with this filter, if we try to replace it entirely with a computer, then the congressman, the secretary, the decision maker himself must provide all of the filtering apparatus, and he probably simply does not have the mechanical skill to do this. My own personal feeling on the solution is that we should retain the staff and the computer and that the people with mechanical skill will be the members of the LRS, the congressional staffs, the Department of State bureaucracy, and so on.

A problem related to that of data base management is the invasion of privacy. We have not mentioned this here today, but it is in the press a great deal. This is a problem that we have created by our technology. Ten years ago it did not exist because it was almost impossible to put together enough information to constitute a threat. We might almost draw the analogy to atomic energy, in that technicians have created the problem and thrust it upon an unsuspecting public. We have some mechanical controls that we can impose on information

117

systems, but the manner of their use, I personally believe, is a public problem, and not one solely for the data processing industry. We should not sit back and wait for the programmers to solve this problem.

The other side of this coin is how to make sure that we get all the information we want in a data base, and that it is current. This is a big problem, and it usually occupies a great many people. The user of information does not always know what is present and what is not. If he fails to retrieve some information he does not necessarily know why he failed to retrieve it, and he may assume that it does not exist rather than that it is not present in his computer.

Let me now summarize quickly. The computer is here to stay. It has an obvious value to Congress and to any other large information-using organization, but the application of automatic information retrieval must be done with great care and great skill. It is far too easy simply to use the machine as a high-speed filing device, which may compound problems rather than solve them. We have to think very carefully about these problems and avoid simply creating a new problem in place of the old one.

I mentioned the obvious points of *cost, speed, accuracy,* and *data control,* and reviewed some of the points brought up earlier today; *communications* between the builders and the users; *skill* on the part of the user, an absolute requirement; *attention to other systems* that we must interface with, and the ability to change our own; making sure the data-processing system really *performs the function* we want it to perform, without which we have wasted our money; finally, the *management of the data base,* of which privacy is perhaps the most talked about subject.

COMMENT ON MEADOW PAPER

Col. Aines: First of all, I enjoyed your professional talk. Of course, one can quibble with individual points, but I don't propose to quibble. I would just like to get an expansion of your views on standardization.

Before you answer that, let me point out that we are doing a lot of work in the executive branch, trying to coordinate many different information systems in the executive branch, some of which are constructed without consideration for other systems. We are using IBM computers and every other make available, and we recognize that that time is approaching when there has to be some kind of an interchange of this information among agencies. As we depart from a manual mode, where people exchange information and depend upon machines to do a lot of this, it appears that there is a basic requirement for getting a high degree of compatibility to communicate without writing elaborate programs to go from one type of machine to another.

Now, I don't know the attitude of the various computer firms in this respect. I don't know whether they have any attitudes. But, from the point of view of the Federal Government seeking to solve a very difficult problem, because it's not only a national problem but an international problem, it appears to me your feeling about standardization needs some amplification.

Mr. Meadow: I have possibly misstated my case here. I am not opposed to the obvious need to work toward compatible ways of dealing with information. What I am saying is that we very often hear people say, "Well, here are a number of data handling systems that are all different, that can't speak together, what we will simply do is convert them all to one common form," without realizing the enormous task that this implies.

In the ordinary libraries there are the two common indexing or cataloging systems, that of the Library of Congress and the Dewey Decimal System. It would be convenient if there were only one, but the enormity of the task of converting existing systems means that we end up continuing the two. This is really all I meant. We find this problem repeated endlessly in many other areas. Surely, it would be nice to have a single language in which to express the many concepts on which computer files are maintained, and it is expensive not to have such a language. But, no language exists that will handle equally well all requirements, and, even if it did, conversion of existing files might be prohibitively expensive.

I don't have a position that is opposed to the idea of standardization. I have a personal position that standardization, by itself, is not the solution to the problem. A maturing industry can and should make progress toward standardization, but in the process, we must not stifle progress. So, I am not opposed to the basic principle.

Dr. Janda: I would like to ask you about one of the analogies that you used in here and ask you to comment on a different analogy that you might have chosen, but perhaps didn't choose because it didn't support your point.

You asked the question, how difficult should this system be to use? And you pointed out that you don't expect every Tom, Dick, and Harry to be able to fly an airplane, and, as a result, we get better airplanes. But, what about the automobile example that was used earlier today? We do expect almost any Tom, Dick, and Harry to be able to drive an automobile. Now I take it that one of the implications of your line of argument was that you really wouldn't expect a congressman himself to use an information system. Instead, he would depend either upon his staff or maybe staff at another level. But, if you follow the automobile instead of the airplane analogy, then you see another kind of system developing. Can you comment more on that?

Mr. Meadow: It is personal opinion and I might say it could as easily go the other way, but I think when we look at automobiles compared to airplanes, we're in an awful mess. We do allow anyone to drive and it's a hazard to simply walk down the street. Many states are calling for tighter licensing rules, for periodic re-examination. They are not getting very far because none of us wants to give up the freedom we have, even though we may be incompetent drivers.

My point is simply that retrieval of information from a large system is a very complicated process. It requires a degree of intelligence, and it requires a great deal of very specialized training. Even if we reach the point where we can communicate in English there is still a question of how do you communicate in English? What do you say?

As long as the systems are performing such a highly specialized function, we ought to recognize that using them is a special skill, not to prevent other people from using them but to recognize that best use demands a high skill.

Dr. Saloma: I think our discussions of this morning and this afternoon have tended to encompass a wide range of informa-

120

tion and functions. You say you have to define the information and functions that you really want from the system and that this will require people who are trained especially to work on analysis of large banks of data, "analysts" who are comparable perhaps to the professional staffs of the committees today. But I would agree with Ken Janda that there probably will be a bers should be able to retrieve simply from the system. range of information, including many of the points that have been raised today, fairly routine information about the legislative process that an individual congressman or his staff mem-

Just as you have to take a driver education course or be taught by your parents to drive an automobile, so there will be a certain restructuring in the education most congressmen receive. Already this is happening in educational and business institutions that use computers. I think that there is a level of learning that most educated people will in the future, as a matter of course, acquire.

Mr. Capron: Following right along on the airplane and automobile now, there is certainly a cross-benefit question that is involved here, whether we happen to agree around this table on the particular judgment that is made. If you could make an airplane at not too much cost that any of us could fly, so that you wouldn't need years of experience to be a safe pilot, that would be fine and we would do it and a lot of people would be flying. Society is making judgments and it is re-evaluating them right now, as was indicated.

But, I think the other point to pick up here is that there really is a distinction, although it is a continuum, really, between raw information retrieval and the need for an answer to a question. The answer I know has already been worked out. I just want a library function separated from the analytic function. If we can get the cost down, it would be fine to have a very simple library service system that my kid could use literally, where he could dial the library and get the right part of the library and get on the screen a book, a page, the pages that he would use for his homework. But, that's quite different from asking a question which has not been answered before anywhere. That requires analytic talents and we don't expect congressmen to be able to do this.

121

Mr. Chartrand: I would like to ask Lester Jayson to discuss briefly the occasion when we at LRS elected to use the University of Pittsburgh system. It seems to me that this is a good illustration of exactly what we are talking about here, how good the user has to be in getting information back.

Mr. Jayson: Bob refers to the fact that we had an inquiry from a member of a committee of Congress which was considering repeal of the death penalty under all the federal laws. He wanted to know what provisions of the U.S. Code would have to be amended if we abolished capital punishment as a federal penalty.

This meant a search of all of the provisions of the U.S. Code, not merely the penal code, to see what provisions of the code provided for a death penalty. We thought this would be a good subject on which to try the Pittsburgh system, so we talked to Pittsburgh about making a search of the U.S. Code on their tapes to see where the death penalty is provided for. In the course of discussion with them they asked for a list of key phrases to assist in retrieval and we gave them "death penalty," "death sentence," "hanging," and so on, a whole series of these. On the basis of this they went ahead and put this list into the computer. In the meantime we went about doing the same search manually.

They came back with a readout that was very voluminous and obviously had a great deal of irrelevancy, particularly with reference to the compensation laws. We examined it, and then we finally realized what had happened. We had given them the words "death sentence," and in going back over these compensation law readouts we found that they included provision of law stating "where injury results in death" and so on, and so on, and "where injuries occur as stated in the prior sentence" then "so and so, and so and so." Wherever those two words appeared in juxtaposition, "death" and "sentence," we had compensation laws thrown at us. The result was we had an enormous amount of read-out material. Of course, once we discovered what had happened, we were able to screen out that material and bring it down to what we needed. We found the . . .

Mr. Capron: May I just interrupt to get this: Did they go back and reprogram this so that they got just what you wanted?

Mr. Jayson: Not that I know of. The end result was that, with regard to the provisions of the law that we were really interested in, they had picked up one or two provisions of the Code that we had not picked up manually and vice versa. We picked up one or two that they had not picked up on the machine for some reason or other.

Now, we tried this simply as an experiment to see how useful it might be to us. Of course, we did prove to ourselves that if we had the machine on the premises for this sort of search of the Code, which we are doing very frequently, either a search of the Code or a search of the various states' statutes, this would be a great aid. But we haven't gone any further with it because we simply don't have the money to pay for the searches. The various outfits that do have the various codes on tape haven't got any formalized program charges as yet that we can fit into our budget.

Mr. Hugo: I would like to recognize specifically an important yet very simple tie-in between the substance of Mr. Meadow's talk and some of the things that were said by Mr. Knox this morning. That is the interface between basic technical developments and political questions such as access and exploitability. The conversion of information into machine-readable form has very substantial implications for the political balance between the legislative and the executive branches, because once bodies of data are translated into machine-readable form the rationale for availability, accessibility, exploitability, changes dramatically.

There is an immense difference between having 500 file cabinets which Congress wants access to and two reels of magnetic tape. This is not to say that Congress will ever develop the capability to read what is on the tape but the question becomes entirely different. Also, as Mr. Jayson pointed out, when the information resides exclusively within the executive branch there is always the danger of their "summarizing" it and giving it to you "selectively."

The problem becomes entirely different when Congress says, "Don't select it, just give me the tape and I can look at the whole thing." Congress may not have the technical capability,

123

but all of the rationales and the political factors are entirely different now that you are dealing with a couple of reels of magnetic tape, with standardized data and documentation, with thousands—perhaps millions—of individual reports rather than 200 or 300 file cabinets.

Mr. Capron: Mike, I don't understand in the terms you are discussing the difference between 500 file cabinets and two reels of tape. I just don't get it.

Mr. Hugo: Take the raw data underlying the federal budget. Now that the detailed budget schedules are on magnetic tape, sources outside of the executive branch can reconstruct the budget to answer any questions they want to ask.

Mr. Jayson: How much money are we spending on education? A congressman wants to know how much money we are spending on education in the South, or in my state? How much money are we spending on research for farms?

Mr. Capron: You see, each of these questions is analytic.

Mr. Jayson: Well, this is where we get down to some of the things that we haven't been grappling with thus far. The congressman doesn't want the raw material. He wants the end product. He wants something that is concise. He wants something he can use in making his decision after you take the raw material and analyze it.

Mr. Hugo: The machine-readable data gives him the possibility of getting the end product from his staff.

Mr. Jayson: It gives him the raw material, but does it go any further?

Mr. Hugo: It won't go any further if he will never provide the staff resources. The point to be stressed is the provision of the staff resources. The problem becomes entirely different once you are dealing with one complete federal budget on a reel of magnetic tape instead of an unmanageable number of reports from the agencies to the bureau.

Mr. Jayson: I agree with that 100 percent, but again it is still a first step. If you're a congressman, you've got to have the same material that is available to the executive in determining or evaluating the alternatives there are. You are reading it differently from the way the executive does.

Mr. Hugo: But machine-readable data introduces another element, and that is the understructure of documentation, coding, and classification which, I think it's very safe to say, seldom existed in such quality before you had the common denominator of the International Business Machines Corporation. This is the common denominator, if the Congress wants to use it, between the data that the executive has got and the data that the legislature will get.

Mr. Capron: I'm still lost a little bit here. Is this just a cost question, or is it . . .

Mr. Chartrand: It's a resource question.

Mr. Capron: Yes, but wait. The data in there is put on in some code. If anyone can find a number that he is asked to get out of 500 cabinets, he can find it off the tape. But if the congressman is put in the room or his staff doesn't have the code or doesn't understand the code, he can't pull the right file drawer open and pull the right manila envelope out, nor can he go to the machine and pull it out.

Mr. Hugo: With the advent of machine-readable data, Bill, it's much more likely that such a code will exist. The Budget Bureau of the United States did not have a comprehensive coding structure, at least for budget data which was made public, until they had to develop one in order to put the budget schedules on magnetic tape.

Mr. Chartrand: To recapitulate, I think that you have essentially three steps: You mentioned the first one. That's the existence of this raw data. The second would be the coding scheme or schemes that went along with it. And the third, which several people have implied here, but haven't really said yet, is the degree of usefulness of the programming, the programs that are written especially to massage this data. Everyone here knows that the ability to retrieve and to take various cuts at this data obviously is only going to be as good as the programs that are written.

Mr. Hugo: I didn't mean to get into the budget per se here, Bob. But in answer to Mr. Capron, the sophistication of the coding system in the federal budget document has changed immensely in the last three or four years. The responsibility for that change lies largely if not solely with the introduction of data processing within the Budget Bureau. It was forced to develop a coding classification system.

Now, Congress may not use that. It may never develop the capability, but at least it's there and it wasn't two or three years ago. Machine-readable data is responsible for this, and I am sure there are many, many instances similar to this throughout the executive. Congress, of course, may decide that it wants to live with its present capabilities.

Mr. Jayson: It is likely that once they know that these tools are available they are going to want to use them.

Mr. Chartrand: Certainly those of us who have spent some time in the intelligence community have seen steps taken, where in order to process and transmit certain information more efficiently and with controlled security, codes were devised and selective data were placed in a format that made the information easier to handle. We still are on the threshold of applying these techniques and procedures to data of concern to the Congress.

COLONEL ANDREW A. AINES

Integration of Public and Private Archives for
Government Decision Makers

I FEEL a little bit abashed following some of the speakers
who have been on. I had no idea, as I prepared my essay,
of the work done by Ken and by some of the others in
this room. I would have been wiser and perhaps written a
little bit differently had I known. I say this as a compliment
to you gentlemen. I am amazed when I read in his paper,
however, that the computer becomes a means of restoring the
legislature to its proper equal status with the judicial and
executive branches of government. From the standpoint of
a person in the executive branch, I never had that feeling that
there was any status lost that had to be regained by Congress.
[Laughter.] I have always had the greatest respect for
Congress, although I am not sure I call it the first branch of
government, as the American Enterprise Institute's book
indicated, *(Congress: The First Branch of Government:* 1966).
I call it one of the most important branches of the government.

I want to indicate that I see some communication problems
that I find fascinating. For example, about three months ago
a gentleman, who is the dean of a Midwest university, met
with me and said, "Andy, we have some money and we are

127

trying to think of what we might do in our university in terms of a new bold educational approach. We are getting tired of running over the same territory that all of the other universities are doing."

I suggested to him that his university might endow a chair dealing with communication in government at all levels, among, up, down, and lateral. He thought about it and thought about it and said, "This must have been done by somebody." I said, "Conceivably, but I am sure of this, you are going to hear a lot more about this proposal in the future, and it's a good idea to go back and make a real determination, not on this offhand way I have thrown it at you, as to whether or not this is a viable thing for tomorrow. I have a feeling that the fate of our government will be tied to the need of better communications in the future. This is a feeling which is visceral rather than based on facts." He came back and said that he tried to sell it to his superiors and they thought it was a real good idea, and maybe they'll consider it next year. Which means, of course, that it is dead right now.

The reason why I feel that I learned something today is that I just didn't realize, and I should have, that there are communication mores of Congress which will perhaps find themselves attacked sharply by the coming of new technology. It occurred to me, in my typically brave, free-wheeling spirit, that Congress would be delighted to capture the essence of new communications and try to make it work. As an optimist, I still have that feeling. Sure, there are going to be people who won't fight at the bastions, but I have a belief that the views of the people like Representative Schwengel and some of the others I have heard today will ultimately prevail.

I have been asked to talk about the integration of information facilities in and out of the government, an eventuality that would provide real gains for decision makers in Congress and the executive branch. To be real parsimonious with words, I could say I am all for it, and add that I am ready for your questions.

But you know, I am inclined to believe that if we want Congress and the executive branch to obtain better information for decision making and problem solving, this can only happen if both institutions are ready to develop systematically internal information systems to take advantage of the many sources of information available today and more tomorrow.

I suspect that this is not going to be as easy as it sounds, that there are forces at work which encourage the communications lag, and this is unfortunate. I say it is unfortunate because there is a possibility that more internal concern shown in Congress for better communications would signal other public and private groups to quicken their pace of development and encourage them to standardize and integrate their efforts so that information could flow faster and better.

What could Congress do to improve the situation?

Before I answer this, I want to make it clear that general improvement of communications is a highly complex operation, and that gains take time and come in small fractions. In addition, I would like to have the record show that I believe that Congress has been rather understanding and generous in providing resources for information handling in a variety of fields, such as education, libraries, and health. There have been gains in executive agency information operations almost across the board. I do not have any hard evidence to offer you, but I estimate that over a half-billion dollars a year is invested in scientific and technical information programs alone by the federal agencies. There is some overlap, I am sure, but I would estimate that close to a half-billion dollars a year of government funds are going into all kinds of libraries.

Yes, one would have to agree that Congress has been anything but pinch-penny when it comes to providing funds for improving and maintaining information facilities. But there are things that Congress can do to improve the situation. Let me try to list a few of them, not necessarily in order of importance or priority. I think it was David Sarnoff * who pointed out that the modern building block today is information. Actually, he has re-packaged an old truism. Countless generations have been taught that knowledge is power. After the Russian Revolution, for example, it was Lenin who counseled his disciples to organize modern and efficient information-gathering and information-disseminating activities

---

* General David Sarnoff, Chairman of the Board, Radio Corporation of America.

in the Soviet Union. VINITI * was the result. The lesson was not lost to all countries in the world, including the United States. I think David Sarnoff's observation is important, because modern communications technology, a field in which the United States is an acknowledged leader, has raised the ante, given us new dimensions of speed and ability to manipulate large masses of data, and provided us with information tools utterly unlike those of yesterday.

I believe that every government official in the United States needs to be schooled in modern communications methods and that Congress ought to encourage and even insure that we move in this direction without delay. That my congressional friends and their staffs will be among the first students, along with some of my executive branch colleagues, is my earnest hope.

At this point, I want to make it clear that I am not only talking about improved knowledge in the mechanized handling of information, based on the computer. I also refer to the art of communicating. The art of communicating has nothing to do with machinery; it has to do with motivation and attitudes and reward-penalty systems. It matters not how elegant a mechanized information system application is if the people who are supposed to use it do not. First comes the knowledge, then the understanding, and after that the kind of sophistication we are going to need if we are going to be able to live with the horrendous "problem-explosion" that this generation faces and needs to harness.

There is another reason why we all have to improve our communication skill, I believe. Our young people will be so much better trained than our generation in the use of modern communications that it behooves us to do our best to learn how to communicate with them. People like McLuhan ** may mystify us with some of their mystic views, but they do us a service by reminding us that there are two worlds of communication—and ours is comparatively linear and square. At least this seems to be the view of the generation now in our schools and colleges, who will, before long, be taking our places.

* Name of Soviet agency in Moscow responsible for collecting, translating and disseminating scientific and technological information.

** Herbert Marshall McLuhan, and Q. Fiore, wrote the book called *The Medium is the Massage.*

Having mentioned McLuhan, I would like to take a page out of his book and do a bit of probing on my own. At another time and place, I have pointed out that we can consider the federal agencies as huge information-accumulating, -handling, and -disseminating establishments. The same can be said about Congress. If this is so, I believe that it is proper to ask the question: How have we organized ourselves to process information in the most efficient way open to us?

I suspect that many members of Congress and my colleagues in the Legislative Reference Service have asked this question many times and have been dissatisfied with the answer that comes out. I would find it fascinating to turn loose a group of creative information systems people with the instruction that they are to come up with an ideal congressional information system, without consideration of its current customs and traditions in information handling.

Let me be specific. It may be unfair to describe it this way, but as I wander through the halls of Congress sometimes I can almost feel the breath of the ghosts that more customarily inhabit courtrooms and town halls of an older generation. Now, what would you get if you instructed the information systems architects to build a structure more like modern laboratories or communications centers? What if you asked Bell Telephone Labs, IBM, and other groups of modern communicators to build you a workshop functionally designed to maximize communications, instead of what you have today, which, I will admit, is stately, formal, and beautiful?

You may disagree with me, but I am inclined to the belief that a different kind of an environment might result in some interesting gains. Picture consoles, closed television, micromedia readers, and the like in each of your rooms. Picture calling a colleague in another part of the building and showing him, on a screen, a document or a passage of a document you want to discuss with him.

Imagine providing each congressman with the capability of video-tie-in with the Executive Office of the President, agency heads, laboratories, statehouses—you name it.

Picture giving each member of Congress access to a series of scientific, legal, economic, and other information banks.

Imagine staging conferences and meetings of very busy and important people in place—almost anywhere in the country and even the world.

131

I cannot help but feel that doing business in this way is the shape of things that has come, and that Congress should join the executive branch and seek to reside in this new world.

A moment ago I mentioned the possibility of having access to a series of information banks through an office console. Quite possibly you would want to be tied to a number of computers—the nodes of a national information network from which you obtain information on a real-time basis. You might want to be attached to a switching center, operated by Legislative Reference Service and the Library of Congress, to any point in the world with specialized data you need. In COSATI —the Committee on Scientific and Technical Information of the Federal Council for Science and Technology—we have done a considerable amount of pioneering work in the early development of national information systems in science and technology. We need the help of Congress in providing necessary authority and resources to move more rapidly in this area. In this connection, I would like to add yet another thing that Congress can do. We simply have to get more understanding and support to bring a few more people aboard to help structure national information systems in conjunction with other groups in and out of the government. We need creative people to help get sharper focus on the many problems we face and help find solutions.

Three weeks ago, President Johnson and President Frei announced from Punta del Este, Uruguay, that a 150-inch reflecting telescope, the largest in the Southern Hemisphere, will be built in the Chilean Andes. It was further announced that the design and construction of the new telescope will be a joint effort of the University of Chile, the National Science Foundation, and the Ford Foundation. The two United States institutions will jointly finance the telescope to the tune of $10 million. The news release went on to say that "the center of our own galaxy, as well as our nearest neighbor galaxy, the Magellanic Clouds, can be seen only from the Southern Hemisphere," and that "when built astronomers from both hemispheres will be able to use this new scientific instrument of unprecedented power." I think we can all applaud the enlightened generosity of the United States, but I cannot help but note the need for the same kind of enlightenment on the Hill. It is not necessary to use a telescope to search out the many unfinished tasks this generation has before it, tasks that might become easier if congressional communication were improved by "new scientific instruments of unprecedented power."

An expert study team from the Systems Development Corporation suggested to COSATI in 1965 that a "capping agency" was needed at Executive Office of the President level to help provide leadership in the development of urgently needed national information systems. As they saw it, some 250 people would comprise the agency and would be needed to more actively help structure the growing national network of scientific and technical information centers and activities. The Federal Council for Science and Technology invited the Office of Science and Technology to take preliminary action. Whereupon, OST asked Congress for a few additional spaces and dollars to help it get started on this program of vital importance to the country.

We have stimulated groups all over the United States and the world to move more rapidly into national information systems, including the Soviet Union. But we are stymied, not necessarily by the lack of interest and concern on the part of Congress and the President but by what I suspect is the bureaucratic slowness that largely comes as a result of a communications system designed for a less hirsute era than the one in which we live. As a consequence, it should not surprise us if we will have to expect to pay a huge price for renovation of information systems that will have grown without harmony and integration. I have no doubt in my mind that, in a year or two, some members of Congress will rake us over the hot coals because we did not move more rapidly in this field. They may even point out that $10 million was raised—a share from the government—to build a telescope in Chile so that we could explore the Magellanic clouds.

I dwell on this case, because I sense that it belongs to the same family of problems that Congress faces as it surveys its own communications. I would like to urge you to remember that communications is the tie that binds peoples and institutions together, provides the background knowledge that makes problem solving easier and faster, supplies the maker of decisions with the information and data that he needs. It is too bad that we have no way to measure the cost of *not* investing more in modern information systems; it might scare the daylights out of us.

As you gather, I am saying that it will be necessary to make sizable investments in new information systems in the future, and we have to add to that the cost of resources needed to integrate public and private information repositories. If we do not undertake this kind of an operation, there is serious question as to our ability to make optimal use of them for our own decision making. More important, perhaps, the repositories or information centers will not be able to interact efficiently with each other and their users. It is the same old problem of different rail gauges or telephone systems, making communication and transportation interlinkage difficult or impossible.

To the limit of our resources, COSATI has sought to develop some interim standards to help ease the situation. We have one on microfiche, on descriptive cataloging, on subject category lists, on corporate author listing, and we are working on others. But it is very evident to us that there is a need for lots more action, especially as we move in the direction of worldwide information systems to exchange scientific, technical, and other kinds of information. As nations converge in the direction of fairly uniform information and data exchange programs, we are naturally interested in the widest adoption of our techniques and systems. Congressional understanding and support would be useful to help the systems grow in a coherent fashion, and, just as important, congressional information gathering from the complex of information centers would be more fruitful. I cannot stress the need for compatibility too much as we move forward.

The government is already supporting hundreds of information analysis and data centers, and they continue to grow with each passing day. It is widely recognized that these information centers will be expected to sift and purge the literature, extracting that which is best, and identifying and discarding that which is outmoded or of poor quality. The larger, more general libraries, will probably take on other functions, like cataloging and archiving. As centers of excellence where the latest information in given areas is stored, the information analysis centers will take on real importance to the educational and research world, as well as the world of managers and decision makers.

Congress will also want to take advantage of the potentialities of the new project-reporting systems that our Federal R&D agencies are now developing. Obtaining information and data on all kinds of programs will be aided by developing congressional capabilities to get read-outs rapidly and efficiently. Since the executive branch needs to develop management information systems to get its job done, it seems to me that Congress should be able to tap in for data it wants as needed, rather than seeking to duplicate the huge data bank that will exist in the federal agencies. Considerable time and money will be saved if we work closely together in the common quest.

Let me say in conclusion that, despite the many problems we face in the development of modern information systems to improve communications, one thing is clear. There are many opportunities being afforded us and we cannot afford to tarry in taking systematic planning and implementing steps. It will take the best we have from all of us, and I know that my colleagues in Congress are just as anxious for progress as are we on Pennsylvania and 17th.

COMMENT ON AINES PAPER

Mr. Capron: You may not agree with the premise that I am going to state, but, even if you don't, I think my question is one that you can respond to. I am one of those who feels strongly that diversity and competition at the R&D stage is very desirable and that we pay a real price in most technologies if we overcentralize or centralize too quickly. But there does come a point at the application stage where there may be tremendous economies and efficiencies gained by this.

I gather from your main theme, if I understood it correctly, that you think that in the information-handling technology as it is developed that we are now at a point where a more systematic planning and integration of national information systems, to use your phrase, is appropriate. Do you think there are any risks here or dangers that you will actually slow down progress in some areas by forcing systems that are at a pretty early stage into some sort of a format?

Col. Aines: I think that is a splendid question. It is very much in keeping with my concepts. Science and technology have to be open-ended endeavors. Obviously we must agree science and technology have to be open-ended or no progress would be made. But whatever our state of knowledge is today, if, God willing, we are able to build on it for the next 40 or 50 years, certainly great progress will result, which may make our present era look comparatively like the 1900s in terms of progress.

Information systems, as I see them, must be similarly open-minded, so that they do not close the open-endedness of science and technology. We can't possibly let the information-systems managers, for example, develop systems in such a way that it would be impossible for us to be able to be free in our research and our experimentation. Your inference in that respect I find relevant. It is one to which I subscribe.

I don't feel that, as Bill Knox said earlier today, we are concerned with and talking about a monolithic kind of an operation where everything falls into a certain pattern or "off with their heads." We are thinking more in terms of what we call a harmonious array of information systems that will grow, because they are being built to serve agency missions and discipline groups, if you will.

We don't feel that anybody has enough brains today and in the foreseeable future, frankly, to sit down and work out a centralized national information system. What we do feel is that there has to be some guidance and some measure of acceptable control at the highest level, and I hope Congress joins the executive in seeking this reasonable good.

If we accepted all of the requests for program support of professional societies, of EDUCOM,* of all groups that now would like to move into national systems, there wouldn't be enough R&D dollars left to do any research and development, particularly since they are all moving into costly mechanization to handle the large masses of data, and increasing the numbers of people who make up their organizations.

There is much work to be done with the infrastructure to provide necessary lubrication and search for areas of systems compatibility. We hope that information research and development funds will be able not only to take care of one system,

---

* Inter-University Communications Council.

but perhaps a half a dozen applications might profit from one bit of research. We are entering an era in which I expect there is going to be much experimentation. Some systems will be started. Some will fail. I hope we will have a good batting average.

I see our present effort as a search for criteria and understanding of what kind of traffic lights we need that could flash red, amber, or green at groups that are looking for government support in building individual information systems. We are concerned with developing a general framework and a common objective toward which these people can move. I believe that all we can do now is to draw a hazy outline of directions to go. I do not believe that we have the talents to do very much more than that.

However, we feel very strongly that the best way to get good information systems is to have them bubble from the ground up. This is going to be expensive at times, and we feel that we have to monitor the funds with intelligence. I have already mentioned that a lot of money is going into this. And, if we are going to monitor funds, we had better know a damned sight more than we do now about the best way to do it.

Mr. Armer: You know, there are some things I liked very much about your talk and some things that I didn't like. Let me focus first on some things I didn't like. You suggested that it might be nice to turn loose a group of creative information-systems people with instructions that they are to come up with an ideal congressional information system, without consideration for its current customs and traditions in information handling. As someone from the information systems side of the house, maybe not a creative one but at least from that side of the house, I guess I should feel flattered. But your suggestion bothers me.

I am reminded of the story that used to go around the operations research community many years ago about the operations research specialist who came into the mess hall and noticed that they had provided three barrels at the exit for the troops to wash their mess kits in. One of these barrels had soap in it and the other two had clear water for rinsing. There was quite a queue at the soap barrel. So he insisted that they put soap in two of the barrels, leaving just one barrel with

137

clear water. The mess sergeant remarked afterward that it was fortunate that the operations research specialist left after two days because all the men in the camp got sick from the soapy water, since their mess kits weren't getting rinsed very well. So I believe that you must involve the people who really know the problem in the design of a congressional information system. You can't just turn the information people loose on this.

Secondly, I believe that if you did design the system without worrying about present customs and traditions, it would be only an interesting academic exercise, since I suspect that the political problems of getting from here to there are such that there just isn't any way of getting from here to there. Thus, I feel we should ask ourselves just what are the steps we can take under the present environment?

What I liked very much about your talk was your early statement that every government official in the United States needs to be schooled in modern communications methods, and that Congress ought to encourage and even insure that we move in this direction without delay. One of the notes I wrote to myself early this morning was that it seemed to me we were mostly talking about the problem and trying to convince each other of its seriousness. I was on the point of saying, "Let's admit that it's a serious problem that does exist and ask ourselves what can be done about it?" I think, to some extent, that now we have gotten off into a discussion of what can be done about it, but I would hope that before we leave tomorrow we do try and focus on what strategies can be evolved, what can be done. I don't think we need to convince each other of the problem.

Col. Aines: I am flattered with the second part, but let me reply to the first. I think you are right. I hope you will recall my opening comments and that I said that I had written an essay. You will remember that I said somewhere in my talk that I am not interested in elegant applications. I think we have to get something that's usable, and I think your colleague to the left made the same point, and virtually everybody has. My main point is that, to obtain progress, we might profit by getting away from the traditional ways of looking at the problem.

As an example of the kind of problems we face, I will be going to New York tomorrow to talk to the Federal Bar Association about copyright legislation now before the Congress. Providing copyright protection for authors, as new computerized networks are developed, brings us to a crossroads unique in history.

There is a growing need and effort to look harder at the problem and the possible effects of legislating before we really have the answers. Virtually all groups—publishers, authors, computer people, and educational people who came to a meeting at our office—agreed that we ought to know more about the problem prior to legislating in this particular sector.

It seems so clear to me that thinking through a problem can be helped by giving it a fresh approach. The reason I am not unhappy about the appearance of a man like McLuhan is that he tends to shepherd us away from our ordinary Euclidean-Cartesian way of looking at things and makes us look at it a bit differently. I don't agree with much of what he says, frankly, but anybody who helps me look at problems from additional angles is appreciated.

What I am saying is that I prepared this talk as an essay in which I set up an idealized approach, because I felt that this may be needed if Congress is going to try to structure a new communications system. Somebody is going to have to give somewhere. So, maybe a little bit of this treatment might be useful.

Mr. Jayson: I just wanted to mention the possibility of an obstacle here when Congress attempts to tap into the systems information the executive has available. That is the problem of executive privilege and classified information. Congress may have problems in getting the answers when it needs to know about something on which it is legislating.

I don't know what impact this has. I just throw it out as another force, just as we raised the point of privacy before, because it is an element that has to be taken into account. In other words, we don't know to what extent the executive branch will be censoring the information that is put out.

Col. Aines: I would say that the same problem exists right now in the executive branch. It exists everywhere. You talked about the chairmen . . . some of you talked about people within Congress who hold onto information that might be useful to other members of Congress. This is a human problem. It is no different in the executive department than it is in Congress, and, really, the only hope that I have, and it's a matter of hope and not knowledge, is that these new systems will cause us to discard some of the withholding of information.

I think we are coming into an era in which you can't hoard information as in the past. I want to assure you that one reason why it may be difficult at times to get information out of the executive branch is not because of a desire to hold back but because we may not have organized ourselves properly to pass it on to Congress.

I have seen this, as a research and development man, many times. In the old days, when we tried to get a fix on geographical spread of funds, we simply didn't have any communication mechanism constructed in the federal agencies to do this easily. I think we are moving in the direction of more openness. I think that with the help and·encouragement of Congress more information and data will flow than ever before, because the success of government operations requires it.

I also hope that information from Congress will flow just as easily in the direction of the executive as you would like to see it coming from the executive. It should be a two-way flow, and this calls for a permissive attitude. Our fighting chance is that with new communications technology we can do it.

Thomas S. McFee, Department of Health, Education, and Welfare: I haven't said very much today. I think I am the only one in the audience that is a member of an operating executive department, and consequently I have some of my own prejudices on the subject.

We were discussing the problems of an information system for the Congress today. I think after tomorrow, when you hear about some of the developmental work in PPB (Planning-Programming-Budgeting) information systems within the executive department, my point may be better made; but I am not going to be here tomorrow, so I might as well make it now.

The point that we have been talking about today is, "How can Congress make use of information and information systems?" One of the things that I've learned, being in the information system business, is that organization for application of this technology is sometimes more important than the technology itself.

In other words, I have found that it's very difficult to organize to make use of this technology. I have studied many problems that, on the surface, have been thought of as information-system-design problems. You end up looking at an organization and saying, "They ought to reorganize, in order to make use of this technology." Then the guy says, "What are you doing studying organization, you're supposed to be studying information systems?" But we all know that they are very closely related.

This is why I have a gloomy feeling about Congress ever being able to exploit this technology with its present organization. Paul made the point that its present organization is reality, and I don't see any other way, right now, for Congress to reorganize to perform its primary function. So, what I am really saying is that it is going to be very difficult for Congress to build an integrated information system fully exploiting this technology.

Now, the executive department has some of its own problems of organization and management. The proposals that Andy Aines alluded to are possible ways in getting the executive department organized. This is my own personal comment and surely not a position of the agency: I think Congress, in the long run, would be further along in getting the kind of information it wants if it would support an integrated development of an information system in the executive department and work very closely with the executive department to take the cream off this type of information system. This would be more fruitful than an attempt to devise or build its own information system.

That is the point I would like to leave, and I know it's a controversial one. I feel that, after your session tomorrow, maybe you will be convinced that some of the structuring and cataloging of information, being forced on the agencies by the development of the PPB system, is going to be one of the answers to getting the type of information that Congress needs to do its job.

One other thought I'd like to leave is a question, and I would like it answered for my own use. What particular need does Congress have for information that is not also a need of the executive department agencies, in order to run and effectively manage their own programs? My own feeling is that there is no difference, and that's why I think the premise, that we should support this effort in only one area, is a good point.

Mr. Chartrand: There will be several hours for discussing this, and I think that was very well taken. We have time for one answer.

Mr. Casselman: I think the danger in creating one information system for both the executive and the legislative branches is that you are going to interfere with a delicate balance-of-power system. You are going to take away from Congress its ability to exercise independent oversight of the executive branch. Granted that the executive branch may have the same use for information that Congress has and that Congress doesn't effectively exercise its oversight function now, but this is not a valid reason for combining the information systems of these two branches of government.

If I may reflect further on what Col. Aines has said as a point of essay: As soon as we talk about creating legislation in an ideal laboratory condition, we change the premise of our discussion. We assume we are working with a perfect political model, with perfect individuals elected to Congress and the White House. This isn't the case, and, for this reason, the founding fathers created a system of checks and balances and separation of powers to prevent abuses and insure the independent and vigorous functioning of each branch of government. Certainly, the maintenance of separate sources of information is basic to this concept. Indeed the House and Senate rules of procedure—as amended by the 1946 Reorganization Act—which provide for a committee system with investigatory and oversight functions, are based on the idea of Congress having, insofar as possible, independent sources of information and evaluation.

In short, information handling, as a political tool and especially as a means of combining the efforts of the executive and legislative branches of government, would appear to me to be inimical to the proper functioning of government. On the other hand, information handling primarily as a housekeeping tool, as proposed in H.R. 21, would seem to have a more immediate and beneficial application to the work of Congress.

Part Two

Implications for the Congress of the Planning, Programming, and Budgeting System (PPBS)

WILLIAM CAPRON

Development of Cost-Effectiveness Systems in the Federal Government

I WILL SET the stage for our discussion by laying out very briefly some background on the planning-programming-budgeting system, which is commonly referred to as "PPBS" or, more briefly, "PPB." I will also attempt to clear up some of the quite natural misunderstanding, which a number of people in Washington, and I think especially in the Congress, have, regarding the administration's purpose in establishing the system. Before I talk directly about the reasons for adopting PPBS, it may be useful to trace briefly the major developments in the history of executive budgeting.

The Budgeting and Accounting Act of 1921 established an executive budget, and required the President each year to submit to the Congress his budget and his specific recommendations and requests for appropriations for all of the executive branch. This was a major change in the system which had existed prior to 1921, in which each department went individually before the Congress, and specifically before the Appropriations Committees. The Chief Executive then had to rely on his general control over cabinet officers and independent agency heads to impose his will on budgetary decisions. In fact, the President exercised budgetary control only occasionally and spasmodically, so that each department and agency had a large measure of independence. In other words, no presidential view of federal program and budget matters was ever presented to the Congress. It was to correct this that the Congress, itself, initiated the move to an executive budget.

After World War I, government activities were becoming much more complicated, and federal expenditures were more significant—although compared to today, of course, federal expenditures then seem miniscule. The Congress itself, I think, had the sense of a kind of rudderless ship down at the other end of Pennsylvania Avenue, and recognized that a presidential budget could potentially provide a powerful lever to bring cohesion and direction to the executive branch. The 1921 Act established the Bureau of the Budget within the Treasury. The next significant date in the evolution of executive budgeting was 1939, when President Roosevelt recognized that the budget was one of the key elements of leadership and control. He moved the bureau into a newly created Executive Office of the President, emphasizing that this was a staff function in a staff agency directly responsible to the President.

The period since 1939 has seen a growth of the technical skill in control of the budget and, I think, in the quality of the system in serving the President's needs. However, those of us who served in the bureau in the early 1960s were increasingly aware that the information the system was generating was not of a sort directly useful to presidential budgetary decision making—nor was it well organized for that purpose. The fault here was really the Bureau's, since it was in response to bureau request that the information came from the departments and agencies.

The President is not primarily concerned with the budget as a device for the detailed control of various programs, but rather as an instrument for decision making and overall guidance on policy and programs. Yet, it is fair to say that the Bureau of the Budget, in its early years, was preoccupied with control. One of the reasons for congressional interest in developing an executive budget system was concern over the various laxities in the administration of the budget. Congress couldn't really hold the President responsible for this laxity, since he had no system, no formal "handle" on fiscal action.* This new means of control was created with the Budget and Accounting Act. It is not surprising, therefore, that the early emphasis in the activities of the Bureau was on making sure that tax dollars were spent for those items for which the Congress had appropriated these dollars. It is not surprising, either, that the "green eyeshade" accounting vision of the Bureau of the Budget was created during this period and has stuck with it since then.

In explaining the dissatisfaction that was felt in the White House and in the executive office with the information that the existing system was producing for presidential program and financial decisions, we can identify two or three key sources of that dissatisfaction that are worth mentioning, because they help to explain some of the elements in the new system. In the first place, all of the information was input-oriented: How much an agency proposed to spend on personnel, how much for travel, how much for new typewriters, and the like. Very little attention was paid in the submission to the Bureau to the purposes of department's and agencies' programs. These were taken for granted and there was no basis for making the following kind of judgment which typically has to be made by the President or by his staff: What will happen if I have to cut this agency's request by 10 percent? Since there was no relationship between the inputs and any kind of indication of the purposes or the output of that agency's activity, this was a decision that had to be made in the dark. As a result, the charge sometimes made on the Hill by defenders of a particular program that the cuts recommended by the administration in a given agency's request were capricious and ill-informed was justified.

The executive budget process, as an information system, was not serving its key function, which I am asserting is to provide a framework and guidance for executive decisions with regard to programs and the sources necessary to implement those programs. No options were explicitly offered to the President. There were no alternatives presented to him in any kind of systematic form. The recommendations came into the Bureau

---

* PPBS has nothing to do with fiscal policy, at least directly and overtly, and the whole line of development, summed up in the phrase "the New Economics," is not a subject for our discussion here.

147

of the Budget in a take-it-or-leave-it kind of fashion. The President had a very difficult time in asserting his own judgments and will, except on an *ad hoc* basis.

One explanation for the *proliferation* of programs that concerns many people, and I think rightly, is that the easiest way, given the old budget system, for the Executive Office of the President and the White House and the President personally to impose his own ideas and directions on policy was to start afresh with a *new* program, which could be developed in the Executive Office and White House. In many cases, if the information system had been better—and it is hoped that with PPB it will be—new programs would only have been introduced when it became clear that modification and revision of existing programs couldn't do the job.

To summarize, I think that we can say that the existing budget was preoccupied with control and management considerations. It was input oriented. It was heavily oriented toward organization units in its structure, and it had very little to offer a President (or the "presidency") in terms of the kind of decisions that have to be made. The same things could be said for the major departments. The cabinet officers and major independent agency heads were captives of the same system and, in turn, had faced a problem comparable, in many respects, to that faced by the Chief Executive. PPB was introduced not only to improve the quality of the final decisions with regard to the recommendations the President would make to the Congress in January, but, also, with a view to strengthening the executive role of the cabinet officers in taking real responsibilities for developing and guiding the programs of their departments. Indeed, the problem of developing budget and financial information suitable for decision making *and* management and execution purposes was acute down the line within departments and agencies.

As a footnote to this discussion, I will say that in the period when we were developing the PPB system there was little concern or consideration with the implications of this for executive-legislative relationships, because the purpose of PPBS was to improve things on the executive side, and it was assumed that the Congress would continue to get recommendations in the form that they requested. It was also recognized, from the outset, that it would be very probable that, at least for some time, the Congress would wish to continue to deal with the appropriations process in the same format and with the same information as usual.

Also, it was recognized that, for the *execution* of the budget, we needed information broken down and structured and organized in the pre-PPBS form—namely, we needed an *input*-oriented, *organization*-unit-oriented budget for administration. Managers of a particular program, at the bureau level in a department, do not buy "output"; they buy people and they buy travel and the like, and they need to know what they have available for those objects. So, the object class or input-oriented budget was necessary for the executive branch, as well as for the Congress, quite apart from PPB.

PPB can be considered an additional slice or look at the organization of budgetary information for the specific purpose of improving the information available for making program and budget decisions. It is not a substitute for the old format, which is necessary and useful in the actual execution of the budget. I think that's a point that deserves some emphasis because, at least in the early days of PPBS when the Bureau of the Budget publicized this hoped-for modification in the system, this point wasn't emphasized sufficiently and it did get lost.

I won't dwell on the major significance of Mr. McNamara's success in the Pentagon since 1961 as an influence on the President's decision to call for a government-wide PPBS system in August 1965. That story is fairly well known. The planning-programming-budgeting system, which Mr. McNamara and Charles Hitch had begun to introduce in 1961, had been one of the key tools that the Secretary had used in asserting for the first time effective civilian control over the defense establishment. There is no question that personally the President was very much influenced by that record made "across the river" in the Pentagon.

For our purposes we don't need to dwell on all of the elements that make up the new PPB system; however, it would be useful to look at the major components. First of all, there is a *program budget structure.* As I have indicated, the structure is meant to focus on *objectives* and, where possible, to measure or develop indicators of the output of programs, rather than to structure the budget strictly on organization lines and strictly on input lines. The second element is the development and

149

periodic updating of a *program and financial plan*, known in the shorthand and jargon as PFP. The most important element in PFP, in relation to what has been done before, is that federal agencies are required to lay out their programs, not for the next budget year but for a period of several years ahead (typically five). Since many of the decisions that are made today in a program and budgetary sense have significant implications for the future, this is potentially one of the most significant modifications that PPB represents.

As a continuing activity, agencies are required to undertake, at the secretarial, bureau, and sub-unit level, *special analyses* of their programs and *evaluations* of their programs. The results of these analyses are to be reflected in the budget process. Such analyses are "fed" into the process in two ways. The studies themselves, of course, are made available, not only to the agency heads and cabinet officers but also to the President and the Bureau of the Budget. In some cases they focus on new programs, but more typically they will focus on an evaluation or re-evaluation of existing programs looking for new directions. It is here that the major emphasis is placed on the development of options or alternatives and looking at the cross-program tradeoffs that are involved.

This information—the program and financial plan and the special analyses—is summarized annually in a *Program Memorandum*. Each agency, each major department, will identify something like ten to a dozen major program areas, and for each area a memorandum will be written, summarizing the major recommendations of the cabinet officer to the President. Each program is then reviewed at the top level and modified by the Bureau of the Budget and the President. The *Program Memorandum*, after this review, will then serve as the basis for the *annual* budget submission, which, as before, will be made in the fall of each year to the Bureau of the Budget.

The actual preparation of the estimates and requests that the President will make in his budget message each year has not really been changed very much. It's just that it is made from a very different and, it is hoped, a very much improved, information base. Although there will be a five-year look in the executive branch at the implications of program and budget decisions, PPB involves no attempt or proposal, that I know of, to disrupt the annual budget appropriation cycle.

150

One of our major interests today is going to be on PPBS and the Congress and the implications of the new system. I do not want to anticipate the discussion to follow, but I will make one point: I think from the executive branch point of view the impact that PPBS has directly on the Congress, and more specifically on the dialogue between the Congress and the executive branch, is very much in the hands of the Congress. So far as I know, there is no attempt to "push" PPBS on the Congress if it is uninterested or unwilling to accept it.

One further point which is directly related to the implications of PPB for the Congress: The planning-programming-budgeting system does not, in a true sense, represent an increased centralization of power in the presidency. He will be better able to make those decisions which he is required to make by law, but it will also, to the extent that it works, strengthen the effectiveness in negotiating and bargaining between the departments and agencies and the executive office, since they are the primary producers of the new information and the new analyses. The power which information and analysis gives will not be concentrated in the Executive Office of the President or the White House, because the new information comes from the agencies.

There is little question that the quality of the dialogue in the bargaining process is going to be changed within the executive branch. I suspect that it may change the quality of the dialogue between the executive branch and the Congress, but that is not certain. We may be a little clearer, at least in the executive branch, about what is being done. And in some areas where mistakes are made, because of the exigencies and pressures of politics, we will undoubtedly go ahead and make that type of decision in very much the same way.

ROBERT N. GROSSE

Cost-Effectiveness as a Tool for Decision Makers
in the Executive Branch

Mr. Capron: To start our exploration of PPB, we have someone who is actually working with the system; Robert Grosse is the Deputy Assistant Secretary for Program Evaluation of the Department of Health, Education, and Welfare. He has a key responsibility for the development and implementation of PPBS in the largest nondefense federal agency. It is very important that we hear from someone who looks at PPB from the departmental point of view rather than the Bureau of Budget point of view because in the longer run the departmental level is not only where the real problems are but is also where the real payoff is going to be.

Dr. Grosse is going to focus on one of the major elements, namely, the analysis side of the total system. But I think it would be useful, Bob, if you would begin by placing the analysis function in perspective within the total system.

L ET ME TAKE a few minutes to discuss some of the problems of the decision-making process prior to last year, and what we are engaged in doing this year in terms of the system schedule and emphases. Programs and budgetary allocations were developed essentially from the bottom up. When a year's budget was to be formulated, a call went out from the Secretary's office, in turn to the Surgeon General of the Public Health Service, the Commissioner of Education, and so forth.

Generally, little guidance was given as to the particular thrusts and patterns which the leadership would like to see. The flow of ideas came from the bottom; they usually suggested increasing modestly the activities that were going on. We have had two major processes operating at the same time, the so-called budgetary process, which covered these programs and funding levels which had been authorized by the Congress, and the development of new legislative proposals and significant changes in authorizations. There has been little systematic planning of the department's programs. There was "thought" as to how to get across certain new concepts or how to get more funds for existing programs, but no tradition of carefully studying our interrelated program needs and evaluation of programs.

I didn't think that Bill Capron's description of a budget which is input-oriented quite fits HEW. One of the steps we had to take in the program-budgeting system was to develop a dimension which classified inputs such as training, research, and construction. Our appropriation classification has been described as a "laundry list," which largely represents our organizational structure—a line-item budget for a bureau or for a division or for an institute. In some cases these can be analogous to inputs but usually not. It is difficult to pull out, for example, the amount of money to be spent on training or the amount of money to be spent on construction. This planning is further complicated by the fact that the Department of HEW operates very few programs. Ninety-two percent of our new obligational authority is expended in grants-in-aid. If you are trying to evaluate a project, and the program is actually administered by institutions other than the Federal Government, it is very difficult to relate what happens in any systematic and useful fashion to our expenditures. So the fact that we lack good evaluation, analysis, and planning is not due only to the lack of appreciation of these as useful tools.

This year the first problem that we addressed was the pulling together of the budget and the legislative systems. Our office, Program Coordination, together with the Comptroller and the Assistant Secretary for Legislation, attempted to identify and lay out a planning schedule for the year. The first decision was to postpone the budget operations. Generally, budget development gets underway in our operating agencies in January and

February. We send out a call around March for this information, package it, bring it to the Bureau of the Budget in May or June for spring preview, and then send out agency ceilings in July. The postponement was to permit time for the development of plans and analyses and to feed them into the process. Experience indicated that significant budgetary decisions do not have to be made until quite late in the year. We then asked that the leadership in the Office of the Secretary and the offices of our commissioners seriously concern themselves with planning. I will outline the actual steps.

First, we agreed in the Office of the Secretary (after conversations with the Budget Bureau, the White House, and our operating agencies) on the significant issues on which studies would be performed. We defined these, and our office undertook to see that they were done, either directly under our research supervision or with us assisting and monitoring the operating agencies.

Second, we issued a call for basic information for the fiscal years 1966, 1967, and 1968, whose budget had already been sent on to the Congress by the President. For each program we asked questions about purposes, about target groups, and elements of the population affected by various programs. We also classified these into activities, essentially input dimensions such as research, training, construction, and so forth, and asked a number of other questions such as: Through whom are you doing this program—universities, hospitals, state governments? We asked for both cost and indicators of output and program impact.

We then sent to each operating agency head two funding levels for 1973. We asked them to submit their preferred programs under each constraint level, and to do this using the same classification of programs as in the information base for 1966–68 (although with less detail). These program objectives were reviewed by the Office of the Secretary and integrated program objectives for 1973 in health, education, and social services, and income maintenance were approved by the Secretary. These plans were assisted by the analyses which were nearing completion. The Secretary's 1973 objectives (in program terms) and 1969 budget ceilings were sent to the operating agencies in mid-August. Agencies were asked to prepare their 1969 budgets, 1969–73 Program and Financial

155

Plans, and legislative requirements to implement the plans. Departmental review to assure conformance to the Secretary's guidance was then followed by the transmission to the Bureau of the Budget of Program Memoranda explaining our choices, a Program and Financial Plan through 1973, and our fiscal year 1969 budget. Accompanying these were program analyses.

The objective of the analytical effort was to examine, in depth, areas about which major decisions need to be made. These decisions are required because of expiring legislation, important social problems, or a large money area. These analyses look at a number of alternative moves toward the solution of social problems and attempt to identify what the difference is if you go in one direction as opposed to another. As I am sure you are aware, in most of the social planning areas we lack data and we lack models but we made a try.

You might be interested in some of the studies we have done in HEW. The problem of deciding what to study and how to study probably takes up more time and is more critical than the actual performance of the calculations themselves. Figure 1 attempts to describe a way of thinking about the health area. We start with a social situation, a description of society in terms of the existing physical and social environments, the demographic structure (who is who and where are they, how many people are poor, how many of them are in trouble of one sort or another). "Personal Development" refers to the health status of particular individuals. From these we hopefully identify health problems. You can think of these, for example, as diseases that people may suffer from, such as cancer, tuberculosis, syphilis. Having identified the health problems in society, we attempt to determine what might be done to cope with them. I have illustrated two possible programs; environmental health and medical care and services.

In order to have these programs, resources must exist and be applied. So we may need to develop or increase the stock and quality of our resources—knowledge, manpower, facilities, and equipment—and bring these to bear on the problem. We have to assure that they are organized effectively and financed so that the delivery of medical care takes place. We look at this structure for society and its constituent elements and attempt to analyze how the Federal Government can best help within institutional and resource constraints. We may

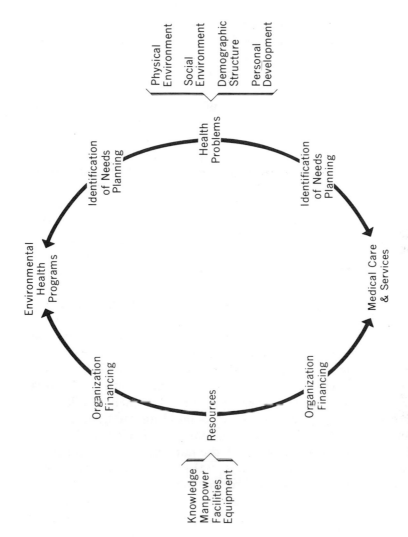

FIGURE 1. Identification of Health Problems, and Applicable Programs.

157

develop a program of research on environmental programs such as air and water purity, or we may help finance medical care—by such programs as Medicare and Medicaid.

We have a number of questions about each of the programs that we develop. What is it for? What does it accomplish? Who is being helped? How is it being carried out? How much does it cost? Who carries it out (both in the Federal Government and elsewhere)? How is it funded? These questions lead to the development of a program information structure. Figure 2 gives some insight into the way in which our structure arrays our programs. In the left-hand column are the names of possible program objectives or purposes such as the provision of medical care, consumer protection, development of basic skills, income maintenance, social services, and the like. To answer the question of how we carry these out, we subdivide programs into activities. A sampling of these is listed: innovation, the training of personnel, the delivery of beneficial services, the construction of facilities. For each we are interested also in whom you are doing it for—the target populations. So in this three-dimensional diagram we also look at what is being done, for example, for the handicapped, the aged, and migrants.

A particular program, from the program manager's point of view, may appear simply as a cell in the structure. And he asks "I filled out these forms and all I see is I'm in a box and it doesn't help me to decide anything at all." He's probably right. What we're interested in, of course, is building with these boxes insight into what takes place. We can add other activities to this cell, which was concerned with building facilities for the medical care of the handicapped, and we can pick up the rest of the medical-care activities for the handicapped and get some more understanding as to whether they are reasonably in balance or not for what we are trying to do. We can go further and pick up what we are doing in the area of medical care for the various target groups. Another way of looking at it is to ask the question: What are we doing for a particular target group in all programs, in this case for the handicapped (Figure 3)? Table 1 illustrates a way program information might come out. For a target group—children and youth of low income families—we can identify these programs—the educational programs, the specific health programs which are aimed at children with respect to child development, crippled children,

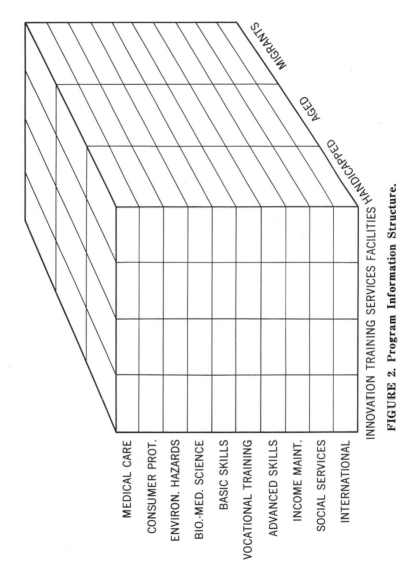

FIGURE 2. Program Information Structure.

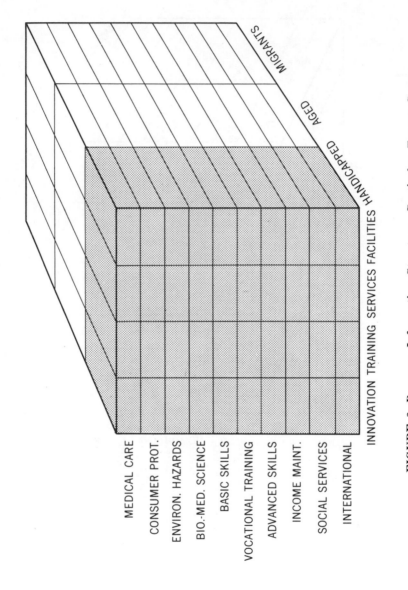

FIGURE 3. Program Information Structure—Particular Target Group
(Handicapped).

early case finding and treatment, various social services and money payments, as well. We can begin to look at programs from the point of view of the recipients of the benefits of these programs.

TABLE 1: Program Information Structure—Sample of Results

TARGET GROUP: CHILDREN AND YOUTH-INCOME
UNDER 5,000 (AGE 0–21)

EDUCATION PROGRAMS
  IMPROVING THE EDUCATION OF THE DISADVANTAGED
    Educationally deprived children (ESEA TITLE I)
    National teacher corps
    Educational opportunity grants (HEA TITLE IV-A)
    Educational talent contracts (HEA TITLE IV-A)
    College work study grants (HEA IV-C)
    Vocational work study grants (HEA IV-C)

HEALTH PROGRAMS
  HEALTH PROBLEM CLASSIFICATION
    Child development
    Crippled children
    School and pre-school children
    Maternity and infant care
    Maternal and child health
    Comprehensive maternal and child care
    Early case finding and treatment
  GENERAL HEALTH CARE PROGRAMS
    Hospital care
    Physicians
    Dental services
    Nurse services
    Home health services
    Out patient

SOCIAL SERVICES PROGRAMS
  INDIVIDUAL AND FAMILY SERVICES
    Day care
    Foster care
    Other child welfare services
  STRENGTHENING RESOURCES AND ORGANIZATION OF SOCIAL SERVICES
    INSTITUTIONS
    Juvenile delinquency

INCOME MAINTENANCE PROGRAMS
  OTHER INDIVIDUAL AND FAMILY SUPPORT
    Aid to families with dependent children

Now, I'd like to describe some of the approaches to resource allocation problems. For example, we asked the question, "To improve the health of poor children, what should be our policy

161

and programs?" We studied a number of alternatives. One of these was to provide comprehensive health care for mothers, or mothers-to-be, and children. We could do this for children up to the various ages. We also examined other approaches such as one which we called "Early Case Finding and Treatment." This would not be comprehensive care, but looks at the children after birth and at ages 1, 3, 5, 7, and 9. The object is to look for handicapping conditions, and do something about them. Table 2 displays some of these programs in terms of what could be bought for each $10 million per year. We looked at the comprehensive health care programs up to age 18 and up to age five, and at the case finding and treatment program in terms of the number of maternal deaths prevented, premature deaths prevented, infant deaths prevented, mental retardation prevented, and handicaps prevented or corrected by age 18.

To reduce handicapping conditions, we got very much more out of a program which was aimed at that specifically. For physical handicaps, we could take care of almost 2,000 as compared to about 200 to 250 under the comprehensive-care programs. But we were not able to affect maternal and child

TABLE 2: Resource Allocation Alternatives—Health Depressed Areas

YEARLY EFFECTS PER $10,000,000 EXPENDED

	Comprehensive Child Health Care Programs		Casefinding and Treatment
	Up to Age		
	18	5	(0, 1, 3, 5, 7, 9)
Maternal deaths prevented	1.6	3	
Premature births prevented	100–250	200–475	
Infant deaths prevented	40–60	85–115	
Mental retardation prevented	5–7	7–13	
Handicaps prevented or corrected by age 18:			
Physical	260	195	1870
Vision problems: all	350	195	3470
amblyopia	60	117	1140
Hearing loss: all	90	70	7290
binaural	7	5	60
Reduction in number of 18-year-olds with decayed and unfilled teeth	2275	0	

deaths and mental retardation. What we did was to recommend several programs. One was the program of early case finding and assured treatment. A second recommendation was to experiment at about ten centers for comprehensive health care. These centers would experiment in the training and application of unconventional paramedical personnel in the area of child care. There just aren't enough pediatricians and physicians to do this kind of job throughout the country. We need to develop new approaches to the manpower problem. We also suggested other programs. If we're interested in reducing the rate of infant mortality, the cheapest way of doing this is by programs of family planning and we so recommend.

In the area of dental health we looked at three things one might do, again for each $10 million expended in health-depressed areas—measured in terms of the reduction of number of 18-year-olds with decayed and unfilled teeth (Table 3). We can take care of about 300,000 with fluoridation. If we have comprehensive dental care without fluoridation, we can take care of only 18,000 for this cost, and if we have a mixed program of fluoridation and comprehensive dental care, we can more than double that to 44,000. We recommended a mixed program and Table 4 illustrates the translation of these decisions into a program and financial plan. This went to the Bureau of the Budget in the form of a program memorandum; and to the White House in the form of a legislative proposal. The legislative changes are being introduced into the Congress this year and budgetary changes are being made.

A second study in the health area was on disease control programs. Table 5 illustrates one set of diseases, cancer. We looked at cancer of the uterine cervix, breast, head and neck, and colon-rectum. We estimated cost per examination, the

TABLE 3: Resource Allocation Alternatives—Dental Health

REDUCTION IN NUMBER OF 18-YEAR-OLDS WITH DECAYED AND UNFILLED TEETH PER $10,000,000 EXPENDED IN HEALTH DEPRESSED AREAS

Fluoridation	294,000
Comprehensive dental care without fluoridation	18,000
Comprehensive dental care with fluoridation	44,000

TABLE 4: Recommended Dental Health Program

MATERNAL AND CHILD HEALTH CARE PROGRAM
AND FINANCIAL PLAN

	Federal Expenditures (millions of dollars)						
	1966	1967	1968	1969	1970	1971	1972
Existing Programs [1]							
Maternal and child health services	45	50	55	60	65	70	75
Special project grants for maternity and infant care	30	30	30	30	30	30	30
Special project grants for school and preschool children	15	35	40	40	40	40	40
Crippled children's services	45	50	60	70	80	90	100
Training professional personnel for care of crippled children	0	4	10	10	10	10	10
Research projects related to maternal and child health and crippled children's services	4	5	7	9	11	13	15
New Programs							
Comprehensive maternal and child health care demonstrations	0	0	33	65	98	130	163
Early case-finding and treatment of chronic conditions	0	0	50	100	150	150	150
Family planning [2]	0	0	10	30	50	70	90
Treatment of Selective Service rejectees	0	0	5	5	5	5	5
Fluoridation	0	0	1	15	17	20	22
TOTAL	139	174	301	434	556	628	700

[1] These programs are the programs identified as "Maternal and Child Health Care Programs" in the DHEW Program and Financial Plan.

[2] Additional support for family planning services, estimated to be $3 million in fiscal year 1966 and approximately $5 million annually in fiscal year 1967 and hereafter, is included in Maternal and Child Health Services and in special project grants for Maternity and Infant Care.

NOTE: These figures are illustrative and do not report the actual Department's position beyond fiscal year 1967.

number of examinations that would be required before a case would probably be found. From this was derived the number of cases that would be found, and estimates of the cost per case found. An estimate was made of the number of deaths that could be averted by the treatment following the detection of the cancers. Then we calculated the cost per death averted, which

TABLE 5: Resource Allocation Alternatives—Cancer Control

CANCER CONTROL PROGRAM—1968–1972

	Uterine Cervix	Breast	Head and Neck	Colon-Rectum
Grant costs ($000)	97,750	17,750	13,250	13,300
Number of examinations (000)	9,363	2,280	609	662
Cost/examination	$10.44	$7.79	$21.76	$20.10
Examinations/case found	87.5	167.3	620.2	496.0
Cancer cases found	107,045	13,628	982	1,334
Cost/case found	$913	$1,302	$13,493	$9,970
Cancer deaths averted	44,084	2,936	303	288
Cost/death averted	$2,217	$6,046	$43,729	$46,181

ranged from about $2,200 in the case of cervical to $46,000 for colon-rectum cancer. These are also shown on Figure 4 which plots the cost for a five-year program on the vertical axis, the number of deaths averted on the horizontal, ordering them from the cheapest to the most expensive. We're about to begin answering questions such as—"If we have a budget to spend over this time which is $75 million, what do we do?" If we have only $75 million, we ought to put the money in cervical cancer; if we have, say $115 million, we could pick up both cervical cancer and some work on breast cancer detection. Head and neck, and colon-rectum cancer seem to be much too expensive. We recommended that these be restricted to research and development rather than large-scale control programs. We made such calculations for a number of diseases and Figure 5 shows estimates of the cost and deaths averted from 1968 to 1972. We see that cervical cancer is one of the higher payoff programs, as are the largely educational programs in the use of restraining devices in motor vehicles.

Number of deaths averted was unsatisfying as a sole criterion. For example, arthritis is one of those studied where fatalities are quite low but the problem of crippling is significant. We also are concerned with the difference in saving lives of people in their early forties to early fifties, as opposed to people in their seventies. Does it matter whether the person whose life is saved has 30 or 40 more years of life left, or five to 15 years?

We made another estimate which attempted to project the prospective productive earnings of the people affected. Figure

165

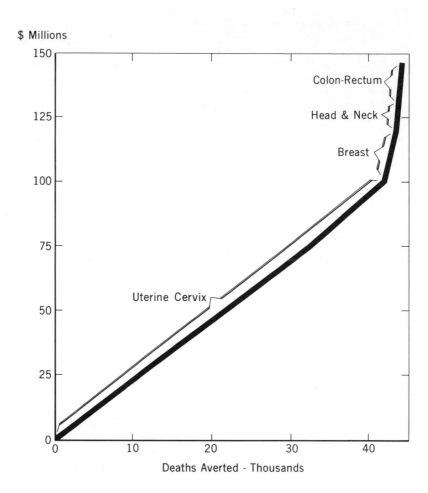

FIGURE 4. Resource Allocation Alternatives—Cancer Control.

6 uses savings in billions of dollars as the output. We are now able to introduce arthritis into the calculation. We found that the cervical cancer and syphilis programs reverse positions. To implement these conclusions, we developed a list of priorities as to where new money, additions to the budget, might be

166

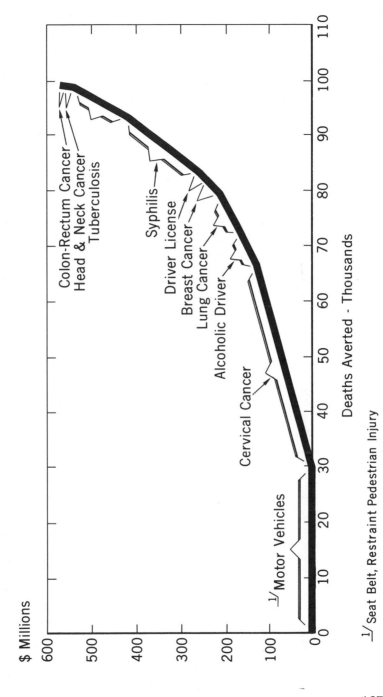

FIGURE 5. Resource Allocation Alternatives—Selected Diseases.

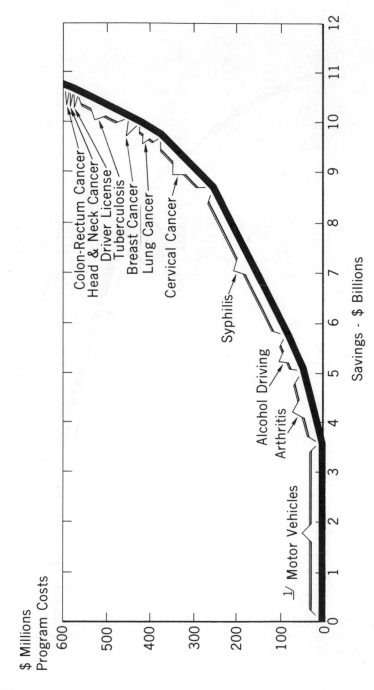

1/ Seat Belt, Restraint Pedestrian Injury

FIGURE 6. Resource Allocation Alternatives—Selected Diseases.

168

placed. This violates the zero-base budgeting concept of program budgeting, but it remains a fact of life that it is very hard to reduce an existing program with all the commitments that have been made. We used analysis to gain insight as to where additional monies should go and we recommended that cervical cancer, syphilis, and arthritis control programs ought to get money before we expanded some of the other programs.

Our conclusions were again translated into the program and financial plan shown in Table 6. To give a few other examples: In vocational rehabilitation, if we relate the costs of the program to the increases in earnings of clients, the increase in earnings is 12–13 times the cost of the program (Table 7).

TABLE 6: Program and Financial Plan—Selected Health Hazards

REVISED FIVE YEAR FINANCIAL PLAN
BENEFIT/COST ANALYSIS
($ millions)

	1967	1968	1969	1970	1971	1972	1968–1972
Total	$49.8	$64.2	$77.3	$83.4	$88.1	$89.9	$397.7
Motor Vehicle Accidents	3.4	6.7	9.8	10.1	11.5	12.1	50.2
Seat belt use		(.7)	(1.0)	(1.0)	(2.0)	(2.0)	(6.7)
Restraint devices		(.3)	(.5)	(.5)	(1.0)	(1.0)	(3.3)
Motorcyclist helmets		(1.7)	(1.6)	(1.6)	(1.6)	(1.6)	(8.0)
Pedestrian injury		(.2)	(.2)	(.2)	(.2)	(.2)	(1.1)
Alcohol and driving[1]		(3.8)	(6.5)	(6.7)	(6.7)	(7.3)	(31.1)
Cancer (Selected sites)	13.2	19.8	26.9	30.9	32.8	33.0	143.4
Uterine cervix	(8.5)	(12.4)	(15.4)	(15.4)	(15.4)	(15.4)	(73.8)
Lung (smoking)	(3.0)	(5.2)	(7.3)	(9.7)	(12.2)	(12.5)	(46.9)
Breast	(.7)	(1.3)	(3.2)	(4.8)	(4.2)	(4.2)	(17.8)
Head and neck	(.7)	(.7)	(.7)	(.7)	(.7)	(.7)	(3.5)
Colon-rectum	(.3)	(.3)	(.3)	(.3)	(.3)	(.3)	(1.5)
Arthritis	2.3	4.2	6.5	8.5	9.7	10.5	37.6
Syphilis	10.2	11.4	11.4	11.4	11.4	11.4	55.0
Tuberculosis	20.7	22.7	22.7	22.7	22.7	22.7	113.5

[1] Includes funds ($23 million 1968–1972) for evaluation and surveillance of entire motor vehicle program.

NOTE: These figures are illustrative and do not report the actual department's position beyond fiscal year 1967.

TABLE 7: **Vocational Rehabilitation and Adult Basic Education:**
Costs and Benefits

Vocational Rehabilitation		
Cost	Increase in earnings	Increase in earnings
(millions of dollars)		per dollar of cost
157	2,000–2,600	12–13

Adult Basic Education		
	(per 1,000 individuals)	
Cost	Increase in earnings	Increase in earnings
		per dollar of cost
$341,000	$3,800,000	11

Adult basic education appears to give a return of almost 11 times cost in terms of increases in earning power (Table 7). We recommended an expansion of this program. In the area of work experience training we cannot yet tell the payoff of the program. What we did was to take some case studies in which we looked at the age of people and their pre-existing schooling. We estimated what the cost per participant would be for bringing up their ability to handle English. We estimated what their earnings would probably be in the absence of the program and made a break-even analysis, estimating how much of an increase in their prospective earnings would be necessary for the program to break even (Table 8).

In secondary vocational education, we found that the apparent payoffs were smaller. Table 9 estimates the incremental costs of training in a vocational over a general high school. Average annual difference in earnings is estimated to be about $300 a year. We were concerned with how long it would take before the benefits disappeared. We estimated that differences might remain for 10 years or for 20 years. In the 10-year case the increase in earnings relative to increases in cost was between 1.3 and 1.6, depending upon the cost estimates that were used. If we assume that they stayed over 20 years you might get between two and one-half and three times the sum in earnings relative to the cost. We recommended an expansion of research into various vocational education approaches to see if we couldn't develop ones with higher returns.

We recently have been considering what studies to perform this year. It may be of interest to you to indicate what we plan

TABLE 8: Work Experience Program—Costs and Benefits

PROGRAM COSTS, EARNINGS, AND BREAK-EVEN POINTS FOR WHITE MALE PARTICIPANTS IN THE WORK-EXPERIENCE PROGRAM KENTUCKY

Age/Education of Participants	Program Cost Per Participant Col. (1) [1]	Estimated Future Earnings Per Participant Without Program Col. (2) [2]	Percent Increase in Future Earnings Required for Program to Break Even (1) as % of (2)
Age 25			
Elementary 0–7	$1,064	$56,577	1.9%
8	1,064	75,938	1.4
High School 1–3	1,064	88,577	1.2
4	1,064	99,652	1.1
Age 35			
Elementary 0–7	1,064	52,719	2.0
8	1,064	69,555	1.5
High School 1–3	1,064	81,378	1.3
4	1,064	91,596	1.2
Age 45			
Elementary 0–7	851	40,532	2.1
8	1,064	53,041	2.0
High School 1–3	1,489	61,569	2.4
4	851	68,977	1.2
Age 55			
Elementary 0–7	638	22,325	2.9
8	851	29,149	2.9
High School 1–3	851	33,789	2.5
4	1,064	37,694	2.8

[1] Includes public assistance costs.

[2] Computed from data in U.S. Bureau of the Census, *1960 Census of Population*, PC(2)–7B, Table 1 and PC(2)–5B, Table 4; and U.S. Public Health Service, National Vital Statistics Division, *Vital Statistics of the United States, 1961*, Volume II-Section 2, *Life Tables*, Tables 2–3. Future earnings were discounted at 4%.

to be studying in the next months. One group of studies we call "Exits from Poverty." These are concerned with re-examining programs to raise earning capacity, such as vocational education, vocational rehabilitation, and work experience training; programs to limit family size; and income-support programs.

In the area of health we are studying the delivery and financing of health services to the poor; a review of our previous work in disease programs, plus kidney diseases, and narcotic addiction; alternatives for increasing the supply of nursing

171

TABLE 9: Secondary Vocational Education—Costs and Benefits

RELATION OF INCREMENTAL COSTS OF SECONDARY
VOCATIONAL EDUCATION TO BENEFITS RECEIVED

Cost Per Year	Total Cost of Training Per Student	Average Annual Increases in Earnings	Benefits Per [1] Graduate	Benefit-Cost Ratio
Assuming Constant Benefit Over Ten Years				
$400	$1200	$300	$1970	1.6
$500	$1500	$300	$1970	1.3
Assuming Constant Benefit Over 20 Years				
$400	$1200	$300	$3505	2.9
$500	$1500	$300	$3505	2.3

[1] Discounted at 4 percent.

services; health-facility requirements; an examination of costs and benefits of alternative solutions to the air pollution problems; and studies of consumer protection activities.

In education we are working on four studies: (1) examining alternatives in improving the education of deprived children, largely an analysis of the results and possibilities of Title I of the Elementary and Secondary Education Act; (2) an examination of proposals for general support of elementary and secondary education; (3) an analysis of how best to finance higher education; and (4) the evaluation of new developments in educational technology.

Finally, we're working on one problem which relates to where I began. I began with the question of the status of society. What is the physical and social environment, what is the demographic status of people, how are people getting along? We have undertaken to develop a set of social indicators, partly statistical, partly narrative analytical in nature. We are dealing with health and population vitality, opportunity (including education, barriers, and social mobility), levels of living, participation (civil, political, communal, and cultural) and the physical and social environment.

Reaction to the development of social indicators has been varied. Senator Mondale has introduced a bill to enact a "Full Opportunity and Social Accounting Act." The *New Republic* has reacted with skepticism, quoting E. E. Cummings who in 1926 wrote:

> While you and i have lips and voices which
> are for kissing and to sing with
> who cares if some oneeyed son of a bitch
> invents an instrument to measure Spring with?

COMMENT ON GROSSE PAPER

Mr. Capron: I would like to make one comment which I had meant to make earlier. I think it's not surprising, in the initial thrust to impose a planning-programming-budgeting-system throughout the domestic agencies, that the President and the Bureau of the Budget were almost forced to do a little bit of "overselling." Any change which has the magnitude and implications of PPB is terribly difficult, from the point of view of a bureaucracy, particularly one as big and entrenched as the federal bureaucracy.

The early announcements and instructions from the Bureau of the Budget about how soon the system was to be in operation and so forth were very ambitious. I think many of us who were involved at that time recognized they were quite unrealistic. But the decision was made that the only way to get the system going was to start. If we had said take a year to tool up and prepare for it, at the end of a year nothing would have happened.

Dr. Grosse has illustrated in his remarks that we have to recognize that this new program, or new budgeting process, is going to take several years before it's really operative. As a footnote to emphasize this, it is worth recalling that in the Defense Department Secretary McNamara began to install PPB in 1961. The system is still not fully implemented across the Department.

The Defense Department had one tremendous advantage: It was building on some 15 years' intensive development of intellectual capital, drawing from places like the RAND Corporation and some of the other organizations which have been trying to develop a different approach to defense planning. A great deal of experience had been accumulated and a lot of knowledge on the part of civilians about military operations and equipment had been developed.

In the HEW program areas there is almost nothing comparable on which Dr. Grosse and his colleagues can draw. They are having to start at a much more rudimentary stage, and it is unrealistic to expect that they are going to be producing a completely satisfactory information system and analytic system which is going to meet all of the objectives that are hoped for over the longer run from PPBS.

Mr. Armer: Could you comment on your effort to bring mechanization via EDP (electronic data processing) into this?

Dr. Grosse: Yes. EDP plays a role in two ways. First, we use EDP in some of the studies where we are concerned with examining a large number of perturbations. For example, in the current study on financing higher education, where we make varying assumptions about population, income, and a whole host of things and develop models, we have been using a computer.

A more sizable effort has to do with the data handling of the program and financial plan. Last year we did this by a very simple-minded EAM* system which worked reasonably well in providing us the listings cut various ways. It had no real retrieval flexibility or capability. This year we wrote up specifications for data processing and are just about to announce formally the selection of a contractor to give us report writing and retrieval capability. We get our numerical information from the agencies in formats which permit us to punch these fairly readily.

Our program structure is a multidimensional system. Each operating program or piece of an operating program is linked to a purpose category of six digits, to an appropriation category, to a target group, to a program recipient, to a functional activity, and to the resource impact. The reason for all of this is that the kinds of questions we want to ask about our program are varied. If we ask, "What are you doing for poor children?" we want to cut it very differently than if we are asking, "What are you doing for the health of the nation?" You have to reassemble the pieces. So far it hasn't looked like either a very enormous program or one that is beyond the state of the art.

---

* Electronic accounting machines.

RICHARD F. FENNO

The Impact of PPBS on the Congressional
Appropriations Process

E VERYTHING I have to say this morning about congres-
sional-executive relations in the area of appropriations
rests on two basic assumptions concerning the subject.
The first is that no budgetary reform is neutral. Or conversely, every change in the budgetary process has an effect
on the distribution of power within the political system, on
who wins and who loses conflicts over policy, on whose prefer-
ences are granted legitimacy, on who gets what in American
society. If anyone needs proof of this proposition he can find
it in the effects which the planning-programming-budgeting
system has had in the Department of Defense, where it has
resulted in a centralization of power in the office of the secretary and has aided the cause of those people in the department
who favored the development of general-purposes forces and
wanted less reliance on strategic retaliatory forces. The point
I want to make here is simply that PPBS inevitably has
political consequences and cannot be viewed simply as a matter
of efficiency. Least of all can it be so viewed, if one considers
it from the perspective of the Congress. What may be at
stake for Congress in this budgetary reform is nothing less

175

than its capacity to exercise its constitutional and historical functions of control over the executive branch of government.

And this leads me to my second basic assumption—that when we talk about the appropriations process we are talking about the most important source of legislative power. More particularly, the power of the purse is the key to the institutional power of the House of Representatives within the American political system. The single most serious blow to the House as an institution would be to reduce its share of the money power. The House now makes and enforces an independent judgment on appropriations matters, and it will scrutinize PPBS in the light of its continuing desire to do so. The institutionalization of the executive budget helped bring about a profound change in the balance of legislative and executive power. Congressmen are well aware that budgetary reform begun in the executive is not only not neutral but potentially quite detrimental to them. My point here then is that for Congress the stakes in any use of PPBS are very great; Congress can be expected to weigh its reaction very carefully, to view PPBS in terms of its potential for our system of checks and balances and, therefore, to see whether PPBS can be made to work for the Congress as well as for the executive.

Within the Congress, the House of Representatives exercises the dominant influence over appropriations matters. Within the House almost all appropriations decisions are made by the Appropriations Committee — whose recommendations are accepted in nine cases out of ten. And within the Appropriations Committee effective decision making lies in the hands of its dozen or so subcommittees—whose recommendations are normally reported out by the full committee without change. In largest part, therefore, the "Executive-Legislative Appropriations Interface" involves key administrators and budgetary officials of the executive branch and members of the appropriate subcommittees of the Committee on Appropriations of the House of Representatives. Since there is a top-heavy representation of executive viewpoints in this seminar, my discussion of the "interface" will be written primarily from the perspective of these subcommittee members. The bulk of my remarks will be devoted to describing the interaction, which presently exists, in the belief that we need to take account of where we are before we can say anything relevant about where we might go.

In order to understand what subcommittee members do, we ought to know a few things about them as individuals—things which we know, intuitively, perhaps, but sometimes forget. In the first place, each member has a view of the public interest which he seeks to implement through service in Congress. Like the rest of us, that is to say, he favors certain programs, opposes others and, in general, tries to implement his set of values through legislation. In the second place, he wants to make a career in the Congress. Thus, he wants to be re-elected—to further both his career and his version of the public interest. This desire for re-election, as we know, keeps him reasonably responsive to the wishes of his constituents—at least those wishes that are strongly and widely held and those wishes (typically individual or small-group complaints) that he can gratify without losing electoral support in the process.

In the third place, he not only wants a career in the Congress but he wants to be an influential member of the House. He wants power *inside* the House; and it is this desire that led him to the Appropriations Committee in the first place. This desire for "inside power" distinguishes the members of the Appropriations Committee (as well as the Rules and Ways and Means Committees) from the other members of the House. And in this sense they are atypical congressmen. It goes without saying that to the degree that a congressman has power inside the House his ability to further his values and his re-election is thereby enhanced. Finally, the necessary condition for meeting these three individual goals is that the Appropriations Committee be powerful. If the committee is influential as a collectivity, the individual member will be influential—or so, at least, the members believe. Thus, their desire to maintain committee influence becomes a key to their behavior in the appropriations process.

To their colleagues in the House, Appropriations Committee members argue that the power of the House of Representatives depends heavily on the power of the Appropriations Committee. Obviously, it serves the individual aspirations of committee members to expound such a belief—but the fact is that House members, by and large, accept the argument. House members believe that only by acting through committees can the House act independently and effectively in any policy area. Both Committee members and House members, therefore, see the Appropriations Committee as the custodian of the House's power of the purse—the custodian, that is, of that function that makes the House an important political institution. When committee members say "We don't want to be a rubber stamp for the executive," they do so with more conviction, more urgency, and a greater sense of responsibility than most other congressmen.

The appropriations system now in existence in the House must be seen as a solution—not the only solution, but a solution—to the individual career aspirations of the committee members and the institutional goals of the House. The system has been in operation since the Budget and Accounting Act of 1921, and has, thus far, been found satisfactory to the House. They are not likely to change it without being convinced that a new solution will be equally advantageous or no more disadvantageous to them.

Some of the important characteristics of the existing appropriations system are as follows:

(1) Committee members support almost all of the ongoing programs of the federal government. Their view of the public interest, that is, does not vary greatly from the national consensus which supports most existing programs. They remain very sensitive to changes in public support for various programs, and register those changes in their appropriations decisions. Appropriations Committee members want to know, always, who supports what program; and they are responsive to changes in patterns of support.

(2) Secular trends in public support for programs cannot be affected by the Appropriations Committee. The committee, as the organ of a representative body, follows those trends. Thus, the impact of Appropriations Committee decisions will be marginal for most programs. The committee makes incremental additions or subtractions to ongoing programs, and does not make wholesale reallocations of national resources.

(3) Within the larger budgetary and appropriations sequence, which extends back into the executive branch and forward to the Senate, the House Committee conceives of its

178

job as that of guarding the federal treasury by eliminating all unnecessary federal expenditures. They see their job, essentially, as the negative, conservative one of reducing executive budget estimates wherever possible. Basically, it is only by prescribing this job for themselves and by carrying it out that the committee and the House can be powerful. To rubber stamp executive requests would not be the road to influence. Nor could they make their mark, they believe, by boosting all budget estimates, since this would increase the power of the executive and since they cannot force the executive to spend money in any case. Experience has shown committee members that budget cuts and threats of budget cuts are their most formidable sources of control over executive activity.

(4) Most of the time the subcommittees make incremental reductions in executive budget estimates.

(5) Sometimes, in response to constituency interests or in pursuit of personal sets of values, subcommittees make marginal increases in executive budget estimates.

(6) And once in a while the subcommittees make large, crippling decreases or huge, beneficial increases in executive requests.

(7) Subcommittee members develop a great deal of expertise in the subject matter of the executive agencies for which they appropriate. This expertise is deferred to within the Appropriations Committee and deferred to on the House floor. The relevant point to note here is that a subcommittee's members are experts relative to other subcommittees and relative to most other House members.

(8) Once a subcommittee decision has been arrived at, subcommittee members stick together in support of their decision, thus adding bipartisan unanimity to expertise as the grounds on which they ask full committee deference. Similarly, once the full committee has made a decision it normally sticks together on the floor—thus increasing the likelihood that its recommendations will be accepted by the House. Committee members believe that if they remain unified across party lines they will maximize the chances of getting their way on the floor. Ability to win on the floor, of course, is the mark of a

179

powerful committee. So subcommittee and full committee decision making is accomplished by bargaining and compromise cemented by tacit agreements to "stick together on the floor."

(9) The committee exercises its influence on the executive by formally changing budget requests, by formally specifying limitations on the expenditure of money, by informally stating opinions in committee reports, by informal conversation with executives and by virtue of the fact that executives anticipate committee reaction in drawing up their budget requests. It is this latter kind of control, by anticipated reaction, that I would stress as being especially important. Committee members believe that someone must let the executive bureaucracy know they are being watched, someone must keep executives on their toes. They believe that they are equipped to do this by virtue of the fact that they can hurt the executives and the executives know it. Would the executive branch behave just as it now does if there were no legislative group wielding the power of the purse? Committee members think the answer is no—and no one, I am sure, would question that judgment.

To sum up, then, an appropriations system with these characteristics meets the individual aspirations of committee members and the institutional goals of the U.S. House of Representatives. Doubtless that is why is has remained substantially unchanged for 47 years.

The question now arises: On what basis do appropriations subcommittees make their decisions? Perhaps the most important aspect of their decision making is the fact that, though these particular congressmen work harder and spend more time at their committee duties than most, they make their decisions under conditions of scarce time and scarce information. They cannot know all there is to know about the activities of an executive agency, nor about the likely consequences of a decision they may make. Compared to the witnesses that come from the executive branch, therefore, they are relatively inexpert. Unable to undertake a comprehensive analysis of agency programs, they make their decisions on the basis of a *sampling* process. Committee decision making becomes a matter of sampling very limited aspects of agency behavior and drawing inferences from those samples about total agency performance. The process is one whereby committee members reason inductively from knowledge about a few activities they can comprehend to judgments about a universe of activities which they cannot comprehend. The sampling process relies on a few techniques which long experience has proven are useful indicators of wastefulness or inefficiency.

Committee members sample for three kinds of information— *program* information, *confidence* information, and *support* information. They want to know about agency programs, of course, to see whether those programs accord with their view of the public interest and to see how effectively such programs are being carried out. Here, subcommittee members sample by focusing their attention on that part of the budget request which represents a change from the previous year's appropriation. By assuming, in the absence of evidence to the contrary, that most ongoing programs are both necessary and being efficiently run, legislators free themselves to deal with manageable increments of the budget instead of all of it. Thus, they deal primarily with new programs and expansions in old programs. However, should they uncover serious problems in this portion of the budget, they may begin to work their way back into the budget base and scrutinize existing program levels.

Perhaps the most consistent thread in subcommittee decision making is the sampling they do for the purpose of deciding whether or not to tender their confidence to an agency. Given the fact that their information is imperfect and given their large zone of uncertainty about what the agency "really" needs, committee members must necessarily act on the basis of confidence, trust, or faith in agency officials. What they want to know, above all else, about an agency or an administrator is "Can I believe what he tells me? Will he do what he says he will do?" So, they sample for information that will determine the degree of confidence they should have in an agency—by "sizing up" an administrator at the hearings, by asking detailed and specific questions of witnesses to see if they know their job, by checking agency performance against last year's promises, and committee directives. If subcommittee members are satisfied with the results of their sampling, they will willingly take agency statements as fact. If they are not, if the agency does not pass the test, legislators

181

will remain extraordinarily suspicious. Confidence is the cumulative product, obviously, of countless interchanges, formal and informal, between committee and agency personnel over extended periods of time.

The third kind of information desired by subcommittee members pertains to the size, shape, and intensity of outside support for agency programs. As members of a representative body and as individuals responsive to their constituents, subcommittee members want to know who is affected by a given program and how they feel about it. Who is helped and who is hurt by the program? How widespread and how intense are support and opposition? Answers to these questions bring political information of the most important sort to legislators who must make their decisions in the light of it. Here again, they sample. Constituency reactions are often used to conduct test borings for support-type information. Or, constituency reaction may be regarded as a useful sampling of outside attitudes toward the program. Disagreement among executive officials also provides congressmen with useful information about who is being helped or hurt. Committee members, in short, are perpetually tuned in to see "who is hollering" about an agency program. They are sensitive to the slightest indication of dissatisfaction, and will seize upon it as an important lead in their investigation of agency performance.

From the perspective of executive officials who deal with the Appropriations Committee, their primary concern is for the funding of their program. And what seems to bother them most about their confrontation with the committee is the degree of uncertainty or unpredictability in it all. Decision making by sampling may be helpful to the samplers; but it remains frustrating and unnerving to those whose activities are being sampled. And this is so, of course, because a dissatisfied subcommittee has the power to hurt the agency. A great deal of that executive budget activity directed toward Congress should be viewed, I think, as aimed at uncertainty reduction. The maintenance of year-round, informal contacts between administrator and subcommittee member or between budget officer and committee staff member, the rehearsals held in the agency prior to committee hearings, the tending of subcommittee member complaints, the careful obedience to the language of intent in last year's committee report, the

THE IMPACT OF PPBS ON THE CONGRESSIONAL APPROPRIATIONS PROCESS

reading of last year's testimony for clues, the attentiveness to clientele complaints, the attempts to compromise intra-agency or interagency conflict and enforce loyalty to the executive budget—all these kinds of activity can be viewed as part of the agency effort to reduce the uncertainty at the executive-legislative appropriations interface. Executives try, in every way they know how, to anticipate committee interests, to forsee committee complaints, and to hedge against every possible type of sampling. To the degree that they succeed, they believe that they will get the kind of committee decisions on funding which they want.

Insofar as PPBS is oriented toward the committee on appropriations, it can usefully be seen, I think, as another uncertainty-reducing device. Basically, it is an ambitious effort to structure the content of executive-legislative conversation. What executives want most to talk about with sub-committee members is their program. What executives least like to talk about are object expenditures—personnel, travel, and equipment. At the present time, executives cannot be sure whether their conversations will involve one or the other. The point is not that subcommittee members ignore program; the point is that they can, and they may. And a conversation about personnel is likely to be more disadvantageous to the executive than a conversation about program. From the executive's perspective, therefore, much of his uncertainty would be reduced and his trouble over if he could structure his conversations with the subcommittee along programmatic lines. Obviously, the form of the budget determines what the conversation will be about. And, he who determines what executive-legislative appropriations conversation will be about has an enormous intellectual advantage. He fixes the frame of reference, determines the alternatives, sets the agenda for discussion, reduces his own uncertainty, and increases his chances of winning. This, from the congressional perspective, is what PPBS is all about.

One long-standing executive branch criticism of the Appropriations Committee holds that they spend far too much time inquiring into and acting upon the specifics and details of agency activity, thereby impeding the implementation of programs. The executive view has been that the committee should make only the broadest kind of program judgments, and then allow the executive flexibility and discretion in matters of administrative detail. Executives have felt that a program budget might force Appropriations Committee inquiry into the realm of broad program judgments and steer them away from the detailed investigation of the items highlighted by an object-classification budget. The truth of the matter, from the committee's standpoint, is that the only way they can effectively find out what is going on in the executive branch is through detailed and specific inquiry. That is what the committee's sampling techniques are all about. Furthermore, the only way the committee can effectively influence the executive branch is through detailed and specific intervention (or threat thereof) in the processes of administration. It is precisely the committee's capacity to affect the implementation of programs in so many formal and informal ways that keeps the executive continuously attentive to legislative wishes. It is a beguiling notion that the committee should restrict itself to making broad programmatic decisions; but it has long been advanced by people whose perspective was executive and not congressional. As the committee views the world, if it is relegated to the realm of overall policy making, it will become more impotent relative to the executive.

PPBS or no PPBS, the Appropriations Committee is going to want to proceed by inquiring into and by acting upon the specifics and details of executive programs, just as it has in the past. Its members are going to want to get and use program information, confidence information, and support information. They will get it by sampling and they will act on the basis of their samples. They will insist, too, on doing all of this annually. They will not and cannot undertake comprehensive means-ends analyses or comprehensive means-ends decisions. They will continue to leave the bulk of program planning and analysis to the executive branch. They will view their task as the traditional one of guarding the Treasury. They will guard the Treasury with a continuing sensitivity to patterns of political support. And they will continue to have but· a marginal impact on most national policies. For the committee, the questions posed by PPBS are threefold: Will PPBS in any way keep appropriations subcommittees from having the kind of sampling-type conversations with executives which legislators find advantageous? Will PPBS help subcommittee members to pursue their traditional mode of decision making? Will PPBS open up new types of legislative-executive conversation that will be advantageous to subcommittee members?

Perhaps none of these questions can be answered until we have had some experience. If they can be answered now, the task will have to be undertaken by someone more knowledgeable than I in the field of budgeting. Offhand, however, I can see no reason why PPBS would impede traditional operations —so long as the committee can insist upon and receive an alternative budget cast in the form most familiar and most agreeable to them. I can see no reason, also, why the committee should not ask for a program budget with the intention of familiarizing itself with it and experimenting to see what hand-holds it may provide. The subcommittee member's problem is always one of obtaining a fragment of information that will give him some purchase with regard to the executive branch. He should neglect no potential sources of information —least of all the program budget. Insofar as he is interested in program information, he may find it more accessible and meaningful when budget categories correspond to programs. And surely he can pursue his traditional sampling of incremental increases and decreases in terms of output as well as input categories. Program interest seems to vary from subcommittee to subcommittee, so that experimentation might profitably begin on a selective basis among the more interested subcommittees.

It is in the areas of confidence and support information that PPBS may prove the greatest help to the Appropriations Committee—both in pursuing traditional lines of action and opening up new ones. For example, subcommittee members will want to know for every program category who the responsible administrators are and what administrative structure is carrying them out. They will want to know precisely who it is they are being asked to trust when they fund a given program. Thus, they will want to be able to convert program structures into administrative structures. In this process, committee members may discover things they never knew about—who is doing what to whom in the executive branch. It may be that they will insist that administrative structure dovetail with program categories as the advocates of PPBS desire. Or, it may be that they will, in response to constituency and clientele interests, help certain existing administrative units to resist reorganization within the executive branch.

In any case, the committee can listen closely to see who among their constituents, clientele interests, and executive officials support alternative relationships of program and administrative structure. By inquiring into these relationships, subcommittee members may get more confidence and support information than they now get. They may uncover more internal bureaucratic conflict with which to get a hand-hold on agency activities. PPBS, in short, promises to raise very important questions of administrative structure. The Appropriations Committee should be vitally interested in these questions, for they are political questions of the first magnitude. Decision-making structures, obviously, help determine the kinds of decisions that emerge. Advocates of PPBS seem divided on the question of how much change in administrative organization will be required to implement changed budgetary procedures. In its pursuit of waste, inefficiency, and unnecessary expenditures, the Appropriations Committee should involve itself in these controveries. It should search out all possible consequences of organizational change versus the organizational status quo.

An aggressive Appropriations Committee in the land of the program budgeters poses some problems, obviously. Perhaps the most basic one involves the amount of internally generated information that will or should be made available to the committee. How far back into the executive's decision-making processes should the committee probe? At the present time, one very important legislative hand-hold comes via a series of questions designed to find out how much money a given agency requested at the departmental and budget-bureau level. Such information usually comes hard for the committee (at least publicly) as executives loyally defend the President's budget. Under PPBS, it seems to me, the committee might want to ask the executive to define the program alternatives or program level alternatives as they were faced within the executive branch. And surely the committee will want to know the reasoning whereby sub-program x was placed in program category y instead of program category z. Should the committee, equipped as it would have to be with computers, be given sufficient information to simulate executive decision making? These problems will be solved, as they always have been, by a combination of bargaining, political pressure, and self-restraint. But a vigorous committee, it seems to me, should be in the business of posing them.

It is my personal opinion that it will certainly be damaging for the Committee on Appropriations, it may well be damaging for the House of Representatives, and it could even be damaging for the American political system as we know it if the committee fails to equip itself with some staff members who are capable of understanding PPBS, as well as those executive officials who have created it. Since the committee's staff is normally recruited from budget offices in the executive departments, time alone will probably produce this result. But, in my view, the committee should proceed far more aggressively than that. It is during the transition period in the executive branch that the committee is likely to get the most important kinds of information and leverage. It should move immediately to make certain that its staff members know exactly how the program budget is put together, and are capable of analyzing it specifically and in detail. Surely the Congress, as a whole, cannot afford to slip far behind the executive branch in its ability to comprehend systems analysis, operations research, cost-effectiveness analysis, and the planning-programming-budgeting system. If no one in Congress can understand what the executive is doing, the legislature as a whole will suffer and surrender still more of its power to the executive branch. If the Appropriations Committee does not do it for the Congress, which committees will? If other committees become the acknowledged experts on PPBS, the Appropriations Committee will surely lose its reputation, its prestige, and its power within the Congress. To my way of thinking, a loss in the influence of the Appropriations Committee would be unfortunate—not because I agree with their budgetary decisions but because they are among the few congressional committees whose members, regardless of party, place a very high value on maintaining the institutional influence of the House of Representatives within the American political system. And I share that value.

187

COMMENT ON FENNO PAPER

Mr. Capron: I would like to ask Mr. Dan Donoghue from (California) Congressman (Craig) Hosmer's office if he would comment on this view that we have had from Professor Fenno, because you can speak to us with the perspective of the Hill.

Mr. Donoghue, Assistant to Congressman Hosmer: Of course, Congressman Hosmer is not on the Appropriations Committee, which limits my perspective somewhat. However, it seems in order to observe that more and more agencies and programs are authorized in advance by legislative committees. If this trend continues, much of the power that you described, which is inherent in the Appropriations Committee, will have been transferred to some extent to these legislative committees.

Would you comment on what effect you see that this will have in the relationship between PPBS and the Hill?

Dr. Fenno: I agree with you about the trend. It doesn't always have the consequence of decreasing the influence of the Appropriations Committee. I think foreign aid is one of the best examples of the case where you do have annual authorization and still I would say the appropriations subcommittee has the most important influence on the program.

I was speaking only about the Appropriations Committee. If I were a member of the Joint Committee on Atomic Energy, as Mr. Hosmer is, or if I were a member of the Government Operations Committee or the Science and Astronautics Committee authorizing NASA appropriations, I might take a similar view and try to develop staff competence in this area. I think I would.

I do think, though, that the Appropriations Committee is somewhat different from those committees, leaving aside the Joint Committee. The tendency for most of the authorizing committees is to be very much in favor of the program for which they are authorizing. Congressmen seek membership on those committees precisely because they are interested in pushing these programs forward, and are somewhat less inclined to take a critical look at what the executive is doing.

I think that the best chance for a critical look still rests with the Appropriations Committee. It is more likely to take a critical view, and I would cite the experience in foreign aid and the experience with NASA.

Mr. Capron: I think that the authorizing committees—the legislative committees—are probably going to find a program budget more useful for their purposes because they do tend to look at bigger slices at one time. They are interested in trade-offs in a way that the appropriations subcommittees are not.

For example, the language of the President's Budget Message, as distinct from the specific appropriations request, is really much more directed to the legislative committees than it is to the appropriations committees. In fact it's pretty clear, if you review appropriations subcommittee hearings, that the budget message in some years apparently didn't exist as far as anything that was said in any discussion that goes on, because the focus is so different.

Dr. Saloma: If you can look at the House of Representatives as almost having a dual committee structure with the Appropriations Committee paralleling the authorization committees, then PPBS may bring you to a situation where you are developing alternative budgets for the two separate committee systems. The advantage would accrue to the authorizing committees, although the Appropriations Committee is still the only single-focus committee that could coordinate and in fact make the ultimate use of this kind of coordinating device. The authorization committees can use the budget within their areas, but when it comes to subject matter that crosses committee jurisdiction we know that problems are going to come up between the various authorizing committees.

What may happen is that the innovation will come through the authorizing committees, and then you will see a really interesting tension between the two. The logical distinction, between program policy on the one hand and appropriations on the other, is difficult to make. A program budgeting system might bring this distinction to an almost unbearable tension. How does the Appropriations Committee keep from becoming too powerful when it masters this technique? How does the rest of the House counter the power that this budget information system confers? I suspect the built in competition between the two types of committee systems will provide both an impetus toward the adaptation of this system and a check on the Appropriations Committee as well.

Dr. Fenno: I think that's a good point. The mere fact that annual authorization has been developing is a symptom of legislative committee dissatisfaction with the Appropriations Committee. It gives two committees information rather than one, and it may well be that the Appropriations Committee will be persuaded to find out what this is all about, which is really all that I am asking at this point.

I don't think this activity ought to be going on in the executive branch without the Appropriations Committee knowing what is happening. It may well be that they don't find it useful, but the consequences of their not knowing what's going on would be extraordinarily grave. Now, it may be that the pressure will increase when the authorizing committees equip themselves to deal with this first. Then the Appropriations Committee, faced with another committee of the Congress, may be pushed to do it. I would hope that it wouldn't take pressure from an authorizing committee.

My view of the authorizing committee is that by and large it would tend to be much more favorably disposed, much more friendly, far less suspicious, and far less ready to move in and check the executive branch than the Committee on Appropriations, which has a tradition and a built-in institutional reason, as I tried to point out, for checking and watching the executive. In other words, I see the Appropriations Committee as the point of the lance in dealing with the executive branch.

Dr. Saloma: The dilemma in this is, as you point out, that the power of the Appropriations Committee has been dependent on this kind of detailed control. Now the power is going to shift toward analytical ability. I disagree with you that the only way the Congress has effect is through this budget cutting ability of the Appropriations Committee. Congress will have increasing power through the ability to affect alternatives in program choices which it has left to the executive up to now but which will come up for much more intensive congressional review. So you may find that the authorizing axe becomes a really important technique of control in the future rather than the appropriations axe.

Mr. Chartrand: Dr. Fenno, you reflected on the recurring need of many of these congressional elements for what we might call information in transition, going back into the budgetary process. I thought perhaps you might have a comment regarding the elements contained in the Legislative Reorganization Act of 1967, which calls for GAO to undertake what is in the eyes of most people a new role. That is, that GAO would provide a systems capability and automatic data processing center and would make available to the members or the committees of Congress, upon request, current budgetary information. I might say parenthetically that many of the people in that agency are rather appalled at the new responsibility that is being suggested here.

Dr. Fenno: I can only say that GAO may well be the place where this kind of analysis will be carried on, and it might be carried on in a central way for all congressmen. If that were to be the case, then there would have to be some sort of careful translation from what the GAO would produce to what the committee staff of Appropriations would use; and I think here particularly of the very close relationship which holds between a subcommittee chairman on the Appropriations Committee and a staff member.

That information which the subcommittee chairman doesn't want—he won't take. What he does want typically is the information that his staff member gives to him. I'm not sure what use would be made of GAO by the appropriations subcommittee if, somehow or other, the committee's own staff weren't worked in as a very close intermediary. My concern here is with equipping the committee staff. I am appealing to Chairman George Mahon to hire two or three staff people as the first and minimal sort of step here, people in whom he has confidence.

As you know, the Appropriations Committee has an unlimited budget for staff. It's the only committee that has an unlimited budget for staff and congressmen frequently tell them to hire more staff. The reply of the staff that is now there is, "Well, I can't even get my subcommittee chairman to listen to all that I have to say as it is, and if we hire ten more staff people, he'd still be the funnel through which information would have to pass." So I guess my only comment is to locate data processing in the GAO. However, if this meant a radical separation from the staff people in the committee, it might not enable the committee to make use of the information.

Dr. Werner Hirsch, University of California at Los Angeles: To provide data-processing capabilities is not necessarily the same as providing Congress with the analytic capability to match an integrated program coming from the executive branch of government. Moreover, GAO has not only an "accounting," but an "exposé" tradition—trying to catch the fellow running away with the money. It's the same problem in many companies today where you have the auditor and accountant versus the planner. So, whether the GAO will offer a good home intellectually and otherwise to support Congress in the analytic phases and the review phases in planning, I don't know.

Mr. Chartrand: I think you are very perceptive in pointing this out, because we have heard reverberations regarding this recommendation from the executive and legislative branches. I think it would be fair to say that during the deliberations of the Joint Committee on the Organization of the Congress, a couple of things concerned the executive and legislative branch groups very much. One was the span of control, which you have reflected on today, for the subcommittee chairman who would like to feel that he has everything at fingertip control. He is wary about going one step further and turning over this type of control to a group such as GAO. In the executive branch there has been scant enthusiasm on the part of agencies to release "raw budgetary data" prior to departmental approval, much less Bureau of the Budget approval, thus making this accessible to the congressional subcommittees.

Mr. Capron: I am quite sure on the last point that this will literally take an act of Congress, because this completely destroys the whole concept of the separation between the roles of the Congress and the executive. In my opinion, the subcommittees on appropriations already administer too much in the way they appropriate, because they simply don't trust the executive.

I would like to raise another issue, though, for Professor Fenno's reaction. The subcommittees have two very different sorts of roles in the implementation of PPBS. One you discussed, which is the way they go about their business. But the other, and this is a very live issue in Washington right now, is whether or not they will give the executive branch the wherewithal to implement the system.

Some recent subcommittee appropriations actions, which are not yet final, sharply cut or eliminated additional positions for program analysis, because of the apparent distrust of a couple of the key subcommittee appropriations chairmen of the whole PPBS effort. I think it is virtually impossible for them to stop PPB, but they can cripple and slow down the development of an effective system. They are apparently going after the program analysis function in particular. This is because this is the newly identified function. A lot of PPB can be done by people who are in the budget shop, and it is very hard to separate them.

This has gotten involved, incidentally, with another perennial issue with some subcommittees, concerning the agencies and departments over which they have oversight. That is the role of the buerau vis-á-vis the Office of the Secretary and the traditional unwillingness to allow the Office of the Secretary to be properly staffed. HEW is a classic example. To someone sitting at this end of Pennsylvania Avenue, this resistance is often seen as a desire on the part of the subcommittees not to allow an effective, strong, central executive at the departmental level to develop because the subcommittee has a very comfortable relationship with the individual bureaus.

Dr. Grosse: Let me say one thing with respect to congressional reaction. We have found that the reaction to hiring people for PPBS activities at the bureau or at the operating-agency level, and at the sub-bureau of an operating agency is equally severe.

Mr. Capron: Yes, because they are suspicious of analysis. They don't think it does any good.

Mr. Donoghue: One of the comments that Professor Fenno made points up the reason for some of this congressional antagonism. This is the McNamara attitude. Alternatives he poses are based solely on cost effectiveness and not really on the basis of military effectiveness. You are then substituting a cost judgment in place of a military judgment. Everything is reduced to getting the most for your money, which is McNamara's theme, replete with charts. Just the other day Congressman Holifield made a speech on the launching of the aircraft carrier Kennedy, in which he pointed out that it was an obsolete naval vessel already. He said that what is really going to count, if the time ever comes when the carrier will have to be used in war, is going to be military effectiveness, and not cost effectiveness.

Mr. Capron: Bob Chartrand and I, at least, would want to take really strenuous issue with this distinction, but maybe this isn't quite the time to get into this debate. I would just say that there is a difference in judgment about military effectiveness. The Joint Chiefs will argue just as strenuously that their recommendations are cost effective, but they have a different military judgment from Secretary McNamara's, for example.

Dr. Hirsch: I think it would be the difference between good and thoughtful cost effectiveness analysis versus a poor one and not a military versus an economic one.

WERNER Z. HIRSCH

Congress and Program Budgeting:
Problems and Potentials

It is commonly held that program budgeting originated in the U.S. Department of Defense when Secretary Robert Mc-Namara introduced cost effectiveness analysis and new budgeting procedures in 1961. It is also commonly held that the success of these new procedures led to the wholesale introduction of program budgeting into the Federal government following the Presidential directive of August 25, 1965. However, this is only part of the story; program budgeting has much deeper roots.

Perhaps the oldest and deepest roots are found in industry. DuPont was already using something very much like a program budget system by the time they made their investment in General Motors, and apparently introduced this system into General Motors at that time.[1] One of their publications, *General Motors Budget and Finance Procedures for the Year 1924*, is an interesting document of early program budgeting. Another root of program budgeting is found in the development of a wartime control system by the War Production Board in the early days of World War II.

---

[1] David Novick, *Origin and History of Program Budgeting* (Santa Monica, Calif.: The RAND Corporation, October 1966) P–3427, p. 2.

However, program budgeting has made most of its progress in recent years; and only in the last dozen years or so have professional economists begun to research the area.[2] The executive branch of the Federal Government, especially the Bureau of the Budget, has played a leading role in the development of program budgeting. Congress, too, has taken a strong interest. For example, a thoughtful report was issued in 1963 by the Joint Economic Committee that re-examines the federal budget as an economic document.[3] A recent House report, covering Treasury, Post Office, and Executive Office appropriations bills, stated, "The Committee concurs that the executive branch ought to take full advantage of every feasible means in making up the budget to identify program objectives, develop dependable estimates of their cost, and present clear alternatives to enable top management to make wise choices concerning the future activities of the government. As government increases, the need for such a system increases. The planning-programming-budgeting system which the President has directed each federal agency to initiate could, if properly pursued, go a long way in meeting that requirement."[4] The House committee backed up its position by recommending an increase in personnel for the Bureau of the Budget, particularly in the planning-programming-budgeting activities area.

Program budgeting is a complex planning and management process. Perhaps a better term to describe it would be effectiveness planning and budgeting. The structural component of program budgeting is the budget itself, its chief feature being an output orientation. It is structured to allow the activities of several agencies or departments to be assembled and expressed in terms of specific output packages—programs and subprograms—of various convenient levels of aggregation.

---

[2] David Novick, *Efficiency and Economy in Government Through New Budgeting and Accounting Procedures* (Santa Monica, Calif.: The RAND Corporation, February 1, 1954) R–254; *A New Approach to the Military Budget* (Santa Monica, Calif.: The RAND Corporation, June 12, 1956) RM–1759; Arthur Smithies, *The Budgetary Process in the United States* (New York: McGraw-Hill Book Co., 1955); Jesse Burkhead, *Government Budgeting* (New York: John Wiley & Sons, 1965); and David Novick (ed.), *Program Budgeting* (Cambridge: Harvard University Press, 1965).

[3] Joint Economic Committee of Congress, *The Federal Budget As An Economic Document* (Washington, D.C.: U.S. Government Printing Office, August 14, 1963).

[4] U.S. House of Representatives Report 1412, 1967 (HR 14266), p. 16.

196

A second component of the program budget is an analytical process. Analysis (and evaluation) of the budget includes a study of objectives and alternative ways of achieving them, and of possible future environments and contingencies of these environments and how to respond to them. One of the most important analytic techniques is a benefit-cost analysis (often referred to as cost-effectiveness or systems analysis).

Finally, the administrative-organizational aspects of program budgeting relate to effective and flexible means of administering and possibly revising the budgetary decisions that have been reached with the aid of the program budget and analysis. A major role is played by an information system and monitoring procedure.

Ideally, we need a national program budget which relates national programs (security, education, health, welfare, science, resource development, etc.) with economic growth and employment policies in such a way that the President and Congress—and through them, the American people—can make informed judgments and decisions. In short, program budgeting should assist the executive and legislative branches of government in judiciously allocating scarce resources among competing programs; in coordinating interrelated decisions; in considering full cost implications of current decisions; and in articulating relevant alternatives, measured in terms of their trade-off values. There is, obviously, a tendency for activities to be distributed among various government departments. As a result the total scope of programs, as well as overlapping and duplicating activities, often remain hidden. This is well summarized in the caption of a cartoon published some time ago in *The Saturday Evening Post:* "Briefly, the problem is this: the State Department has five million to stabilize their government, and the CIA has ten million to overthrow it." [5]

Program budgeting assists decision making on three levels. On the highest level it can be used to help select a budget mix composed of such large program areas as national security, social development, economic development, law and order, and administration—and still give special consideration to the major programs within each of these areas. Explicit articula-

---

[5] Cartoon by Lee Lorenzo. Reprinted with permission from *The Saturday Evening Post* © 1965 The Curtis Publishing Company.

tion of virtually global choices and their thoughtful discussion are major assets.

On the second level, program analysis can help to determine the best mix of subprograms and sub-subprograms, regardless of whether they are parts of one or more larger programs. For example, the decision maker might want to consider trading off retraining programs for programs that create new employment opportunities or programs that supplement income. These are all subprograms designed to aid the poor although they attempt to do so in different ways, sometimes under different national programs.

And finally, there is the relatively low-level decision concerned with inputs, i.e., determining the most efficient way of obtaining a given program objective. Input trade-offs pertaining to vocational retraining may relate to both the education and welfare fields. For example, a decision may need to be made as to whether vocational retraining is more efficiently attained through on-the-job training or in the classroom.

Although Congress should mainly address itself to the two higher decision levels, it is rather ill-equipped to do so effectively at the present time. Deficiencies in at least three major areas prevent Congress from more fully benefitting from program budgeting in making decisions: lack of analytical information; lack of a method to integrate information to give an overall perspective of the budget; and lack of a procedure to review and evaluate the performance of the various agencies and the specific programs within the agencies.

Former Budget Director Kermit Gordon seemed to believe power stems from knowledge when he said, "Analyses become powerful weapons in the arsenal of persuasion." If this is true and the executive branch were to establish a strong capability in program budgeting for which there was no counterpart in the legislative branch, the balance of power between the two branches of government would favor the executive branch.

What can be done to remedy this situation? Two steps come to mind. Various congressional committees could hire budget analysts to assist members of Congress in their dialogue with different departments and the Bureau of the Budget.* Efforts

---

* The number of persons with these analytical skills is relatively small, as discovered by the Bureau of the Budget and different departments during the last two years. With the aid of the Civil Service Commission, and close cooperation with universities, further steps could be taken to train specialists in this area.

in this direction would be extremely useful and they could possibly be supplemented by the establishment of some congressional unit to coordinate the work of some of these specialists.

Furthermore, the Federal Government has many missions that are neither contained in a single department nor handled by a single appropriations committee; for example, science (or research and development), education, regional development (Appalachia), or urban affairs. It might be desirable for Congress to ask the Executive Office of the President to prepare an annual report on such missions which sets forth the substance, organization, costs, goals, problems, and progress of the mission. The report could review the recent past, indicate the present state of affairs, suggest the directions the mission should take in the short- and long-term future and specify the rate of investment and other commitments that are likely to be required. Both the roles of private and governmental sectors could be dealt with in terms of support and performance. The underlying philosophy of the mission should be included, as well as a qualitative inquiry and quantitative information.

Such a report could be patterned after Defense Secretary Robert McNamara's annual presentations to Congress. He has been giving the legislators a sort of systems analysis of national security problems for the future, explaining how he proposes to deal with them in terms of projected programs and subprograms. His presentation has been followed up with budget information relative to the financing of next year's increments of the Defense Department's projected plans.

Armed with such information, Congress (and others) may be able to view such large national programs as science, education, or regional development, within an integrated context. Such information could be the basis for public hearings held by joint committees of Congress; could sharpen the dialogue between the legislative and executive branches of government; could be invaluable to the private sector and to state and local governments because it would relate to their own programs, problems and aspirations; and could force a nationwide awareness of specific problems of major concern.

The second deficiency, one of perspective, relates to the process of authorization and appropriating funds. Even if the executive branch of government could succeed in developing a comprehensive, well-integrated program budget and make splendid programmatic presentations to Congress, their efforts may come to naught because of the characteristics of Congress' present deliberation process. There is no mechanism which provides for an overall congressional perspective of the budget. Congress tends to cut the budget submitted by the President into small pieces; various portions of the budget are sent to specialized authorization and appropriations committees, which are semi-autonomous, exercise great power, and are deeply enmeshed in tradition. Committees tend to act as a loose confederation of principalities. At the same time, they're headed by subcommittee chairmen, who, by reason of their office as well as their knowledge and hard work, tend to be major powers. This system can lend itself to inconsistencies: one department's program may grow rapidly under the benign guidance of a generous chairman while another may be starved by a hostile one.[6]

At present, there is no way to carefully put the budget together again after various committees have looked at its separate parts; nor is there any assurance that the various parts add up to a meaningful total. Since rather limited consideration is given to appropriation bills on the floor, there is little opportunity to take a broad and critical view of any one bill, or to weigh choices between major program areas and individual programs within them.

This situation is not easy to remedy, but a number of improvements suggest themselves. In 1946 Congress enacted legislation that provides for a Joint Budget Committee composed of key members of the revenue and appropriations committees, and that is designed to conduct an overall financial review. The committee has not been established, partly because the House of Representatives appears reluctant to share its constitutional and traditional prerogatives in financial matters with the Senate, and partly because the various committees and subcommittees are anxious to retain full control over their present areas of jurisdiction.

The Committee for Economic Development recently recommended that the House Appropriations Committee invite the

---

[6] Kermit Gordon, "Reflections on Spending," *Public Policy*, Vol. XV (ed. by John D. Montgomery and Arthur Smithies) (Cambridge: Harvard University Press, 1966), p. 19.

House Ways and Means Committee to sit with it to hear the initial testimony from the Budget Director, the Chairman of the Council of Economic Advisors and other key officials.[7] If this materializes, these joint hearings will be held immediately after the executive budget is received, and at their conclusion the two committees will adopt a joint resolution, or two separate ones, outlining revenue and expenditure targets for the coming year. The targets thus adopted would guide the Ways and Means Committee in recommending taxes; and the Appropriations Committee in its recommendations for total spending levels, which in turn would help establish consistent patterns among various subcommittees. This procedure would give the House a mechanism for developing rational relationships between revenues and expenditures, and also a forum for reviewing the impact of the budget on the national economy. Key Senators, or their senior staff members, could be invited to attend the House joint committee hearings to improve communications and mutual understanding between the two Houses.

Another step to revitalize the appropriations process would be to reactivate the full Appropriations Committee. This Committee could review the broad budgetary strategy of the executive branch, appraise it in a meaningful manner, and suggest revisions while keeping in mind the need for a well-integrated set of programs. The Appropriations Committee could hold hearings on the proposed presidential allocation of resources between programs and agencies. It could seek testimony from heads of departments on their overall programs early in the year, similar to the testimony presently given by the Budget Director to the Appropriations Committees of the House and Senate.

Appropriations are currently made on an agency-by-agency basis, although parts of many programs can be found in the several agencies. For example, more than 40 Federal departments, agencies, and bureaus have funds in their budgets for education. The program budget approach would make appropriations in terms of programs rather than agencies, and or-

---

[7] Committee for Economic Development, *Budgeting for National Objectives* (New York: Committee for Economic Development, 1966), pp. 46–48.

ganize appropriations subcommittees in both Houses along programmatic rather than agency lines.

Finally, the third deficiency area in Congressional budgeting procedure is the lack of a continuous review of how well agencies perform and how well their individual programs are carried out. At present the task of reviewing and appraising agency performance is assigned mainly to the Government Operations Committees of each House. This enormous task appears to have been beyond the capability of these committees. The General Accounting Office was established in 1921 to help Congress with the financial audit phase of performance evaluation, but this office provides mainly spot-check evidence in strictly monetary terms concerning general levels of expenditures. These are effective checks against the illegal and dishonest use of appropriations, but they do not provide a government-wide view of agency financial operations and efficiency.

A number of steps can be taken to provide Congress with a continuous review of governmental agencies. Instead of overburdening the Government Operations Committees with the overall review responsibility, much of the review functions could be assigned to the legislative committees and subcommittees responsible for long-term program authorization. These committees could be provided with a larger staff of competent personnel to monitor and evaluate specific programs.

Billions of dollars are spent annually on national programs, and yet there is no provision for funds to design and implement an effective monitoring and evaluation system. Such a system is essential, not only to check the efficiency with which programs are administered, but also to evaluate the appropriateness of a given program. For example, a number of different housing acts have been passed since the early 1950's. Some tore down slum areas in the heart of our cities, while the most recent one is designed to "guild our ghettos" by improving the existing housing, providing new community services, etc. An evaluation of the results of these two approaches could guide future legislation and funding of housing programs.

The monitoring and evaluation of agencies and programs could be coordinated by a bureau in the General Accounting Office, which in turn could provide relevant information to specific committees responsible for long-term programs.* Important recipients of this information would be appropriations committees as well as the two Government Operations Committees, and to some extent the Joint Economic Committee, which could concentrate on reviewing interagency programs and functions. Specialized legislative committees could receive the annual reports suggested earlier in this paper to be prepared by the Executive Office of the President and hold hearings on the programs which cut across departmental lines. (For example, the Subcommittee on Urban Affairs of the Joint Economic Committee could receive a broadly gauged Urban Affairs Message and hold a hearing on it.) In this manner appropriations committees and the public could gain a better perspective of national programs.

While these steps would strengthen the legislative branches' ability to review the performance of agencies, a further step could be taken. In many state and local governments, the legislative branch of government has established what is often referred to as the Office of the Legislative Analyst. The analyst assists legislators in determining if the legislative intent of a program has been carried out and, if so, how efficiently.

A different approach is found in Israel, where a Comptroller reports to the legislature on the expenditure of all public funds, commenting on the efficiency as well as the legality of the outlay. The Comptroller has been able to provide the legislature with a thoughtful review which, once it is published, becomes a powerful weapon. As a result, the legislature is forced to write the specific intent of the law more carefully into legislative acts. The U.S. Congress might consider amending the Budget and Accounting Act of 1921 to give the General Accounting Office some of the functions provided by Israel's Comptroller.

Once Congress is assured of continuous and reasonably effective review and evaluation of programs, it should be somewhat less reluctant to vote for badly needed longer term financing.

---

* Other arrangements could also be made. For example, the development and operation of the information system could be assigned to the Bureau of the Budget or the agency responsible for the program. It might also be argued that the outlook and tradition of the General Accounting Office is inconsistent with the broader review and evaluation visualized here and a new unit reporting to the Legislature should be created.

It should be remembered that federal program budgeting is still in an early state of development. Much remains to be done by scholars to improve analysis and measurement. However, also much further effort awaits the executive branch, and perhaps even more the legislative branch. Some of the problems program budgeting poses to Congress can be transformed into significant opportunities. If Congress takes creative steps, effective program budgeting in the executive branch of government will not change the balance of power in favor of that branch. Quite the contrary. Congress can provide itself with a perspective on the composition of the budget to weigh against the presidential perspective, an advantage it does not have now. Further, Congress would then be able to better assure itself whether or not agencies tend to operate efficiently in ways consistent with congressional intent.

COMMENT ON HIRSCH PAPER

Mr. Capron: You call for the preparation of cross-cutting analyses and reviews of programs in areas like science. Modest attempts have already been made to do this. There are, in the back of the President's Budget, a number of special analyses which undertake this. In addition, there are reports to the Congress from the President in such areas as manpower.

It is my impression, at least as a casual observer, that these have had absolutely no impact at all on the Hill. I think they have been ignored. What is wrong with the attempts that have been made thus far. Are they bad analyses and reports?

Dr. Grosse: I can't answer your direct question, obviously, as to why it has no effect on Congress. I can raise a question about the meaningfulness of this activity by itself.

Science is not an end product. Science, as viewed by the federal government and I am sure more generally, is a tool. It is something you develop and utilize for the accomplishment of further aims; at least I view it as such.

In that fashion, lumping all scientific programs together doesn't necessarily give you a better view of what is going on, or your objectives, or anything else.

204

The development of economic science or of biological science or of physical science may be of tremendous interest associated with other things. For example, to take my department, we are very interested in the development of biomedical research. I think we would be much more inclined to want to view the biomedical research and the development of science in these areas, as they relate to other activities in the health areas, rather than put them into context alongside of other scientific activities of the government.

Mr. Capron: The Bureau of the Budget does conduct what they call a science budget review. This is where they bring together from all over the Executive Branch the R&D and basic science budgets and put them together and look at them.

One of the purposes here is that there are some very scarce resources, and these funds in a sense are competing for these resources. I think that's a useful exercise. It turns out, though, that you can't make much sense out of this without getting into the missions of the agencies. Your basic evaluation on the science budget really turns on your evaluation of the Defense Budget, the NASA Budget, and so forth.

I think that this can perhaps be somewhat illuminating but I don't think it is going to have much impact on the decisions that are made in the appropriations process because there isn't anything called a science program. Our science programs, NSF to the side, which is small potatoes, are all mission-oriented and, in my opinion, should be, as federal science programs.

Therefore, what you are really looking at is the payoff, in the context of our national security objectives, of the science aspects of the DOD program. It is much more meaningful to look at it in that context, it seems to me, than all across the board.

I think the case is a little bit different in some of the other examples which you have raised. The urban one is a good one, I think, and whether the Joint Committee can cool this off in some way—

Dr. Hirsch: I haven't sold this.

Mr. Capron: Yes, I know, but it's an interesting idea.

Mr. Chartrand: I think it might be worthwhile pointing out that in terms of providing the members of Congress and the committees with information that would allow them to address themselves to some of these programs which cut across agency lines, that some two-and-a-half years ago there was formed a group in the Legislative Reference Service, of which I happen to be a member, called the Science Policy Research Division under the leadership of Dr. Edward Wenk.

I think it would be completely accurate to say that the way in which this small group has functioned in addressing itself to selected areas such as oceanography, weather modification and control, to name a couple, gives evidence that the Congress not only was honest enough to admit that it needed that kind of help in order to respond to the kinds of input which it was receiving from the Executive Branch but also that it wanted a sustaining force, that is, a residual capability which it could draw upon and which would allow the education of its members as well as provide one-time research products.

Dr. Fenno: When you talk about the Congress, what do you mean by that? What is the Congress in this context?

Mr. Chartrand: In this case I would refer specifically to those committees and subcommittees which are particularly concerned with various aspects of science and technology.

I think that the actions of Senator Harris's committee, the Daddario committee, and others are fairly well known here. This is not a large number of committees, I hasten to say, although, frankly, there are more than we ever dreamed when the division was formed that have their fingers in the scientific pie.

We also find that there is an increasing number of individual members who are starting to realize that they must become better versed in what technology can do for their constituency in areas that they never dreamed of addressing before. No longer is science just space and defense and atomic energy.

I think this is a very, very critical factor. Less than five per cent of all of the federal R&D dollars at this point in time go into areas such as pollution control and transportation development and so forth. Many members of the Congress are starting to articulate on the floor and in the professional journals, that something must be done about support for Congress in the area of science policy. In order for them to address the problem they have to become better educated, so they turn to us.

PETER SZANTON

The Present and Future of PPBS: Status and Plans

M Y TOPIC is The Present and Future of PPBS: Status
and Plans. Let me first say a few words about its
current status. It is necessary, though perhaps only
briefly, to begin by being quite clear that PPBS is not a more
effective method of keeping the books; it is not a different
accounting system; it is not even a new vocabulary in which
to cast budget requests, leaving decisions to be made in exactly
the way they have always been made. In talking about the
status and future of PPBS, I will be talking about a system
which attempts to do nothing less than radically to change
the method by which—at least within the executive branch—
decisions regarding the appropriate allocation of resources
come to be made.

What instruments are needed to get that job done, and to
what extent are they in hand? One requirement, obviously, is
simply an understanding, within the executive branch, of
what PPB is. I would say generally that after a year and a
half of considerable publicity, lots of talks, some interesting
magazine articles, and a couple of influential books, there is
now a fair understanding of what PPB intends and a general
recognition of its procedures and methods. I should note,
though, that this understanding may be insufficient at some

of the points where it is needed most; that is at the level of the heads of a number of domestic agencies.

A second requirement is some trained people. I don't want to push this point too hard. At least in the early years it does not require many people with very sophisticated training, for initially it is not an arcane science of minute tradeoffs involving esoteric techniques of mathematical analysis. At least for the present, the tasks of PPB are grosser and less rarified. They involve identifying the missions of agencies; determining where, in terms of those missions, the agencies' resources are now going; generating some realistic alternative means of accomplishing the purposes; suggesting the criteria against which those alternatives ought to be measured, recording the agencies' decisions as between those alternatives, and making explicit the rationale for those decisions.

These jobs are fundamental and they are difficult, but there are relatively few points at which they benefit from the application of advanced quantitative analytic techniques. The training required, in short, will not generally be that of a Ph.D. in economics or mathematics, although an understanding of some analytic methodology is helpful. Training efforts have advanced relatively well, I think. The Civil Service Commission has taken a very active role, and together with the Bureau of the Budget has set up two-day briefing sessions on the nature and purposes of PPB, three-week courses in basic analytic techniques, and one-year postgraduate, analytic training programs for people likely to be placed in the central analytic staffs that PPB requires. Something like 2,000 trainees have gone through one or another of these courses in the last year and a half. Something like 1,000 additional people have gone through training or orientation courses which the agencies themselves have set up.

The third requirement has been organizational. It has been necessary to focus an understanding of PPB together with basic analytic ability in specialized analytic staffs—and to a lesser degree in programming and budgeting staffs—both at the departmental level and at the bureau level, and below. These are the staffs charged with producing the two principal documents which PPB requires, the Program and Financial Plan, and the Program Memorandum. As of now, almost all agencies have created such staffs, which in fiscal 1968 will contain roughly 700 professionals. During fiscal 1967 the number has been roughly 500. In many agencies the staffs are probably close to being big enough. They are not close to being able enough. But many of them have proved capable, even in their current situations, of turning out very useful work.

These requirements being largely met, what has so far been accomplished? The first piece of work that everyone faced was that of creating a program structure. As you all know, this involved identifying the major objectives of agencies. It turned out to be hard work. It was particularly baffling for some agencies. The Department of Justice exemplifies some of the resistance to PPB to an extreme and interesting degree, and may be worth a moment's sidetrack. Justice's first reaction to the problem of establishing a program budget was: It can't be done here. It involves identifying objectives, but we're lawyers. Lawyers don't have objectives; lawyers have clients. Clients may have objectives, but we are basically only a service operation. If the Department of the Interior wants us to condemn some land, we condemn it. If IRS wants us to prosecute a nontaxpayer, we prosecute.

The small PPB staff in the Department of Justice therefore established as one of the objectives, and hence one of the programs of the Department, the provision of legal services to other agencies. However, when the current budget was broken down into program categories, that program, to the shock of many people in the Department, absorbed no more than 7 percent of the Department's resources. The moral here, I think, was that many agencies—Justice was only the clearest case—were reluctant to acknowledge how much discretion they had.

Given the program structure, the next problem was that of analysis. No agencies produced consistently satisfying analyses. A number of agencies, however, did generate quite good studies. HEW, OEO, the Peace Corps, Treasury, USIA were among them. By good, I meant better, at least, than the Bureau of the Budget had typically seen in any one year. In relating these studies to decision making, there was less success; a list of the agencies which succeeded on that score would contain a few of those I just mentioned, but it would be a small list.

It should not be dismaying, however, to find few agency decisions—or BOB (Bureau of the Budget) decisions, for that matter—in the current budget, which are both good and attributable to PPB. Getting a system as ambitious and as comprehensive as PPB into effect cannot be done quickly, and the analysis of complex social problems simply takes a lot of time. As you all know, Mr. McNamara's system had behind it, before it was instituted in Defense, 10 or 15 years of intense intellectual work outside the government. In most of the civil areas we've had no such running start. And the problems that government is now addressing are larger, more complex, and more subtle than many of those it has traditionally dealt with. Trying to design an adequate urban transportation system is a good deal tougher than designing an adequate airlift-sealift capability. The notion of adequacy is itself more elusive, and the relations to other objectives—proximity of homes to jobs, land conservation, air pollution, access to employment for the poor, aesthetic values—are subtler and less well understood.

Even with first-rate staffs, adequate funds, better data, and so forth, it is going to take some years to produce analysis of the conceptually more difficult problems that will give us—give the agencies themselves, the Budget Bureau and the President —the necessary confidence that the conclusions they come to will deserve to be acted upon. And by "action" I mean nothing more nor less than a willingness by the executive branch to make recommendations to the Congress, or to revise its own policies when it is free, without congressional action, to do so. The problem of getting changes on issues where political sensitivity is high or congressional involvement is intensive is, of course, a larger and a tougher question.

Let me say something now about the future of PPB. Basically what is required, I think, is more—and better—of the same, but there should probably be some new developments as well. On the "more" side, first, there will have to be some revision of program structures; in many cases these are quite crude and satisfy no one. A lot of work is going to be needed on problems of cost. Our notions of what things really cost, even to a bureau, let alone to an agency or to the federal government, or to federal, state, and local governments together, are still quite primitive and they are going to take a lot of work. And then there are larger questions of full costs to all of United States society of one program versus others. The output measures, the measures of physical output that PPB has required, have not turned out to be very useful, and a good deal of thought is going to have to go into what crude quantitative measures of output are more helpful than misleading.

But, above all, what we need more of is adequate analysis—analysis of appropriate objectives, of likely alternatives, of differing scales of effort, of criteria for decision making. We need analysis that is methodologically more sophisticated, that operates from a wider and better understood data base, that is intellectually more satisfying, and that is better keyed to decisions that must be made by agencies, by the President and by the Congress. And I think there must be more participation in this process by the Budget Bureau, which should be improving its own ability both to stimulate and to evaluate studies, and to make them more relevant to decision making. The Bureau, too, has work to do in improving its ability to make resource-allocation decisions—or recommendations—not in an incremental way but on a programmatic basis. Those are the main points, I think, where what is needed is basically more of the same.

As to the novelties, one can identify perhaps three. One is that additional agencies will become involved. All of the big-spending agencies are currently involved, as you know, but there are a number of smaller ones which have been so far only encouraged but not required to adopt PPB. Most of the agencies not now covered will come under PPB in the next year or two, including some regulatory agencies where the conceptual problems appear to be tough because what is to be allocated is the time of its people. Some of this work has begun through the initiative of the agencies themselves.

Another novelty that I think will be coming up in the next few years is the use of PPB materials for audit or review purposes. PPB will always be oriented principally toward the future; the key question it asks is always: What should we be doing? But one side benefit of answering that question systematically and explicitly, year after year, is that you thus produce a record of what you thought could be accomplished with a given scale of resources, and why you thought so. Once we have that kind of a record, it is going to be useful to go back and see what the accomplishments really were, and whether they varied from the predictions, and if so, why.

This need not be simply a narrow post-audit or monitoring function. It ought also to be a learning process—the review of old analyses, of the assumptions on which they were based, of old concepts of the problem, of the adequacy of the data used. This is a kind of review which, over time, will very greatly improve, I think, our ability to analyze major problems of public policy—to spot reasonable and unreasonable assumptions, to identify the critical variables, to improve the data base, to see the problem in the largest manageable perspective.

The last of these three novelties concerns legislation. PPB so far has had virtually no effect on agency legislative proposals. There are exceptions, and I take it from the cock of Dr. Grosse's head here that HEW provides some of them. But the fact is that the experience of the last few months of 1966 suggested strongly that there was very little connection between the analytic thinking that went into agencies' PPB submissions, and the work that went into agencies' legislative proposals. It's going to be necessary to expand the scope of the required analysis to include those measures which the agency intends to propose as part of the President's legislative program for the coming year, and to make sure that those proposals are consistent with plans for on-going programs.

Let me conclude now with one hypothesis, one factual note, and one hope. The hypothesis is that there is a high correlation between agency success in PPB and the recentness of the appointment of its head. The agencies which have pushed PPB hard—the Peace Corps, USIA, HEW, OEO, the Post Office—almost all had chief officers who had come quite recently to the job. The connection should not be surprising. The questions a new manager wants to ask—What is it we are trying to do? How are we doing it? Why are we doing it that way?—these, of course, are also the basic questions of PPB.

The point of fact is simply that PPB is not something that only the federal government is involved in. Not only does PPB have roots, as has been pointed out, in business practice, but systems very much like PPB, as many of you know, are being developed in other countries: Israel, Canada, Sweden, the UK. At least in the case of Canada, their systems appears to be ahead of ours. Similar systems are also growing up in states within the U.S. New York has a planning-programming-budgeting system; Michigan, California, Pennsylvania are, in varying ways, moving in the same direction. So are some cities, including New York City.

Let me end on a note of unrealistic hope. A professor of business administration, after hearing a talk on PPB, was heard to remark that the last 10 years have seen the professionalization of business, and that the next 10 years are going to see the professionalization of government. We shall see.

COMMENT ON SZANTON PAPER

Mr. Capron: Let me pick up the last note and ask our congressional observers if there isn't a fairly strong resistance in the Congress to the notion of a "professionalization of government"?

Mr. Donoghue: I wonder if you would define that a little more precisely for us.

Mr. Szanton: That's not easy, as no doubt you appreciate. I take it what it means is that there are no scientific ways of making decisions, at least not important decisions, but there are better and worse ways of making decisions. There are more and less systematic, more and less comprehensive ways of looking at data and being explicit about objectives, about the various ways in which one can get at them, and about the criteria which one can use to choose between alternatives. And there are more and less sophisticated ways of calculating costs and benefits. But explicitness may be more important than correctness; that is, it may be more important to set down clearly what it is you are trying to do, what the alternative ways of doing that are, how you can judge between those alternatives, and why you have chosen the way you have chosen. The reason it may be more important is that if you are explicit, you can be wrong several times running but the reasons for that error can, in retrospect, be identified. Review and learning will be greatly facilitated where there is a will to learn. Future decisions may be more soundly based.

213

Mr. Donoghue: In reaching certain decisions, the Congress is subjected to a lot of pressures which are not susceptible of analysis in the same sense that executive proposals can be made on a clear, analytical, and explicit basis. As Professor Fenno pointed out in his discussion this morning, clientele, political, and constituency pressures will come to bear. I don't think Congress would want to be faced with a situation where real rational analysis would interfere with what they might consider their legitimate political or institutional interests.

Dr. Fenno: I would like to expand on that a little. I think Congress has shown a desire to professionalize itself over time and I think you can see this in the Legislative Reorganization Act that has gone through the Senate. They have provided for review specialists and for more staff help. So I don't think Congress is reluctant to professionalize government. They are interested in trying to professionalize Congress to do the thing that Congress is good at doing. In answering Mr. Szanton's original question, congressmen are bound to be concerned about performing their function. The question is: How can we professionalize the performance of the congressional function?

I was trying to suggest that one of the functions is to watch the executive, to try to check the executive. I think that's a value that's built into the political system, and I tend to start by asking: How can we preserve that value? It is interesting that over the years some of Mr. Hirsch's proposals have been made, as Jack Saloma knows, again and again. More coordinating, more integrating, more comprehensive congressional consideration of executive programs— all these have been proposed—yet they have been resisted by congressmen steadily since the Budget and Accounting Act of 1921.

Now, I think we have to assume that congressmen are just as smart as everybody else, and just as much concerned with the public interest as everybody else. If they have resisted it, it may very well be that they don't feel that these proposals and reforms that are being offered to them are likely to help them perform their function any better. This, I think, is the problem. If you present them with a more comprehensive view of a program, is this going to help them to do what they want to do? Or, is it going to help the executive do what it wants Congress to do—namely, consider broad programs in a very abstract way, make a very abstract judgment, and then withdraw. I don't think congressmen want to do that, and the reason they. resist is because they feel that it isn't going to help them do what they want to do.

These reform proposals have tended to be executive-originated and executive-produced proposals. The executive has always been good at telling Congress how it ought to do its job. I agree with Mr. Hirsch that Congress ought to be more creative—but I think the way for it to be more creative is to put staff assistance into the mechanisms that congressmen find most comfortable now, and to beef up the committees which do a specialized, piecemeal, incremental, noncomprehensive kind of analysis.

Mr. Capron: I want to pick up one point: I think it is not accidental but it may be somewhat instructive that exactly the same approach that you emphasize is taken by the subcommittees on appropriations, namely, a sampling approach. It is the technique that is used, to the extent it is done at all, at the secretarial level in the departments and certainly at the Bureau of the Budget. Indeed, as I heard you talking about what the subcommittees do and the way they view their jobs, I felt very comfortable with this because I used to sit in the Bureau of the Budget, and this is very much the posture there. There is a good deal of similarity in the posture and attitude of the Bureau of the Budget toward the agencies and departments, I think, and the subcommittees in this regard.

There are some agencies that the bureau is very relaxed about. There are others that the bureau is, for proper or improper reasons, much less relaxed about. Of course, there are profound differences in what the subcommittee and bureau are doing because the bureau is trying to serve the President of the United States, who has one political role, and the subcommittees are trying to serve the Congress of the United States, which has a very different political role. But there are some similarities here which are instructive.

Mr. Szanton: I think really what we are saying is that Congress is responsive to different pressures than the executive, and that's presumably why we want Congress to have an independent look at policy. That is really what we are striving to get, a different set of interests to play on a policy decision. If this means compromise, then that's good, I think. The more interests we can get to play on a problem, prior to making a decision, the better.

Dr. Saloma: There are two functions or roles of Congress that have been slightly blurred. One is the congressional role in policy formulation, and the other is oversight. Most of the discussion of PPBS has been on policy formulation, and on the nature of decision making in the executive. Here there is a change. In the past you have had a division of opinion between those who felt comprehensive decision making in the budget process was necessary and those who argued that decision making was incremental. Now PPB claims that you can have comprehensive decision making. At the same time, PPB increases the capacity of Congress to exercise oversight. So really you are effecting two things and you have to separate them to see what the total impact will be.

I agree completely that Congress has to define its own use of the new facilities. There are distinctive congressional perspectives in this process and assuming that Congress will continue to be an autonomous or semiautonomous, independent institution, Congress itself has to define how it will adapt to these changes. At the same time there is no reason to assume that the functions or roles will be static. They have changed considerably with the Budget and Accounting Act of 1921, which resulted in a major transfer in decision making and reorientation of functions. The whole oversight function, for instance, didn't develop until after that. Oversight doesn't become part of the statutory apparatus of the congressional role until 1946. So you may see, with PPB Systems, a further change in the function and roles of the two bodies. I don't know that we can predict at this stage where it will lead.

Dr. Grosse: Professor Hirsch made a strong plea which I would support, for evaluation being included in legislative proposals. I want to point out that, with very few exceptions, each of the legislative proposals going forth from our department includes an amount up to 1 percent for the purposes of evaluation. We have also asked for evaluation funds for ongoing programs.

I would like to talk about this question of sampling for a moment. You know, you can sample in many different ways. One is to fish randomly into the marginal things that come up. I think that it was different in my experience in the last year in dealing with the Bureau of the Budget. I don't think it's been the same kind of sampling that might have taken place before. We have had numerous conversations whose purpose was to try to identify those areas which are significant, and we worked very hard at developing an agenda for discussions between the Secretary and the Director.

One of the purposes of the program structure and the analyses which we developed to feed into that structure is to focus on those things that are critical. I think that the sampling is pretty selective today rather than simple tests of whether the man can make a sensible presentation on a particular item.

Dr. Hirsch: I would like to make two short comments on the presentations this afternoon.

I am delighted to be exposed to the optimism that you brought along as a man who has only recently left the bureau and I hope you are right. It is difficult because we might have oversold it in a period where many of our domestic programs were being either held constant or reduced, and that is not the time when you want to show your cards. So far as the agencies are concerned, you don't want rationality at the moment, and also it's terribly difficult. I think on that one you made some awfully good observations, for the structural and analytical sides are very difficult. But I hope you are right. I hope that this optimism is warranted.

Second, I was much interested in your statement on professionalization and I think this is really very common, because even when you look at lobbying these days, it seems that it is no longer merely the arm twisting and the buying of a drink. The sophisticated lobbyist is trying to get himself in a position where he has at least some capability in the benefit-cost area, where he can throw in different discount rates, where he can throw in different estimates of what the costs are or what benefits will really amount to.

Turning now to our concern about program budgeting in relation to the Congress, I see a great challenge to the con-

217

gressional committees, if a good analytic study is generated in the executive branch which says these two or three options seem to be very good ones. I would hope that Congress and certain committees of Congress will have the capability to take these assumptions apart and, by building different scenarios, show that the results might turn out differently and, therefore, choose a different route.

Finally, I am very much in agreement with what Professor Fenno says. I have no illusions about the fact that Congress wants to be terribly rational, but what I am seeking in a sense is new institutional arrangements that will open a wedge. For example, at this moment the appropriations committees are terribly strong, and substantive committees like the House Operations Committee and the Joint Economic Committee are not as strong. Perhaps giving the substantive committees a new mission would also give them a chance to assume new stature beside these strong appropriations sub-committees. I hope this would develop strategies that help improve in a marginal way the comprehensiveness of review and rationality.

Mr. Capron: On the point of comprehensive review, a question of clarification: In your paper, Professor Hirsch, you mentioned two proposals. One is the Joint Budget Committee which, so far as I know, is still on the books, whether it has ever been implemented, and the other is the more recent Committee for Economic Development proposal. My impression is that both of those proposals were not directly germaine to the focus of planning, programming, and budgeting since these proposals are much more concerned with overall fiscal policy issues. Now this doesn't mean that you couldn't use this approach to get a kind of a congressional review of the budget, major item by major item, but that's a somewhat different thrust. Am I wrong about this? Just for the sake of historical accuracy, please correct the record, for this morning, before you came in, I distinguished rather sharply between the fiscal policy and the programmatic and budget details on the micro-side.

Dr. Hirsch: Insofar as the Committee for Economic Development is concerned, its publication *Budgeting for National Objectives* is in many respects concerned with the PPB approach.

218

Dr. Grosse: I have been puzzled by Professor Hirsch's comment about the difficulty of program budgeting at a time when budgets are held relatively constant. I can see this is a difficulty in getting funds for people to do program analyses, but for interest in PPBS the reverse may be true. It is very difficult to sell program analysis and program budgeting to an agency which is fat and happy and getting increasing budgets. What do they need you for? You can hurt them but you probably can't help them.

On the other hand, when they hit a period of financial stringency they may be much more inclined to be interested. Assuming that they have some faith in their programs, which most of them have, they would be much more inclined to seek assistance in demonstration. Our strategy for pushing heavily for evaluation as we go into interchange with Congress is essentially to say this is not the time politically that we can really mount vast, important, and new social programs. Now is the time to take stock. Now is the time to get ready for the situation which may change. These things do take time to understand and to evaluate and maybe we can take advantage of this so-called breathing spell.

Dr. Hirsch: I am no expert in the field but I was told by the people in the Bureau of Budget that the greatest difficulties at the moment are in relation to those departments that feel a little threatened when it comes to their budget. This doesn't mean that these departments do not come forth with new proposals but they are very reluctant to put them into a programmatic form. I can see your point very well because, for example, I feel that those of us who believe in a master plan for a city usually are very unrealistic if we assume that a rapidly growing city wants a master plan. I think it's the one that is stagnant and sliding down that wants a master plan and has the proof for its people.

Mr. Hugo: I wanted to raise a question concerning statistics which Bill Capron brought up earlier, and which is very relevant here. It appears that the bureaus are doing better than the agencies, though both of them may be doing poorly, in accumulating analytic staff for PPB.

Dr. Grosse: Is that bad, do you think?

219

Mr. Hugo: No, I just think that this should be connected specifically to an assumption, which I understand was very important in framing PPB, that the initiative and talent for program analysis and review resided, if at all, at the bureau level, and they wanted to reinstate that balance by providing analytic staff for the secretaries.

Mr. Capron: Yes, I think if we had the figures on a comparable basis, that the greatest increment has come at the central level. I don't mean the Bureau of the Budget but the departmental level. There has been a small increment at the bureau level. But this ties directly to a comment that I wanted to make backing up what Werner Hirsch said a moment ago. It is my feeling that it is just very important that the Congress develop a capability in its staffs, particularly the Appropriations Committees, to scrub these analyses on a selective basis.

We've got a long history of so-called cost-benefit analysis in one major area of public expenditure, the water-resource field, and the average quality is terrible. This is not because the technical side of the analysis is so bad, although there are a lot of criticisms there, but because of the assumptions, which are usually implicit. You can justify any water-resource project, at least almost any, if you make just a few little assumptions and, of course, you don't want to spell these out too loudly. To prevent abuse of this sort we need someone who is asking some of the hard questions.

There should be many more program analysts doing work at the bureau level because they are closer to the data and the real problems. They have direct access to the people who have the intellectual capital and who have been involved in the administrative programs. But you need people at various levels up the line who, on a selective basis, are reviewing these analyses very carefully and asking the hard, nasty questions. This is Dr. Grosse's role in HEW, as I see it. As he pointed out, a lot of these task forces that are working on these analyses this year are wholly or primarily staffed by people in the particular agency. But his responsibility to the Secretary is to make sure that there aren't any kickers in the assumptions that haven't been revealed, which may bias or dominate the results of the analysis. So that I don't think just looking at the wrong numbers by itself is enough, if I understood the thrust of your question.

Mr. Hugo: I would like to address a second question jointly to Mr. Capron, Dr. Grosse, and Mr. Szanton. What guarantee is there that as soon as hard question-askers are set up, these people in turn won't become champions of or captives of the programs that they are assigned to analyze? To a great extent this is a very basic criticism of the present system. The people who are responsible for analyzing and framing alternatives, if any, are really champions of the program. What about the people who are being provided to the Secretary to produce the independent analysis and review of these programs?

Mr. Capron: This is why I second Professor Hirsch's view that the Congress has to develop a capability on a very professional level to take a very hard look at these analyses, these justifications as they are produced.

Dr. Fenno: Oh, I agree completely, that the Congress ought to develop this capability. The question I want to raise and put to people who have looked at it somewhat more from the executive branch than I have is one concerning the information available to Congress. How far back into the executive decision-making processes should Congress go, or will they need to go, in order to get at the assumptions on which executive decisions were based?

Dr. Grosse: I would like to talk on both of these questions. I think there is a distinction to be made between decision making and analysis. I don't say that our analyses are suitable for professional publication, but we have published them. The Legislative Reference Service of the Library of Congress has these, individual congressmen who are interested have these, universities and such have the same basic data and explanations that we delivered to the Executive Office of the President and the Bureau of the Budget.

The difference is that we have not put in these specific administrative recommendations and we haven't recorded the conversations, which I think is a reasonably appropriate split. We may regret this later but right now our feeling is that this is public information in the broadest sense of the term and we hope to keep that one going. We don't have to face the security problem that muddies the defense issue.

221

With respect to the question you asked about the objectivity of the people, I commented somewhat facetiously that things are worse than you think, and by that I meant that things are so bad in terms of analytical capability that objectivity or non-objectivity is not the major issue at the moment. We are trying desperately to find out what is going on. We are trying to find out what the objectives are. We have the problem in our department of trying to get people who have the idea that progress in education, medical care, and social work is a good in and of itself, and needs no further discussion, and then to talk a little bit about what happens if you put a little more or a little less in. We are pressing this. While I see the problem about objectivity coming—and it comes at all levels, I am sure—we get so many other problems of development of information, development of basic data, and such that I think that this is not, in the way you phrased it, a significant issue.

The numbers themselves in one sense are an underestimate. For example, when we do an analysis, the people who are identified as program analysts are a very small portion of the people involved. They tend to be the supervisors along the line. What happens when you do a study is you drag in people from the programs and from outside the Federal Government who are concerned with the problem, and form these into an analytical team with various functions. If you look at the Public Health Service people, let's say, who are given the program-planning and evaluation staffs, their inputs are very modest. But we could put 40 or 50 people, who never show up, in these numbers, who come in for three, four months, and disappear from this. It is a muddy situation in any numbers that you deal with.

Mr. Capron: I would like to comment, Professor Fenno, on the question in your paper of how far back Congress should go into the information flow on the executive side. Let me illustrate the nature of this problem by one of the elements that has been introduced in PPBS, namely, the program and financial plan which, as has been pointed out several times today, includes a forward look of five years or so.

At least when I was still in the executive branch, there was a good deal of soul-searching as to whether or not these plans should be classified because of the political danger to the President of turning them loose publicly. Even though we write on all sides of the paper, "this does not represent (except for the next budget year) any kind of presidential decision or even departmental decision," the President in some areas is going to get "locked in" to those numbers, particularly if a subsequent re-evaluation indicates that some of these implied budget numbers need to be reduced.

The pressure groups and interest groups and the congressional committees most directly supportive of that program are going to wave the five-year plan around and make an awful lot of noise. There is a really difficult presidential decision. The practical response to this point is that there are enough people down the line in the bureaus who have this data that it is going to get to the Hill on this side of the table or on that side anyway, and it may not make all that difference. But if it goes informally and unofficially it can't be used in the same way that it can if it has been formally presented.

Now, Mr. McNamara has handled this problem in the following way: First, it is always him talking and not the President when he reviews the five-year plan. Second, he never talks dollars, except for the next budget year. He talks force structure—the program plan—but not the financial plan, and this is a big difference.

I think there's always going to be a contest between the Appropriations Committee and the President with regard to whether or not a bureau head indicates what he asks for, or a cabinet officer indicates what he asks for. I approve of the President's resistance to revealing this, because I think executive discipline requires loyalty to the President's budget. On the other hand, the facts of life are not going to be changed by PPB or anything else.

As you pointed out in your paper, this is very interesting and difficult. You find some very strong resistance among newly appointed, still-loyal-strictly-to-the-President-and-not-the-captive-of-the-interest-groups-yet cabinet officers, and you find an eagerness, shall we say, to point at the Bureau of the Budget. They never point at the President, of course, they point at the Bureau of the Budget. We wanted more, Mr. Congressman, but they wouldn't let us have it.

Mr. Hugo: You still have the problem of providing the President with the means to challenge the traditional three-cornered basis of support that underlies most programs. You have the bureau's, clientele in the private sector, and the support group on the Hill. Now, for example, if you want the expertise to challenge the merchant marine's operating differential subsidies, where do you go? You go to the Maritime Administration.

Dr. Grosse: That's, in a sense, an argument in my parochial terms for not breaking up the Department of Health, Education, and Welfare into separate departments. You need a layer for domestic programs beneath the President.

Mr. Hugo: But take a forward look at PPB. Aren't you going to have to deal with the problem of establishing and maintaining a truly independent analytic capability?

Mr. Szanton: There is no wholly satisfactory answer, I think. Ultimately you depend on the election every four years or every two years. In descending order of approaches to the problem, you do want strong congressional staffs capable of providing what analytic backup the Congress may feel comfortable trying to use. It is true in this area that staffs at one level imply the need for better staffs at other levels rather than weaker ones. They interact with each other and each is more effective if there are other staffs at other levels to talk to.

At the level of the Secretary you have people who may indeed become champions of programs, but they are different from the traditional champions of programs in at least two senses. One is that the program they are looking at has different dimensions, has a different character than a traditional program. In the Department of Justice there may be, it's possible, champions of the FBI. However, as you look at the program structure of the Department of Justice, there is no FBI program. Investigation is not a program. The programs are things like reduction and control of crime, assurance of civil rights, maintenance of competition, and internal security, and so forth, in each of which there is an FBI role.

This kind of organization, this kind of categorization of what the department is doing, coupled with analytic capability reporting to the agency head, tends to look at the FBI in terms of what it contributes to reduction in crime, what it contributes to civil rights, and so forth. In short, if someone specializes in, let's say, the civil rights program, he may become a champion of civil rights, but his point of view of civil rights is different from that of anybody in the FBI or in the Civil Rights Division or in the U.S. attorney's office. He provides, by hypothesis at least, a broader perspective on the problem and one that is clearly different from anybody else's perspective.

That's one difference. The second is that typically the people you're talking about tend to have much weaker institutional ties. They tend to be young outsiders. They move around a great deal or at least they have no prior loyalty to any other organization. Sure, that loyalty becomes compromised and eventually they will become programmized. Perhaps TFX is an example where loyalty to an agency head may preclude the kind of analysis you want rather than to produce it. Then you are leaning on the Congress and the elections, but you have filtered out a lot of junk, though not all of it, by the device of strong staffs to the secretary.

Mr. Capron: There is a conflict in this issue as I am sure you recognize, Mike, namely, if someone is too objective, he's probably too ignorant to be very useful. That is, you have to spend some time working in an area to build up the intellectual capital to give you the necessary understanding so you can make any sense out of the area. In the process of doing this many people do tend to feel that their particular slant on the approach to that problem area is probably the right one.

INDEX

228

229

Sarnoff, David, 129, 130
Saturday Evening Post, 197, 197n
Schwengel, Fred
  panel discussion on paper by, 99-108
  paper, Problems of Inadequate Information and Staff Resources in Congress, 97-99
  reference to, 128
  reply to comments on paper by, 99-102, 104-106
  statement by, 5
Science Information Exchange, 11, 22
Scott, Hugh
  references to, 2n, 7n, 27, 28
  statement by, 7
Seaborg, Glenn T.
  statement by, 8, 8n
Senate, *see* Congress
States
  data processing systems, 46, 74, 87, 91, 92, 101
  Office of the Legislative Analyst, 203
  planning-programming-budgeting systems, 213
Statistics
  congressional computing centers, 83
  congressional problems, 54
  congressional reform recommendations, 58
  HEW program information, 161-165, 169-171
  scientific documentation, 60, 61, 65
Subcommittee on Domestic Finance, 81n

Systems Development Corporation, 12, 133
Szanton, Peter
  panel discussion on paper by, 213-225
  paper, Present and Future of PPBS: Status and Plans, 207-213
  reference to, 221
  reply to comments on paper by, 213, 215, 224

Truman, David B., 48n

Unidentified flying objects
  Air Force bibliography, 24
U.S. Code
  searching provisions of, 74, 122, 123
U. S. Patent Office, 61
University of Iowa, 97, 101
University of Pittsburgh, 17, 18, 46, 74, 122
University of Wisconsin, 37, 41

VIP Systems, Inc., 93

Wallace, Robert Ash, 82n
Washington Lobbyists, 73n
We Propose: A Modern Congress, 5, 5n
Wenk, Edward, 206
Wheare, K. C., 48n
Winchell (reference book), 22
Woll, Peter, 50n, 53n
Wright, Frank Lloyd, 111

Yale Political Data Program, 23